How to Deal with a Divorce as a Christian

How to Deal with a Divorce as a Christian

Infertility, Adoption, Loss of Jobs,
New Career, Family Relationships,
and Alcoholism

— A Memoir —

Iris Mollen

RESOURCE *Publications* · Eugene, Oregon

HOW TO DEAL WITH A DIVORCE AS A CHRISTIAN
(Infertility, Adoption, Loss of Jobs, New Career, Family Relationships, and Alcoholism)

Copyright © 2022 Iris Mollen. All rights reserved. Except for brief quotations in critical publications or reviews, no part of this book may be reproduced in any manner without prior written permission from the publisher. Write: Permissions, Wipf and Stock Publishers, 199 W. 8th Ave., Suite 3, Eugene, OR 97401.

Resource Publications
An Imprint of Wipf and Stock Publishers
199 W. 8th Ave., Suite 3
Eugene, OR 97401

www.wipfandstock.com

PAPERBACK ISBN: 978-1-7252-9830-9
HARDCOVER ISBN: 978-1-7252-9828-6
EBOOK ISBN: 978-1-7252-9829-3

11/02/22

Contents

Notes From the Author | vii
Dedication | ix
Introduction | xiii
Word Search | xviii

1. My Story Begins—My Childhood | 1
2. Dating | 8
3. Wedding Plans, Wedding and Honeymoon | 11
4. Beginning of Our Marriage | 13
5. Infertility and Coping | 16
6. Friends | 19
7. Our First Miracle | 21
8. Our Second Miracle | 23
9. Raising Boys—Family | 26
10. My Marriage Starts to Fall Apart—and Losing a Job after 25 Years | 41
11. Finding a Place to Live, House Sale and Divorce | 54
12. The Grand Canyon/Rolling Stone's Concert | 59
13. E-Mails Between Me and My Son During my Separation | 61
14. After the Divorce—"Kinks" | 70
15. What Does the Bible Say about Divorce | 74
16. CNA (Certified Nursing Assistant)—A New Career | 84
17. A Friend in Need | 105

18. Another Job Loss—Termination (PP) | 107
19. Worked at Two Other Places (A and LP) | 115
20. Finding the Perfect Job (Home Health Care) 117
21. Choir-Church | 123
22. Family Relationships | 128
23. My First Gentleman Friend | 136
24. The Love of My Life | 147
25. My Birds; My Babies | 155
26. Words of Wisdom | 161
27. Communication with Ex-Sister-in-Law After the Divorce | 164
28. Being a Christian/Emergency Bible Numbers | 167
29. Interview With Christians Who got Divorced | 170
30. Sermons | 173
31. The Lord's Prayer | 183
32. Rehearsal, Rehearsal Dinner and Wedding | 184
33. Alcoholism | 186
34. Baby Announcement and Baby Shower | 191
35. Closing Comments | 198

Answers to Word Search | 205

Notes From the Author

First, I want to send prayers to all of the families that lost their loved ones due to the horrible COVID-19 pandemic. I can never imagine how you must feel. And to those who are still getting sick from the COVID-19 and still losing their loved ones.

I was quarantined for ten days and it was a difficult time for me. I got tested for the COVID two times and the waiting to see if the test was negative or positive was very tough.

I am fortunate to have my Mom, my gentleman friend, my sons and friends who prayed for me.

2020 and 2021 were terrible years and we all have to pray 2022 is better regarding Covid 19 and our Nation.

Like my Mother says, "This Too Shall Pass" and it does. You need to keep the faith, pray, talk to professionals about your feelings, your Pastor, and if necessary, take some prescription medications with your doctor's supervision to get you through this very, very difficult time.

My book is dedicated to my 88 YEAR old Mother who has been my rock.

God Bless.

Live

Laugh

And

Love

Dedication

I dedicate this book to my Mother, who has always been there for me. Her love and being a pillar of strength have gotten me through difficult times in my life. It is because of my faith and her example of being a great Mom that I have gotten through the tough times in my life. She is my best friend. And she is the most honest person that I know, and the sweetest. She buys flowers at an outside stand at Jewel and goes in to buy groceries and then she looks at the receipt, because she thought it didn't sound like she got charged enough. So, she went back and paid the additional $18.00 for the flowers. She said that her conscience would not let her walk away without paying, even though someone made a mistake. I am her daughter. I would have done the same thing. She brought me up as a Christian.

Mom loves cardinals. Why did God make the male cardinal more beautiful than the female cardinal? I think he made a mistake and I will have a talk with Him when I get to Heaven!

And Mom . . . I know you had me over 65 years ago and I came feet first. I have been standing firmly on the ground since then!

I almost lost my Mom the end of 2019. She ended up in the ICU (intensive care unit) with a very low sodium level due to a change in her medications. She ended up having a mild seizure and was pretty sick for awhile. Thank you God she is good now.

I took my Mom to Arizona for her 80th birthday and stayed with my sister and brother-in-law. My niece and nephew live there and it was great to have three generations of family together. We had a lot of fun and I thank God for our time together. There is nothing more important than family and of course, friends.

This is a true story, but fictitious names have been used.

I want to thank all of my family and friends (real estate broker and home staging friends) and my wonderful friends at my church, especially one who is my Stewardship Minister. What is a Stewardship Minister? It is a person at a church that goes through special training to help counsel people;

i.e. divorce, death, illness, hospice care, etc. My Stewardship Minister has recently been diagnosed as having Alzheimer's. At the beginning when my husband asked me for a divorce, I went to see our church nurse. We talked at length and she told me that she had gotten divorced, and then she let me pick out a "prayer shawl," which I keep by my bed. It is purple, my favorite color.

Thank you to the pastor of my church and the associate pastor of youth ministry for their love and support and help with my book.

Thank you to my wonderful doctor who told me anxiety after a divorce lasts an average of one to one and a half years, and he was right.

From 1 Peter 5:7a, 8–11: Cast all your anxiety on Him because He cares for you. Be self-controlled and alert. Your enemy, the devil, prowls around like a roaring lion looking for someone to devour. Resist him, standing firm in the faith . . . and the God of all grace, who called you to His eternal glory in Christ will restore you and make you strong, firm and steadfast. To Him be the power for ever and ever.

Thank you to my wonderful, caring, loving lawyer and her associates for all of their hard work and support during my "nasty divorce." They are all real sweethearts, and females!

My dear friend and dentist, and her dental assistant, and two other friends at their office, one who originally typed my "draft" book for me. God works in mysterious ways. The woman who typed my book overheard me talking to another friend at the dentist's office about needing a typist for my book. She was the one.

My dear hair stylist, JK, who has been with me for years through all of my life's journeys.

And, my dear love of my life for his love and support.

Another friend from work who took two of my cockatiels. What a blessing from God. She gave them a wonderful, loving home. She loves them dearly. She had lost one of her parakeets and it was "perfect" timing. She wanted another bird, but got two of my cockatiels. I had to find a home for a few of my birds as I could not move with eight birds after my divorce and sale of our home. It was hard finding a place to live with birds, even though they are caged. Landlords do not want pets, not even birds. I gave a parakeet and love bird to a pet store I had been going to for years. The birds found a home that day.

My gynecologist who knows everything that happened and thinks my ex-husband is, "An a___ wipe!"

My cleaning lady, friend, and old neighbor from my old neighborhood who was called early the day of the closing on the house to clean out a refrigerator/freezer in the garage. In 2021 she passed away of cancer. She was younger than me. Very sad. At her memorial service, I found out her husband had had two major strokes. He was being pushed out of the bathroom in a wheelchair and when he saw me, he broke down. I gave him a hug.

It wasn't until I left the funeral home that I broke down in tears. We used to hang out in the neighborhood and she would show me her gorgeous flower garden she was very proud of.

I also ran into my old beautician there and caught up on the girls from the ole beauty shop.

Thank you God for saving two dear friends of mine from committing suicide. The one friend, her own mother, didn't help her out during this difficult time in her life, but my friend sought help and got through it. Another friend called me and I could tell that she was in a bad way. She stopped taking her medication for depression, and even though she told me she wasn't thinking of doing anything to herself, I knew better. I suggested that she call the doctor immediately as I thought they would hospitalize her, which they did. She called me and thanked me. I told her that she was the one that made the decision to go to the doctor and get help; I just made a suggestion. She is now going to meetings for depression. She also ended up in the hospital again for her depression.

My churches have always been a huge part of my life since I was very young. Thank you Mom for raising me in the Lutheran/Christian faith!

THANK YOU TO ALL AND GOD BLESS. I LOVE YOU ALL!

Introduction

At first I started writing down my thoughts about everything I was going through before, during and after my divorce. I believe I did it as "therapeutic" self-help; like a diary-journal. God has led me to write this book and I decided to pursue my book to try and help others that are Christians dealing with a divorce and other events that I have encountered, such as losing a job four months after my husband asked me for a divorce. I worked for the company for over 25 years and then decided to start a new career after I was 55 years old. After high school, I attended nursing school to become an RN. I was halfway done with school and got sick with the chicken pox for three weeks and I had to quit school. So, I decided to pursue something in the medical field that did not require a lot of school. I became a CNA (certified nursing assistant). My book also deals with infertility issues and miracles.

You take your wedding vows before God, family and friends, and believe that your marriage to that person you love will be forever. Till death do you part. You never believe that it will happen to you. A divorce. You believe that your spouse will always be there for you, for better or for worse; in sickness and in death.

My husband didn't take his vows seriously. After 35 years of marriage, he asked me for a divorce because he said that, "I don't love you anymore." I had been with him for a total of 40 years, including dating and engagement.

I was devastated, yes. Our last six years together weren't good, but divorce? What was I going to do? Be alone? I got married when I was 21 years old and now I was 55. I had to learn a lot and deal with a lot, being that I was going to be a single woman.

Our vows were broken. It was very painful.
Marriage is a gift from God.

I was afraid of being alone and it was overwhelmingly scary. Our pastor's sermon on Mother's Day was, "The Touch of Jesus." Jesus can remove our fears. Everything is in his hands. How very true. One day I was driving by a church and the sign read, "More of Jesus, Less (of?) with Me."

My husband and I tried counseling many years ago, then for six months and dating after he had asked me for a divorce. People laughed at me about the dating part. I know the dating part sounds funny, but we were trying to save our marriage. We went to comedy shows, but then he'd drop me off at the house, as he had moved out, and then he would drive away, which really hurt me. I cried my eyes out. It was his idea to go to a comedy show which was a great idea. I knew deep down in my heart he really didn't want to try to save our marriage, but he did put forth an effort; I believe for show.

What happened to him? Was it a mid-life crisis? He was very depressed and had been drinking quite heavily.

The last straw that broke the camel's back was when he said in counseling, "You'll be well taken care of. I'm worth a lot of money." That cut me like a knife and I knew that our marriage was over. The security of being married was shattered. I remember saying to him after he made the comment to me, "You are not worth a lot of money. We are." What a terrible thing to say. I had worked my whole married life. This man saying this horrible comment to me after so many years of being together was devastating.

We were always blessed financially, so we never had to struggle for money.

Now we have divorced, sold our house, split our assets, and because he runs two businesses, I got him real good on maintenance, also known as alimony, for ten years. That was based on one-third of the number of years we were married.

This book is about how to survive a divorce as a Christian, my life story, my struggle with getting divorced, and my belief that God was helping me through it all, including finding a new career which I am happy with, and finding my true love.

I know now that getting divorced was the best thing that ever happened to me. It took me a long time to realize this, but like a friend of mine asked me, "Would you have rather stayed in an unhealthy marriage?"

I know that life can be worse. I used to work with a paralegal who died in her early 40's and left behind her husband and four small children.

I remember our senior pastor telling me that a divorce is worse than a death. I believe that is true. Death is final, but when you get divorced, that person you once loved is still around, and in my situation, my ex-husband lived a few blocks away from me for a few years which was difficult. When he sends me something in the mail and I see his hand writing and it still hurts.

I read that the divorce rate is one out of every two couples. I would say that is high.

INTRODUCTION

I never thought I would get divorced. My mom got divorced from my father, my aunt (my mom's youngest sister) got divorced, and then my baby sister. Then it happened to me. It was like a nightmare!

I heard on a program called *The View* that a lot less people are getting married these days.

In February, 2014, I was listening to Channel 9 news. They said there were a lot more divorces the past three years as couples were putting off getting a divorce because of the economy. They also mentioned that it is affecting the housing market because people are searching for a place to live!

Now couples are trying to take a vacation together to try and save their marriage; like a second honeymoon.

Figure out what you have always wanted to do . . . and go for it! Keep busy! Pets are a great help. They give you companionship and unconditional love. My cockatiels knew when I was feeling down and would cuddle with me.

Another suggestion: get help for whatever you need. Help is out there and don't be afraid to ask for it; counseling, medication, whatever it takes, except for, of course, illegal drugs and alcohol. Go out with friends and family. Get involved. Volunteer. Find yourself and concentrate on YOU.

I made a list from the movie with Jack Nicholson and Morgan Freeman, called *The Bucket List*, of things I still wanted to do in my life. I have accomplished all of them, except for traveling to Hawaii, which I will do. I got Invisalign braces, went to see the Grand Canyon, and went to hear The Rolling Stones in concert. I am having fun.

Like my dear sister said to me when she suggested that I not write the book, "Your written book/journaling, served its purpose in a kind of therapy to write it all down so that you could then release it; let it go and move on." She is right to a point, except for just journaling for therapy. She is afraid that some of my family and friends who read my book will be hurt. THAT IS NOT MY INTENTION. My sister said everyone has a story to tell. This is so true. But, who writes about it? My mother also believes that my writing/journaling during and after my divorce was just a kind of therapy.

Right before I was working on the final edit of my book, my sister told me she would not endorse my book; she did not like it; she did not believe it is a Christian based book; and it is about our family.

My Mother does not agree with me pursuing my book either. It talks about our family and she will refuse to read it. She wishes me the best.

I have tried to explain to my sister and Mother that I have spent over ten years working on my book along with a lot of money and I have prayed over this for a year. God is leading me to finish.

I am very hurt by how my sister and Mother feel, but I have to do what I have to do. I wish that I had their support.

A dear friend of mine told me to pursue my book to completion. She told me, "You are a survivor, a compassionate family member and a good friend. Go forth and write your story, Love you."

So, I am moving forward!

I understand there is a dating service out there called Christian Mingle. I don't know anything about it, but it is always a possibility to check into. I have a good friend who met her husband through a dating service and they have been married for 25 years and are very happy.

I recently had a new at home care lady client who almost immediately told me she got divorced many years ago. She called it, "Devastating." Other words; "It's worse than a death, vows are broken, you grieve the end of your marriage vows, it is very painful."

Divorce affects everyone in your life; family, friends, neighbors, your children (younger or older). It changes your whole life.

During my divorce, I was hoping my ex-husband would let me keep my married name after being married for so many years. I did not want to take my Father's last name. I kept my married name. It would have been a nightmare changing my name on all the necessary documents.

An old time friend of mine insisted his ex-wife not take his name after their divorce. They were married for 25 years and she cheated on him!

Look at divorce as a new beginning.

Look at what happened to the three young women in Cleveland who were held captive for a decade before they were finally freed. Miracles do happen. But what an ordeal. How will they ever get through those terrible years? A lot of therapy and love.

I went to see my accountant after I was divorced for a few years. I told her some of the things that happened during the divorce. She made a comment to me, "You could write a book!" I said, "I am!"

Here is my story. I hope whoever reads my book will find comfort in dealing with a divorce and how life goes on after 55. Miracles can happen and with God's help and love from friends and family, you can get through it. I promise. Be strong.

A BIG thank you to my friend, DK in Brooklyn, New York who helped me edit my book off and on for over ten years!

And to my lawyer a big thank you for reviewing the documents from the publisher.

INTRODUCTION

If I have hurt anyone in writing this book, I APOLOGIZE. This is my story!

What would Jesus do? He would love first. Remember, HE is always with you.

Remember, life on earth is just the title page on the book to eternity.

JOY—JESUS ONLY YOU!

I am in need of prayers. After living (renting) a townhouse for ten years, I have to move. It took awhile to feel like home. I love it there. My landlord passed away and her son wants to sell. I cannot afford to buy it, so my broker friend will be looking for a new place to rent.

I hate the thought of moving. I have to relocate my eight birds that have their special aviary room and I am sure it is going to be traumatic for them, and me.

My mother told me, "Well, they are just animals." Yes, but it affects them too.

Alleluia. A friend of mine from choir called me one day to tell me about an apartment For Rent. I called; got approved; moved and I love it. And so do my kids (the birds!).

Word Search

ALCHOLISM
BIBLE
CAREERCHANGE
CHILDHOOD
CHOIR

COCKATIELS
DIVORCE
GOD
INFERTILITY
JOBLOSS

KIDS
LIFE
LOVE

```
                    J  G  H  C
                    D  O  B  H
                    I  D  B  I
        B  L  O  V  E  C  L  B  O  L
        L  H  X  O  J  A  D  O  L  G
        U  I  I  R  C  R  H  K  S  E
        D  W  F  C  O  E  O  I  W  S
                    E  C  E  O
                    I  K  R  D
                    N  A  C  E
                    F  T  H  A
                    E  I  A  L
                    R  E  N  C
                    T  L  G  H
                    I  S  E  O
                    L  B  C  L
                    I  K  H  I
                    T  I  O  S
                    Y  D  I  M
                    P  S  R  G
```

CHAPTER 1

My Story Begins

I believe I had a "normal" childhood, but what is normal?

I am the oldest. I have a sister who is three years younger than me.

My father told me when I was very young that I was choking on a grape. Daddy turned me upside down and there went the grape on the floor.

When I was in kindergarten, there was a cute classmate that had these beautiful black shoes, which I loved and I remember being envious of her. I love clothes and shoes and I guess that was the beginning of loving to dress up.

Mom used to sew clothes for my sister and me when we were young because she couldn't afford to buy us new things. When we were very young, our outfits always matched. My older cousin had beautiful clothes and my aunt would give them to me as hand-me-downs. I was in heaven. Years later, we lost touch with my cousin and aunt. Is that why I love clothes so much and matching shoes and jewelry? I used to work at a small women's dress shop and loved helping the ladies pick out outfits.

Around the time I was in kindergarten, I had to have my tonsils out and my cousin, who I was close to, had his tonsils out at the same time and we shared a room. The things that we remember! I was sick after I had my tonsils out. I recall bleeding from my mouth huge blood clots. At least I had someone in my room that I knew.

Then my parents bought a small house on a busy street in an affluent suburb of Chicago when I was going into fourth grade. I struggled with the move and did not get good grades that year, but at least I passed. I still remember my teacher's name to this day.

My grade school was a few blocks away. I remember at Halloween, the school had a big event. All of the rooms were decorated for Halloween and had games. In the gym, they had my favorite game. Tossing a ping pong ball into fish bowls. I won a goldfish and was so excited!

I was studying one day and my father asked me to come in and listen to something on TV. I was busy studying and told him that, but he thought

I was, "smart mouthing" him and he got up and kept slapping me in the face to the point where my lips were so swollen, I could hardly bear it, or even talk. I told my mom what he did to me and showed her my swollen lips. I think she was afraid to say anything to him.

My Mom had a dear friend, CS. Her and her husband, BS, had two boys and two girls. I had a crush on both of their sons when I was young. We used to go to their house that he built. It was a beautiful home. CS, a fantastic person, years ago had cancer of the voice box which was removed. She had to use a hand-held instrument to talk. It was very sad. I remember my Mom and I used to sit in Mom's kitchen and talk with CS about life. The good ole days!

The removal of the entire voice box is called a laryngectomy and you are no longer able to speak in the normal way. An electrolarynx, which is a battery operated machine, is hand held up to where your voice box would be located, and that produces sound for you to create a voice. It is a very strange sound.

Many years later, we found out a few months before she died, that CS left her apartment, walked out into the street, and someone found her unconscious. She had a major stroke which affected her speech, but the stroke did not affect her arms or legs. She also broke her hip when she fell, but could not have surgery right away because she had a bladder infection. She was in her 80's when she died and was at home where her oldest daughter cared for her till the end. I remember her oldest daughter. A real sweetheart.

I was around 12 years old when my mother asked my father for a divorce. He moved out and my mom kept the house. She struggled raising two girls by herself and working. We didn't even get the "luxury" of drinking pop/soda in those days, unless it was on sale. My father never paid child support. I found out years later that he was a "manic depressant," also known as "bipolar." My mother also told me that my father used to jump from job-to job. He would find a decent job, then quit. One year he went to visit his father in Arizona and came back and told my mother that we were moving to Arizona. She told him she would not move. She had enough. She then asked my Dad for a divorce.

I remember my mother telling me that my dad was in the Navy!

My mother told me when I was a baby, she used to take buses with me in her arms, a stroller, and typing to drop off and get more typing for her job. The home office was in Chicago and we lived in the suburbs. She did what she had to do as my father was jumping from job to job.

One day I received a call from the police that he was a mile from our house, standing in the pouring rain, reading aloud from the Bible. I remember one time he was in jail for something and wanted me to bail him out and

I left him there hoping he would learn his lesson, finally. He was definitely not on his medication

He did move forward in his life. He got remarried; divorced; remarried again and his third wife was lovely. I always wondered what she saw in my father. Love is blind. She was there with him until the end.

I wasn't close to my father. I felt like he favored my sister over me, as she was younger. It took me years to realize that he was my father and that I should respect him. He was sick. I am a Christian and it is called forgiveness. As Matthew 15:4-5 says, "For God commanded, saying, Honor your father and mother."

My dad gave me a hard time when I was at the age when I wanted to get my ears pierced. All the girls were doing it. His reaction to me was, "If God wanted you to have holes in your ears, He would have given you holes in your ears!" After my parent's got divorced, I got my ears pierced.

My mother told me years later that my Dad's biological Father was never found. Someone found his clothes and shoes by a river, but his body was never found. My grandmother got remarried; her husband, who I knew all along as grandpa, adopted my father and aunt.

Ironic; my Dad's biological Father fell off the face of the earth, along with his sister and niece. I tried to locate them, but had no luck. It is very sad. I used to be close to my aunt and cousin years ago.

When our boys were growing up I used to take them to see my father, their grandpa. I remember he was in a facility and my sister and I went to visit him and she went to the ladies' room. While she was gone, the look my father gave me was as if he were saying goodbye. I knew he was going to die. I had a gut feeling. I told my sister and she didn't believe me. Well, he was gone.

Since I was the oldest and my mom worked, I considered myself the "Boss." My sister was leaving one day to walk to our mom's job to pick her up and walk home together. She left too early. I got mad at her because she was leaving way too early and I banged real hard on our dining room window. Well, that was a mistake. My hand went right through the glass window and I was bleeding all over the place. It was painful. I had cut my right thumb, and I am right-handed. I went to our neighbor's house who knew that our mom worked, and she was there for us in case of an emergency. She wrapped my finger up in a kitchen towel and we went to the emergency room. I remember the doctor shooting me in my wound to numb it and stitch it up and it was horribly painful. I had around six stitches. I still have the scar.

One day my mother found out the company she worked for was moving, and she had to buy a car. Before that, she walked six blocks to and from work. That is when her father came to live with us to help us out financially, and bought my mom a 1967 green convertible Mustang. It was a cool car.

When I got my driver's license, I of course wanted to drive, but my mom would not allow it because she depended on the car to get to work. Being a young woman with a driver's license and wanting to drive, my mother and I used to fight over that constantly. Now I understand, but back then I didn't.

When grandpa came to live with us, he took my mom's bedroom and my mom, sister and I shared a very small bedroom together. Let me tell you, that wasn't fun; three girls living in one small room. Plus we only had one bathroom in the house, but we survived.

One year my gentleman friend and I drove by where my grandparents used to live. He was showing me the neighborhoods he grew up in in Chicago. I can't believe I remembered where my grandparents lived. "Memories, like the corners of my mind."

Grandpa worked as a maintenance man at the Dearborn Street Station in Chicago.

When I was very young, my grandmother got real sick with lymphoma. My last memories of her were being so sick and looking awful. She died and I remember having nightmares of her lying in her coffin and getting up and talking to me.

Before my grandmother got very sick, my mom, sister and I used to go visit my grandparent's every Saturday night. We used to watch "Lawrence Welk" and then go back to the kitchen and we each had a fudgicle! Memories.

My dad's parents also lived in Chicago, in an apartment. My grandfather used to spoil us kids for our birthdays. I remember him taking me shopping when I was around 11-years old and buying me a brown skirt with a chain belt and cute blouse. My grandmother never went with us as she was sick. I believe to this day that my father took after her—manic depression, or bi-polar.

My mother told me that my grandfather worked for the Chicago Park District, but she doesn't know what his actual job was or what his job title was. She does remember him bringing home plants for grandma that ate bugs.

When I was a very young girl, I remember going to my dad's relatives' house on a farm. I remember them having a fenced-in area for a beautiful horse and I was envious. My cousin, who used to ride the horse, died at a tragically young age of breast cancer. I also remember hanging out at a gas station across the street from their house. It was like an "Andy of Mayberry" town; small and in the country.

When my sister was around five years old and I was eight years old, we lived in a house that was constantly cold in the winter. There was a creek behind our house, and my mom told my sister never to go back by the water. Well, she didn't listen. She went back by the creek and the neighbor boy, or so my sister said, pushed her into the creek. Thank goodness the water level was low. The boy's older brother helped my sister out of the creek and she came running into the house all wet and dirty. She told our mom the neighbor boy pushed her in. My mom gave my sister a bath and spanked her for going near the creek. Mom told me that the boy, two years later, ended up dying in the creek. He fell in and the water level was high.

My sister and I used to have to help our mother around the house. Clean, cut grass and shovel, not snow-blow, a long driveway. I started working babysitting jobs, and then I got a job as a maid at a local Holiday Inn. Boy, the dirty magazines I used to find underneath the mattresses! I also had a good friend whose mother sometimes got me a job helping out with a catering business. I would walk to work, ride my bike, or sometimes mom would drive me. I was saving to go to college because I wanted to be a nurse. At first, I thought about majoring in music, as I played violin, took private lessons, and played in an orchestra. I was second seat, first violin, which is almost the best. I loved music, but I wanted to be a nurse more. I quit violin in high school and concentrated on studying, working and helping my mother. I was always busy. I never got into trouble.

My mom picked me up from work one day from Holiday Inn. I was being a smart-mouthed young girl to her and she got so mad at me, she pulled over and made me get out of the car and walk home. The walk was around two-miles. By the time I got home, I had chilled out.

Her version of the story: "That day years back when you smarted off at me was when I picked you up from Holiday Inn. Then I dropped you off about half-way home. You were sweet as pie when you got home. Funny the things we remember, right?!"

I had a guy friend that lived two doors down from me. We used to study together, played football and basketball. We got close as we got older and our hormones started to kick in. All we did was kiss. I thought I was in love. He was into building go-carts and I used to watch him build them. He had four other brothers, which at that age I thought was neat. I remember his older brother backing out of the driveway with his car. They shared a driveway with their neighbors (who were our immediate neighbors). I don't remember the details, but when he backed out, I was behind him and the neighbor's car was behind me and I didn't move fast enough and got backed into between the two cars. I remember being rushed to the hospital, but I was okay. No broken bones; just bad bruising. They came to see me at the hospital.

My guy friend had to have surgery when he was younger as he had one leg shorter than the other. I remember visiting him in the hospital while he was recuperating from his surgery. I remember being very upset. Then I found out he had to wear a special shoe. Puppy love! My best friend, who lived a block away, was a few years older than me. I used to hang out at her house more than mine because she had her own room in a finished attic, which I just loved. She also had a pool. When she got her first car, it was a lot of fun driving around with her. It was a white car and had push-buttons for drive, reverse, etc. I remember her father was a baker and he got up really early to go to work. We had to be quiet so he could sleep during the day. We used to walk up and down our busy street flirting with the truck drivers. Those hormones again. And we often went to the corner store for penny candy. We caught lightening bugs and put them in jars and watched them glow.

One day my girlfriend and I were walking by this building where a door was open, and a few cute guys were standing around. We were invited in. What a mistake. We walked down some stairs and there were a whole bunch of guys nude. I stood and stared at one guy because I had never seen a penis before. My girlfriend had to drag me out of there. I drove by the building recently where we saw the nude guys. It is now a hair salon.

Years later, my friend found her father hanging in their garage. How sad and horrible and devastating. I adored her mother; she was like a second mother to me. We kept in touch for many years, but I didn't keep in touch with my girlfriend. She and her husband had bought a new house and my husband and I were buying a home that was being built and, when I showed my girlfriend the pictures of the house, I believe to this day she was jealous and didn't keep in touch. We had friends that had bigger, nicer homes than what we were buying, but I was never envious of them; I was happy for them.

I was also in junior choir at church for years. We used to sing Christmas carols at various houses where members of the church could not get out. How fun: snowing; decorations. I went to church every Sunday with my mom and sister, and went to confirmation classes and got confirmed at my church. I was also involved with the youth group and planned various activities. One cold night we went on a hayride and I remember having a crush on two boys! I adored our pastor. I also taught Sunday School for a few years.

Years later I found out that our pastor and his wife got divorced and he married the choir director. That devastated me. His only daughter's name was Faith. I found out when I got older that the church I grew up in that someone was stealing money. It was unbelievable.

The church building where I grew up is now a Masonic lodge. It is strange to drive by there and see that it is no longer a church.

My sister was the shy one and I was the outgoing one. My sister asked me one day how I could talk to just anyone. I told her, "That's just how God made me."

My mom started dating. I never liked two of the guys she was dating, but it was her life. Then she met a man.

My mom got married to my step-father and he moved into the house with us (I was around 15 years old). He had three sons and a daughter. One son came to stay with us for a while and lived in the basement, which was unfinished. The other two sons were constantly in trouble. Having stepchildren is not easy.

My grandpa that had lived with us for a while moved back to Chicago and lived with his dog, Lucky. Between my mom and my aunt, they checked in on him every day.

My high school friend and I used to listen to the album of the Mamas and Papas and sang along to it. We used to sit on the floor in our closed in back porch. Years later I saw her at one of our high school reunions. It was fun reminiscing.

Funny how when you start thinking of your childhood, you really remember a lot.

My mom sold the house that we moved into when I was going into fourth grade and I was pretty sad. A chapter in our lives that was closed. We lived there for many years.

One door closes and another door opens.

CHAPTER 2

Dating

I was 16 years old. I had a few dates, but that was it. My best friend was dating this guy. They broke up and three months later he called me for a date. The reason why it took him so long to call me was because he was having trouble with his eyes and contacts, or so he said.

So, that was the beginning of our dating

I used to go to local military shows with him. When I first met him, he collected World War II (WW II) daggers and swords and helmets, but eventually he got into buying/selling WW II German postcards. I would help him set-up/take-down his stuff and help at his tables at the military shows. He has been doing this for years and it is a pretty lucrative second business for him. He used to go to Germany to buy postcards. He used to receive phone calls from all over the world because he did auction books once a month so people could bid on his cards. The weird thing is, he used to also have posters of some Hitler pictures. Weird, huh?

I remember wanting to go with him to my high school prom, but he was in Reserve Officers' Training Corps (ROTC) at the time, which is a college-based program for training commissioned officers of the United States Armed Forces, so he took me to their dance and I didn't ever go to my high school prom. I remember my mom sewing me a long gown with big flowers. He did not pursue ROTC because of his bad eyesight.

We used to sit in my mom's living room and watch TV and cuddle. We went to an amusement park called Adventure Land and it was a lot of fun (it eventually closed down).

We used to go to the Indiana and Michigan Dunes and beaches in his 1967 Mustang like my mom had, except it was not a convertible. I have a picture of me when I was 16 in a white bikini. He then worked at a local grocery store in town which years later closed.

When we got older and were able to drink, we used to go to a local club on the top floor of a hotel. They had live bands back then and we danced and had a lot of fun. I remember one night he drank too much and went behind my mom's garage and threw up. It even came out of his nose. How gross is that? The hotel is now a senior living facility.

For a while, before he went off to college, he worked in a factory.

He is a few years older than me, so he went off to college first. He wanted to be a history teacher back then. I became friends with his sister, so we used to party together. Again, we went to a bar with live bands. I met a lot of guys and had a lot of fun, but I missed my boyfriend a lot.

I used to get a lot of love letters from him. I actually found them when I was cleaning the basement out to get the house ready for sale when we were in the process of a divorce. I read a few and cried. I was going to keep them, but I changed my mind. What for? That really, really hurt. But I had to move forward.

One Christmas he gave me a gift certificate to my favorite clothing store. It was called Stuarts. I was in heaven. I loved clothes and I still do.

After we were dating for a while and he got to know my mother, he used to go into the refrigerator and say, "Isn't there anything good to eat (meaning any junk food) in this house?" Wow, did that bother my mother. My sister had a magic marker board on our bedroom door and he used to write all over it. That really made her mad.

When I first met his parents, I was really nervous as they lived in the same affluent town as I did, but... they had a beautiful, huge house and they had money. It was a young woman's dream house.

I graduated from high school in 1974. I received a $500 scholarship for school. I went to nursing school in a small town in Illinois. That was an adjustment. I studied hard and worked at a hospital to help with finances. My mom helped out financially as much as she could. I used to get terrible menstrual cramps due to something called endometriosis. Endometriosis is where the endometrial lining sheds outside the uterus and can adhere to major organs or other areas. When you get your period, the spots on your organs, etc. fill up with blood and cause severe cramping. It is awful. I was working one night at the hospital and got praised by the head nurse for staying, as I was very sick. She even gave me a hand-written note thanking me for staying. I was recently looking through a scrapbook my sister and niece made for mom many years ago. I saw a picture of me with my nursing cap and uniform. I asked my mom if I could get a copy made, to show my friends, which I did. It was from our one-year pinning ceremony.

Speaking of nursing school. I remember one summer I came home and worked at a nursing home. I had to get up really early for work and when I got off of work, I was exhausted. Funny how years later I am working as a certified nursing assistant at a healthcare facility.

I was able to see an OB-Gyn for free because I was a nursing student. He asked me if I was serious about someone and I replied, "Kind of. I have a boyfriend that I have been dating for a few years." The doctor told me that before I could have sex, I would have to have surgery because I had a "crooked hymen" and was not going to be able to have sex without having surgery. So I had the surgery. Having a crooked hymen is rare.

One weekend he came to visit me at school and we got a hotel room, as no boys were allowed in the dorm. We had been dating for a few years and our feelings were strong. I remember that night and the nightgown I wore. It was a long yellow one. I felt so sexy. We were intimate and yes, it happened. We had sex. Wow, I was a woman!

I came home for a visit one weekend. I was fortunate to have a girlfriend in nursing school that was a year older than me, had a car, and lived a few towns away, so I got a ride home from her.

A number of weeks later I came down with the chicken pox and was deathly sick. My sister had been coming down with chicken pox, unbeknownst to any of us. I was halfway done with nursing and had to quit, so I moved back home, got a job in town at a dental insurance company typing checks. I was a fast typist like my mom, who was a secretary. I also learned how to run the massive check printer. Then I got promoted to processing dental claims.

One day we were watching TV and he asked me to marry him. We saved our money, as we were both living at home. We went out and bought an engagement ring together. Now it was time to plan a wedding.

CHAPTER 3

Wedding Plans, Wedding and Honeymoon

We started planning our wedding. Planning a wedding is a lot of work, but fun too. We got the church and my pastor from the Lutheran church I grew up in. My fiancé was brought up Catholic, but converted and became a Lutheran. We booked the hall, hired a photographer, and ordered the flowers, invitations and bridesmaids' dresses. My dress was gorgeous. In 1976 when I bought it, the dress and veil cost $600.00, which was a lot of money back then, but I loved it. My sister got married a few years later and wore my dress, which was touching. All she wanted to do was change the neckline because it was a high neck and she wanted a scoop neck, which she got professionally altered. It was off-white and had French lace on it. I felt like a princess. We found an apartment, bought furniture and my fiancé was living there before we got married. I loved that word, fiancé."

We wanted to buy a beautiful townhouse before we got married, but for some reason, which I don't remember, his parents' talked us out of it. We could have made a bundle off of it if we'd bought it and then sold it. It was gorgeous. Maybe they thought we couldn't afford it.

We took ballroom dance lessons so that we would look good on the dance floor at the reception.

It was time to plan our honeymoon. We decided on a Caribbean cruise. We were all set to go.

My favorite aunt surprised us with a bridal shower. It was great. All of the memories of the fun, gifts, friends and family and the huge umbrella bridal shower decoration. We all had a great time and my aunt, who gave us the shower, has now gone to heaven.

The day of our wedding, in May 1977, the church was packed. My flower girl was my fiance's cousin's daughter. Everything went well. Of course I cried walking down the aisle with my father. Before the wedding we had pictures taken at my mom's house with the bridesmaids, flower girl and our dog and cat. I had to have our pets in the pictures. I grew up with animals!

The reception was perfect. I remember the hall where we had it, which featured a winding staircase where we had pictures taken.

The reception was packed. We had a band and a suite table. When my husband and I walked in as they announced us as husband and wife, everyone stood up and clapped. They clanked their glasses with silverware for us to kiss, so we did. We ate dinner and then showed off with the first dance. It was so much fun, especially since we had taken dance lessons.

I found out that my cousin, who I saw wearing a tight dress, did not wear a bra and panties to my wedding. Boy did that make me mad.

We decided to slip out early as we had to get up early for our cruise. We thought we were being sneaky, but my father, who was drunk, followed us to the car. He tapped my husband on the head and one of his contacts fell out and landed in between where the window goes down. Thank goodness we found it. I remember my father gave us $5.00 for a wedding gift. Sad, huh?

We went back to the apartment for our honeymoon to save money. We opened up all of our envelopes and threw the money all over the bed. We made out like bandits!

The next morning we got up early to catch our plane. I had new sexy outfits and was excited, although nervous. I had never been on a plane before. I am afraid of heights.

We got to the ship and boarded. The first night was, "Meet the Captain Night." It was a big celebration. I remember wearing a sexy, red jumpsuit. They had some crew members walking around with sparklers and it made me nervous with my outfit. Well, I was right. One of the sparklers fell down the back of my jumpsuit and burned it. Of course, I was upset. Eventually I did get reimbursed for the outfit by the cruise line.

The first day we went out sunbathing. What a mistake. I am blonde and fair skinned. I was burned to a crisp. I wore a skimpy bikini and my chest got so burned, I blistered and it was painful. No more sun for me.

The food, entertainment, everything was awesome. We met a few couples that got married the same day that we did. It was a lot of fun.

Now for the bad news. Midway into our trip, the ship lost its stabilizer and rocked back and forth. I was prone to getting car sick and boy did I get seasick. Between that and a sunburn, our honeymoon didn't involve a lot of sex. What a bummer.

CHAPTER 4

Beginning of our Marriage

A number of years after I got married, I started taking private violin lessons again. I played in a duet at my good friend's wedding and my cousin's wedding and played in a local symphony for a number of years at Christmas. I also played at odd jobs with my violin teacher and a few other violinists. I remember playing at a house at Christmastime. The house was beautiful and it was rewarding to play at someone's home. So I did keep up my music, I just didn't major in it.

We rented an apartment the first year of our marriage. When I was looking for a place to live after my husband asked me for a divorce and I knew I would have to sell the house, I checked that particular apartment complex out to possibly move into. What a weird feeling. Then we bought a small house. When I say small, it was small. It had two bedrooms, one bathroom, a living room, kitchen and a laundry room. It was on a slab and got cold in the winter, as we had the old-fashioned metal, crank windows. But, it was a start. We had a good sized backyard and a detached one-car garage. He would cut the grass and I would plant flowers. We were happy. We used to go on a winter vacation every year in December to get away from the cold. It was great.

When we were married about a year, my husband ran in the Chicago Marathon. I was so proud of him. What a great accomplishment. He could never run again because he developed back problems.

My husband bought me a white 1977 Trans Am before we got married. I was 21 and had my first car and the car had a big red bird on the front and red velour seats. It had a powerful engine, so it was hard not to speed. I thought I was hot stuff! After we had the car for a few years, we decided to sell it. I almost got killed in it a few times. It fishtailed on the ice, snow and rain. I wish now we would have hung onto it. It probably would be worth a lot of money. I did love that car.

When my husband was out of town for his job and I was at the local mall shopping (retail therapy), it was already dark outside when I got to my car. I went to put the key in the ignition, but it was broken and the seat was pushed back. Someone had tried to steal our car. I was scared. Thank goodness there was a mall security vehicle and I walked up to him and told him what had happened and he checked out the car. He was nice and followed me to the apartment which was only a short distance from the mall. It scared me to death.

Then one day, while he was out of town working as a salesman for his father, who owned his own business, which my husband eventually took over, I somehow found out about a puppy and bought her. She was adorable. I remember I was gone somewhere and my sister picked up the puppy and brought her to the house. She cried all night. When my husband got home from being out of town, he laid on the floor with the puppy during the night. We used to walk our dog around this big lagoon that was a half block from our house. Life was good.

We lived in our first house for six years, and we did improvements on it such as central air, a new driveway, and remodeling the kitchen and the bathroom. It looked nice. Then we put it up for sale. A young couple bought the house and added a second level to it. It didn't even look like our house anymore.

We were looking for a bigger house and found one out in what was then the country. You could smell the cows. It was great. The house had three bedrooms, two and a half baths and a good-sized kitchen with an area that could accommodate a big table. There was also a dining room, living room, family room, basement and a two-car attached garage. It had a small yard with a deck. The best part was a loft that overlooked the family room, which had a gorgeous fireplace that went from the floor to the ceiling.

I do not remember a lot of the details, but I remember drinking wine at my mom's house a few years after I got married. I got sick from drinking and was vomiting in a big huge pot and I remember saying to my mom, "He doesn't love me anymore." Why? I don't know. But, it happened many years later.

We used to go away in the winter to try and conceive a baby. We visited tropical islands, and even Germany, for my husband's side business, which was buying/selling German postcards. Before he told me he wanted to take me to Germany, I never thought I would visit Europe. It was cold there; we went in November: overcast, but it was great. I bought a cuckoo clock which I brought with me after the divorce as he didn't want it. Many years later I gave it to my oldest son. He complained about having to carry it on the plane on the flight home. I would have loved to have been able to go to Switzerland, but there was no time.

Around six years later, my husband wanted to move closer to work, as he was taking over his father's business and he was traveling to and from work for too long. I told him that we wouldn't move until we could find a house I loved just as much, or even better, as the one we were living in.

We found the house of our dreams and lived there for 25 years. I loved that house, but had to sell if after our divorce.

I call it the house of our dreams. Four bedrooms, 2 ½ baths, big size kitchen, dining room, living room, family room with a beautiful fireplace, full basement. We loved it. Until, the first two years living there, an old house across the street had tons of cats climbing all over the house. The stench that came out of there smelled like death. I called, along with the neighbors, the Health Department. The owner was told to clean it out. This went on for years. His cats would miscarry fetuses on our driveway and our boys at the time were very young. What if they picked one up? It was very sad and I was ready to move again. Eventually, after a number of years, the owner died and the house was renovated. It was very cute after that. Before it got renovated, I got to go into the house. The smell was so horrible I ran out gagging. Now things were great, but it took up to five years.

CHAPTER 5

Infertility and Coping

Now it was time to start trying to have a baby. We went on another vacation. Nothing was happening. We tried to have a baby for over a year. Our doctor at the time told us that a couple is considered infertile if the woman does not get pregnant within a year of trying. I don't know if that is still the case today.

It was the beginning of eight years of trying to conceive. He got tested. He was okay. He made some comment like, "Of course it's not me; I am Italian." It was me. I had something called endometriosis, which for some reason causes infertility. As I mentioned in an earlier chapter, endometriosis is when the lining of the uterus sheds outside of the uterus and can adhere to major organs. It was painful when I got my period. It was horrible. I would get menstrual cramps a few days before my period and I couldn't work. I would lie in bed on a heating pad and took pain pills. There is now a tv commercial advertising a medication for endometriosis. I pray it heals women as it is a very painful disorder. It controls your life.

We tried Lupron (hormone) shots, which my husband had to inject in my upper buttock area, and I remember having all of these fertile eggs. I was miserable. Nothing happened. I had three laparoscopies to laser out the endometriosis. Nothing happened. I was still in a lot of pain. Why me God? HE had a plan.

Laparoscopic surgery, also called minimally invasive surgery, Band-Aid surgery, keyhole surgery, belly button surgery, is a modern technique in which operations in the abdomen are performed through small incisions, as opposed to the larger incisions needed in a laparotomy.

During the eight years we tried to conceive, I had three laparoscopies to laser out the endometriosis.

Nothing happened. I was still in a lot of pain. Why me God? HE had a plan.

We went on a few more vacations. We even went to the Sybaris, which is a romantic cabin type place you go to for romance. They had an indoor pool

INFERTILITY AND COPING

and a fireplace. At least it was fun trying. I was also put on a medication to stop my menstrual cycles for six months. The next month after I was off of the medication, I had bad pain again. Was it ever going to stop? It did. I went through menopause at 38 years old, which is young, and no more pain.

My husband got, yes, marijuana, and we smoked that a few times. It was great sex. Nothing happened. He used to have "premature ejaculation," so he bought me a vibrator to help with our sex life. Since it had been so long since we had sex before the divorce, I asked him, "Can you still get it up?" These things happen to men of his age. He told me he had no problem with that. Sure. I did not believe him.

We were given a low chance of conceiving and if we wanted to try in-vitro fertilization, the odds of success were 25 percent. I had to go often to the infertility doctor before work. It was a nightmare. Were we ever going to conceive? I was all-consumed with this. I used to see young girls pregnant and would cry my eyes out and when I saw tv commercials with babies.

We also tried using my husband's sperm and inseminating me when I had eggs ready for the big day of conceiving, but still nothing.

In vitro fertilization (IVF) is a process by which an egg is fertilized by sperm outside the body. IVF is a major treatment for infertility when other methods of assisted reproductive technology have failed.

I talked to my auto mechanic's wife. They have been trying to have a baby and everything checked out. I asked her if she wanted to talk about infertility and she did. Hopefully I gave her some words of wisdom and support.

I remember telling my husband that he could divorce me if he wanted to because I couldn't give him a baby. He told me that I was "being silly." Funny how things turn out and we ended up divorcing.

We started checking into private adoptions. There was a lot of paperwork and the costs were expensive, so we took a breather.

I remember going to our in-law's house one winter day. We couldn't get home to take our dog out, so we called one of our vet friends to walk her. When we got home, there was a note that our baby was let out to go potty and she ran away. She never did like our friend for some reason. She used to pee on the carpet whenever he would come over

I remember being on the phone with my mom when we finally got home, crying my eyes out that our dog ran away. No pregnancy and now our baby had run away. We were on the phone talking at midnight. We had two side windows next to our front door, with shears on them that were tied in the middle. There she was, wagging her tail. Thank God she was okay. She was full of mud, so we gave her a warm bath. Our baby was home!

Our dear friends were having problems conceiving at the same time as we were and they were also going through some infertility treatments. She called me one day to tell me she was pregnant and I was so happy for them.

My sister called me one evening at the office when I was working late for a lawyer. She was crying; I guessed what it was. She was coming home for a holiday visit and she was pregnant. I told her I was happy for her and that I wouldn't wish infertility on my worst enemy.

One day I was watching a TV show and they mentioned that there are donation sites for couples with infertility, in order to help couples out, because it's so expensive.

Interesting Point—You do not have to have intercourse to conceive. That happened to a friend of mine. She got pregnant and didn't even have sex. Try explaining that to your parents! Her partner had horny sperm!

Point: I am sure that couples that are having infertility problems and that have to have sex on a certain day find it difficult. It seems like stressful work and it is. It is not like you are craving your partner. It is a baby you are working for and that takes the enjoyment away from the sex. It's business, so to speak. The most joyous sex becomes a chore: basal-thermometers, menstrual calendars and ovulation charts.

We were never able to conceive a baby.

CHAPTER 6

Friends

I met one of my dear friends at my first office job. She started after I did and I made her feel at home with her new job and on her first day, I took her out to lunch. We hit it off immediately. She was originally from Indiana. She is my friend who married a race-horse vet and had problems with infertility, but was able to get pregnant and had a girl and a boy. I was happy for her. We lived in the same neighborhood out in the country for many years and used to get together a lot. We had fun times.

Then I met another friend through my sister-in-law. We used to party together when my boyfriend was in college and many years later, we touched base. She was our real estate broker for the house that had to be sold before the divorce.

We used to have get-togethers once a month at a couple's house. It was the couple from Indiana, another friend we met through my sister-in-law who got married, had kids, and we used to have a lot of get-togethers. Everyone was married, except for the third couple (friends of our friends from Indiana). The couple who were having a get together at their house were responsible for providing the meal, including dessert and drinks. We used to have a blast. We played games and drank.

One Halloween party we all dressed up in costumes. I dressed up as a sexy nurse and my friend's husband dressed up as a streaker. I remember he had a fake, large penis underneath his trench coat and there was a picture taken of me holding it as a joke. When I was cleaning the house out to get it ready for sale because of getting divorced, I found the picture and it made me chuckle.

Another year we had a New Year's Eve party at our house and played strip poker; nothing vulgar or dirty. But boy, did we drink, especially tequila. We threw confetti all over at midnight. The next morning I woke up to sticky tequila all over the floor and there was confetti everywhere, but it was worth it because we had a great time. I remember when we moved out of that house, I found confetti on top of the ceiling fan in the family room.

I have friends that I have known for years. It wasn't until we were friends for many years that I figured out that they were lesbians. They helped me deal with the fact that my son was gay.

My father-in-law and husband hired someone to work with them. Let's call him "G." He was let go because of the economy. My husband, "G," his girlfriend and I went to Florida for a business trip. This was before he was let go. We had a good time and became good friends. I remember going into the pool with my husband one night and went skinny dipping. It was my idea. I remember going to "G's" sister's house for a visit and she had the same bedroom furniture as my husband and I. "G's" girlfriend, let's call her "M," home staged our house when I was getting it ready to sell before the divorce and she did a great job. We were hoping that her business cards would get her some more jobs, but no luck. We have kept in close touch since the divorce.

My friend from Indiana and I are still friends after many years. She was recently diagnose as having Parkinson's Disease. Her and her husband, the race horse vet, also got divorced years before I did. He passed away and I saw my ex-husband at the wake. There were pictures on a screen of all of us at our first house. Memories.

Parkinson's signs and symptoms may include:

- **Tremor.** A **tremor**, or **shaking**, usually begins in a limb, often your hand or fingers. . . .
- Slowed movement (bradykinesia). . . .
- Rigid muscles. . . .
- Impaired posture and balance. . . .
- Loss of automatic movements. . . .
- Speech changes. . . .
- Writing changes.

I also found out from my girlfriend that her daughter, who I used to babysit for, stole money from her, unbeknownst to my friend. I do not know all of the details, but she had to file bankruptcy.

Years later they are talking. Her daughter ended up being hospitalized and was diagnosed as being bi-polar. It is so very sad.

CHAPTER 7

Our First Miracle

I was working for a real estate lawyer as a legal secretary at the time. He was a real sweetheart and I loved working for him.

I never discussed my problem with infertility and why would I?

Then, the Big Day finally arrived.

I got back from my lunch break. I'll never forget it as long as I live. My mother-in-law had left me a voicemail message to call her back immediately. I called her and she asked me, "Are you sitting down?" I replied "Yes, what's going on?"

She proceeded to tell me that she knew of someone that put us on the top of an adoption list at a doctor's office where her sister-in-law worked and that there was a baby boy available for adoption. I was in shock. She never said anything to us about this.

She told me who to call at the doctor's office and I called her immediately. I also called my husband, who was out-of-town.

That was the beginning of our new life. I went in to talk to my boss and told him the good news. I finished my work, and had to take some time off to find an adoption attorney. My boss helped us find one. I remember his name to this day.

The process started. We had to prepare for this baby boy in three days! Normally, you have nine months to plan.

I ran out for an outfit for our new son—a Christmas outfit, as this was in December. Then there was formula to buy, furniture, etc.

We were planning a Christmas Eve dinner at our house that year. We were ready to go and we were all waiting.

The lawyer came to our front door and delivered our baby boy. He was perfect. He even had red hair. My husband and I debated on his name, but I gave in with the name he chose. Everyone was speechless. An Italian first name and our son was part Irish!

Our neighbor let us borrow a beautiful bassinette and all was well.

It took six months for the adoption to become legal. Another awesome day when we received the news that the adoption was final. I was 30 years old.

I was a stay-at-home mom. It was great. Our Christmas miracle. It was one of the happiest days of my life, including getting married.

I quit my job working for the lawyer. We had waited over eight years for this day.

On Christmas Day, we went to the home of my husband's family as we did every year. They lived on the second floor and his uncle asked, as we were walking up the stairs, "What do you have in there? A puppy?" "No," I replied. "We have our son." Everyone was shocked. What a fantastically wonderful Christmas present.

My in-law's neighbor had a great baby shower for us and invited my friends from where I used to work (the law office). The girls from the office teased me that my son was, "Well endowed." I was changing his diaper.

We got our son baptized at the church I grew up in. We were happy.

I kept busy being an at-home mom with a new baby. I had doctor appointments, took him shopping with me, looked after our dog, and cooked dinner for my husband every night. Life was good.

I went out to California to visit my sister and brother-in-law when our son was three months old. My niece was four months older than our son, so we had a lot of fun. My sister and I went out one night to a male strip club and had a blast. We had never done anything like that together before. I gave her some single dollar bills to put in the dancer's G-string!

I remember I wanted to try to breast feed our son, since I could not feel what it would ever be like to be pregnant. My husband told me not to because I had enough problems with my body due to the endometriosis. The doctor told me all that we had to do was give me a shot and it would start the mammary glands to produce milk. I look back now and should have done it anyway. But, we got a baby, which we never expected.

Every year when we celebrate his birthday, my mom always talks about the special day our miracle baby arrived at our front door.

CHAPTER 8

Our Second Miracle

I was home one day getting ready for our annual family Christmas Eve dinner. The door-bell rang. It was the woman from the doctor's office that was responsible for putting us on the top of the adoption list. She had a gift and I assumed it was for our son's birthday as he was born in December. She asked him to open the gift—it was a small teddy bear. She asked him to open the second present and proceeded to say, "This is for your future baby brother or sister."

I was in shock, again! Our son's biological mother was pregnant again and she wanted us to have the baby. I told her, "Yes" and called my husband first, of course, and then everyone under the sun.

This time we had more time to prepare for a baby; four months. After I told her we would adopt the baby, I proceeded to call our lawyer. I couldn't believe it. She got pregnant again, only with a different guy. I found out years later she had a baby girl and decided to keep her. We would have adopted her as well in a heartbeat. I was upset; I wanted the girl. I felt the kids belonged together. My girlfriend told me not to be like that. Not to be greedy. She had had trouble conceiving too; ironic, huh? But, she and her husband did conceive and had a girl and then a boy.

I remember her making a comment that I didn't have to go through all of the "pregnancy stuff," and had my babies delivered to the front door! She was just kidding.

Well, our son was born and we adopted again. I was a busy mom with two boys and stayed at home to take care of them. I did miss work, but I was happy. Actually, I did miss typing, taking shorthand and my friends.

Our sons don't look anything alike, though some people have told us they look like us.

Our youngest son was a pill. He had projectile vomiting and had colic and kept me up a lot. I was exhausted. He didn't sleep through the night until he was fifteen months old. Thank goodness he was our second child because if he was our first, I don't know if I would have wanted to go through having another child. We were blessed with our first born son being a good baby.

I remember early one morning our youngest was crying and I brought him down into the family room.

I got so frustrated with him, that when I was lying on the couch, I threw a pillow at the swing I put my son in so that he would hopefully fall asleep. I didn't hit my son with the pillow. I was just exhausted.

To earn some extra money for myself, I did some babysitting for an infant boy, out of our house. One of the lawyers I used to car-pool with from the office needed me; only he was an older child. I also watched my neighbor's adopted daughter after school. My sister and brother-in-law and niece had moved in with us for three months, so things were hectic, but fun. My sister and I used to put the kids in the bathtub together and my niece would scream bloody murder when she got her hair washed. My son would sit in the tub, all happy, and look at her like, "What is your problem?" They are very close even today!

After my sister and husband and niece moved out, I was babysitting for my niece at the time and my sister would bring her to the house around 4:30 a.m. My sister paid me for babysitting. Boy, between our youngest son not sleeping a lot and getting my niece at the door at 4:30 a.m., I WAS POOPED OUT.

One day our dog bit our oldest son in the face. Our dog was 10-years old. I couldn't have that. If she bit our son, she could do it to one of the kids that I was babysitting for. I called our neighbor and she watched the boys. I called the vet's office and was told to come in right away, that there would be a room for me so that I could say good-bye to our dog. I called my husband and told him that I was going to put our dog down.

When my husband got home, he looked around for the dog and asked me where she was. My reply was, "She is in doggy heaven." He wasn't mad, but couldn't believe I had her put to sleep. He didn't believe that I could do it, but I did. They were supposed to have a room at the vet's office for me to say goodbye to my sweetie-pie, but they were so busy, there wasn't a room available. I had to say good-bye in the waiting room in front of all of these people crying my eyes out. Then I had to drive home.

I saw a sticker on someone's car that read, "Your mom chose life." That touched my heart. That's what our boys' biological mother did. She chose life instead of an abortion, two times, which had to be really tough for her and her family.

There is an adoption saying that talks about an adopted child not being of your flesh or bone, but they are yours. They grew in your heart. It is beautiful and touching.

My mom cross-stitched and framed that saying when we adopted our first-born son. I was at a craft show and there was a purple (my favorite color) picture frame with this saying. I bought it and put a picture of my husband and our oldest son, who my husband was holding, and me being given our second baby at the front door by our lawyer. My youngest son loved it so much, I saved the business card and had one made for him for his birthday when he was older. I was touched to see it hanging in his bedroom.

Adoption is a wonderful gift from God.

CHAPTER 9

Raising Boys—Family

Parenthood is not an easy job, but well worth it. I have a friend that I used to work with, a single mom, who was raising a nine-year-old son by herself. I tried to help her with her problems with him. She had to leave him alone when she went to work. Very sad. The dad was not in the picture.

My husband and I were fortunate to have his mom and dad, my mother and her gentleman friend, to babysit for our boys so that we could go away or go out with friends. I remember my mom and the "love of her life," watched the boys. He was great with them. They would play board games, do puzzles together, and even watched my birds.

One Christmas, right before we were having our family over, my husband was on the floor playing with a train set with our oldest son and threw out his back. We had not adopted our youngest son yet. He has had back problems since we were first married; degenerative disk disease. He thinks he hurt it in high school working at the local grocery store or shoveling snow when we were first married. He did finally find something that worked. It is known as prolotherapy. He received around 45 injections of vitamins to build up the muscles in his back. He was going every six months. This was not covered under insurance and cost $500.00 per visit.

He used to go on Boy Scout camping trips with our oldest son and many times he would have to be driven home as he threw out his back and I would have to call the ambulance and have him brought up on a stretcher to our bedroom. A number of times when he threw out his back, he could not go to the bathroom and I would have to give him a urinal before I left for work. When I got home from work, I would have to empty his urinal. Oh, joy in the morning.

One day he threw out his back and went to the hospital. He was in there for a week. I remember his mom coming to visit him and he was screaming in pain. It was unbearable for her hearing him scream and she started crying. She didn't cry often.

He was home for around a day or so. I was sleeping in the next room as he had to have a board under the mattress for his back and I couldn't sleep. He crawled into the room I was sleeping in complaining he couldn't breathe. I called the paramedics. He was diagnosed with a small blood clot in his lung due to being inactive for so long. He was in the hospital for a week and was receiving injections of Heparin, a blood thinner. When he got home from the hospital, he was put on Coumadin, a blood thinner pill, for around six months. It was scary.

I was always there for him.

I remember I used to take something called Metabalife to help lose weight as I wanted to try to be my husband's Barbie Doll. I was on the Metabalife for quite some time and I had to go to the doctor because I developed bruises all over my legs. The doctor sent me to the hospital for a leg ultrasound to determine what was causing the bruises, which were painful. The woman who did the test asked me if I was in a car accident. The results from the test came back and I was bruising due to something in the weight loss pill.

My husband also has an eye disease called keratoconus. He has to wear two contacts in each eye; a hard one and a soft one. It is frustrating for him. He used to lose a contact in the bathroom quite often and asked me if I could look for it. I always found it for him, except for one time I could not find it. A few days later, I went down into the basement to do laundry and I found his contact on the basement floor. He could not believe I found it.

When our oldest turned one-year old, we had a birthday party at the house. I made a teddy bear cake. It turned out adorably cute, except when we went to cut it, we could not cut into it. All I could figure out was I used coconut in the frosting which made it hard. My husband went out to the garage and got the electric saw as a joke. It was one of the family jokes!

While my husband was out of town for his job, our oldest son scared me. He was sleep-walking. I thought that someone was in the house. All of a sudden I saw a shadow in the hall outside my bedroom door. I talked to him, but he didn't respond. I put him back to bed. He outgrew that pretty quickly, thank goodness.

Right before Thanksgiving, my husband would fly to Germany for his side business; buying and selling German postcards. A few years before I had gone back to work as a legal assistant for a real estate company. I needed to go back to work to cover my family for health insurance.

I had a few more scary events happen while raising the boys.

When our oldest was around three-and-a-half to four years old, he woke up one morning with red spots all over his lips and bruises all over his legs and arms. The first thought that came to my mind was leukemia. My mother-in-law's brother had just died of leukemia.

I called the pediatrician and got our son in to see her immediately. He was sent to the hospital. I called our neighbor to see if she could watch our younger son for a while, as I didn't know how long I would be. I called my husband and he rushed to the hospital.

Well, thank goodness it wasn't leukemia. It was something called ITP, Acute Idiopathic Thrombocytopenia Purpura. It's a bleeding disorder in which the immune system destroys platelets, which are necessary for normal blood clotting. People with the disease have too few platelets in the blood.

I'll never forget it. The doctor told us it was a virus that invaded our son's spleen and lowered his white blood count.

When my husband got to the hospital, he cried his eyes out. I told him to compose himself for our son's sake as he needed us to be strong.

He was in the hospital for a week. My husband stayed with him the first night and I went home to be with our youngest son. The next morning my husband told me that our son was down in the emergency room. He was hemorrhaging through his nose and had to have his nose packed. What an eyesore for me to see him in that condition. Poor little buddy. He looked bad.

Our dear friends had come for a visit. My friend's husband had never been to a hospital (he hated hospitals) and I appreciated him coming. He cried when he saw our son.

Our son came home within a week and was fine and never got ITP again.

When our youngest was real little, he was moving on his butt to the beat of "Do You Love Me," by The Contours from 1962. It was so cute. Years later, I went to hear a show called "Motown" with a friend. It was a great show and one of the songs that they sang was "Do You Love Me." It brought back good memories.

When the boys were younger, I took them to a local drug store/gift shop. I had them in a grocery cart and told them both to stay still while I went a few feet away to pick out some Halloween candy. In the blink of an eye, the cart had tipped over and my youngest son was bleeding all over. I screamed out for help and when I went to pick him up, he was screaming hysterically as well. The cart had fallen on his pinky finger and his finger tip was hanging there. Thank goodness it wasn't cut off.

I got a rag and wrapped it, and someone called the ambulance. We went to the emergency room and he was stitched up. We had to go to a specialist to make sure there was no nerve damage, which there wasn't, thank God.

Once, when our youngest was around two years old, he came up to me and said, "Goddammit; son of a bitch." I asked him to repeat it because I could not believe my ears. I told him to go tell his father and grandfather what he said. I then asked him where he heard that from and he responded, "The TV." It was so cute coming from this little blonde cutie pie.

I used to take the boys to church, alone, when they were young. I loved the church, but when we moved when they were still young, it was too long of a drive, so I found the church that I am a member of now.

My husband's father used to come over to see his grandsons quite a bit while my mother-in-law went to Texas to visit their daughter and family. I would ask him to come over for dinner. When our kids were young, our oldest was riding his bike and our youngest was sitting on the front porch with me. Grandpa drove up in his Cadillac and the boys ran to meet him. It was so sweet

Whenever I invited Grandpa over, he would say, "Yes I'll come unless I get a better offer!"

When the boys were young, we used to take them on the train into the city to see Santa Clause at the Marshall Field's department store. It is now owned by Macy's. It was a lot of fun.

It was a beautiful day outside and I took the boys to the park. When I was trying to take my younger son out of his car seat, he was in the back seat, my foot got caught in the seat belt. I remember falling backwards and held onto my son for dear life. I saw stars and passed out for a short period of time. I couldn't move. I asked my oldest son calmly to get a nice lady at the park to help us. I was rushed by ambulance with the boys to the emergency room. I fell on a bunch of rocks on my coccyx bone and badly bruised it.

When our older son was around five years old and our youngest son was around three, somehow our youngest got locked in the bathroom and was crying his eyes out. I couldn't get to him. I had to call the police to get him out. Grandpa came over and our oldest was sitting on his lap. Grandpa adored his first-born grandchild. He waited long enough. That's normal. Grandpa was talking to our oldest son about, "I heard your mom locked your brother in the bathroom and she had to call the police." Our son replied, "No grandpa, the cops." We have it on video. It's adorable. The look they had between them was priceless. Our cute, chubby redhead.

The next day the phone rang and it was my cousin's husband, a Chicago police officer. He disguised his voice and said something to the affect,

"Ma'am . . . we heard that you locked your son in the bathroom and we are investigating this." It scared me to death. Funny. Then I knew that it was him.

I remember one year I had no idea what to buy for my in-laws for watching the boys. They could buy anything that they wanted and I ran out of ideas and my husband was no help at all.

I came up with a Polish basket with all sorts of food and snacks. I thought it was a great idea. My mother-in-law was Polish. She died at 95 years old in 2021 from complications due to covid. I ordered it from a local floral-gift store around the corner from our house that I had been going to for years. I was working at the office at the time and my girlfriend from the floral-gift shop called me and told me that my mother-in-law refused the gift. I could not believe it. Refusing a gift. How rude. I asked my friend to deliver it to our house and we would enjoy it. Needless to say, I told my husband what had happened and he didn't say a word. I was livid.

My Father-in-Law had a company Christmas party one year. Oh my gosh (OMG). My Mother-in-Law ruined the entire night. She was rude to the guests. She complained about her potatoes. What a terrible night. On the way home, I told my husband that I could not believe how his Mom had acted. She misbehaved something awful. He said nothing. Now when I look back, I believe she was starting to go through the beginnings of dementia. Now, years later, she was diagnosed with late stage Alzheimer's. I find it very interesting that I felt something was wrong with her. I was right. I was not a CNA (certified nursing assistant) yet! I guess this was my calling.

We used to go every Sunday to my in-law's house to spend time together so that they could see their grandsons. We used to watch "*60 Minutes*" and other TV shows, and order pizza from our favorite place.

I would take the day after Thanksgiving off and the boys and I would go and pick out a Christmas tree together and then go home and decorate it together. This was one of our traditions. Dad was in Germany for his business. One year my husband brought me back some perfume from Germany, which I still buy to this day.

When the boys got a little older, I worked part-time at a woman's dress shop that was located in the affluent town I grew up in. I loved helping women find outfits and they really liked me.

One year the dress shop had beaver fur coats on consignment from New York. They were such a good deal, I asked my husband to buy me one, saying he would not have to buy me a gift for a whole year. He agreed and, to this day, I still have it and still get a lot of compliments on it. Since it is so old, it costs a lot of money to keep it up; stitching, cleaning, storage. Now it is too old and I can't wear it anymore—the stitching is torn because the skin is too old and dry.

Every few years we drove to the Lake of the Ozarks in Missouri with my in-laws. My sister-in-law and family from Texas met us there. The kids loved it in the Ozarks. My husband had lost one of the accounts he represented right before Christmas and his sister knew it and never said a word. I had a few glasses of wine one night and we went back to our room to talk and I told her off.

One year we went with friends to Disney World and had a fantastic time. My husband did not want to go, but he did it for our kids and he had a great time. He got up on stage during one of the performances of "Raiders of the Lost Ark."

A few years before our 25th wedding anniversary, we went to Las Vegas with my cousin and his wife. What a great place for a vacation. It was my first time at a casino and my cousin and husband went to gamble. My cousin's wife and I went to the slot machines. All of a sudden, she screamed out that she had won $1,000 and we were only there less than a half hour. She asked me to go get my cousin. He didn't believe me, but he followed me. There she was getting crisp, new $100 bills. She treated us to dinner to celebrate our anniversary. We had a lot of fun; sunbathed, saw shows. Oh, the good times.

My husband and I went to Atlantis, off Paradise Island, Nassau, to celebrate our 25th wedding anniversary. What a beautiful place to go, and it's not a long plane ride. There is the underwater City of Atlantis that is under a tunnel type area. You can sit down there and relax and look at all of the beautiful fish. It's gorgeous and we had a great time. It's an underwater paradise of fish.

The island had a black-out which was unbelievably scary. I remember my husband was downstairs gambling and I went to the room to read. I was so scared that I called my mother in Illinois.

Fortunately, my husband and I could afford to send the boys to private grade school and high school. It was my husband's idea. Even though we were raising the boys Lutheran, the best schools were Catholic. I had a problem with this, so I called our pastor. He said it was, "one God," so the boys were off to private Catholic school. A great thing about sending your children to a private school is that they get to wear uniforms, so you don't have to argue with them about what they are going to wear and keeping up with the fashions.

I found out shortly after that my sister and brother-in-law were sending my niece to private school.

I remember having a 50th surprise birthday party at the house for my husband. It was a great party. Boy . . . did I surprise him!

My younger son used to take acting lessons, singing lessons, dance lessons and piano lessons (at the house). It was a lot of fun helping at the various acting shows. I helped in the back room to get the kids changed. Then the teacher started an adult acting class. I was involved in that for three-years. It was fun, but a lot of work.

Some of the shows our son was in: *Titanic, West Side Story, Set the Night to Music, The Wizard of Oz, Hello Dolly, The Secret Garden,* and *How to Succeed in Business without Really Trying.* I plan on making him a scrapbook of his life. I made one for my older son one year for his birthday and really enjoyed making it. What you do for one son, you have to do for the other son, right?

Both boys played softball, soccer and took Tae Kwon Do lessons. I kept busy. While the boys were at Tae Kwon Do, I used to take a long, peaceful walk.

My oldest has always loved puzzles ever since he was young. I asked him if he would put a puzzle together for me of a koala bear because I love them so much. It was so cute, I put a frame on it and have it hung in a hallway.

Then, menopause happened (the big "M."). When I went to the doctor shortly after I turned 38, he told me I wasn't ovulating.

I was studying every night with my younger son and helping him with his homework. When it came to math, we finally got a tutor to come to the house. I was so tired after working all day and had to come home and help my younger son study. The next night he would not remember what we had studied. He was diagnosed with ADD (attention deficit disorder). Oh my gosh. I was going through hot flashes and just was not myself. The hot flashes started in my head and ran down to my feet. So, I insisted on a blood test. When the doctor called me, he told me I was in full-fledged menopause. My response to him was, "You are in big trouble Mr." I was put on hormones and the hot flashes stopped and I felt a lot better. I was around 40 years old by then. This was young to go through menopause, but I didn't care. No more cramps.

My mother proceeded to tell me after the fact that her mother went through menopause early. "Thanks for telling me, mom." Years later, my husband brought up in counseling when we were trying to save our marriage about his terrible time dealing with me when I was in menopause; poor baby. He could have been a little understanding and loving. I really should not have been taking hormones as breast cancer runs in our family, but I did. I felt much better. It's no wonder years ago women were put in insane asylums because back then they didn't know about menopause and hormones. You feel like you are going crazy and have no patience; at least for some women. Some women only suffer from hot flashes, which is bad enough. My younger son now tells me I was, "crazy" during menopause. I don't even remember it.

My husband used to offer to babysit for my niece's good friend, who had a baby when she was young. He never asked me if it was okay and I would find out at the last minute that HE was babysitting. I was working and busy and I told him, since he offered, he could watch the little girl. Of course, I helped and it was a lot of fun. I have to give him credit. He was good with her.

Our older son graduated from high school and took four years of carpentry classes, part-time. He worked for a construction company until the economy went bad. Then he worked for a landscaping company. Now he works for his father in the family business that his grandpa started over 40 years ago.

He then rented an apartment. I believe it was too much togetherness with his, "Pops." Living together and working together . . .

Then our youngest son graduated from high school. He struggled in school as he had ADD. Both boys were diagnosed with ADD, but our youngest had it worse. We had to go through testing for both of them to diagnose the ADD. Our youngest son still is on ADD medication to help him focus. I used to, when he was younger, find the pills on the floor in his bedroom. To this day I can tell when he is not taking his medication. A mother knows these things. He wasn't on his medication for over three months and that was not fun for me. Patience is a virtue. While in high school, they were not giving him the help he needed for his ADD. We pulled him out of private school and sent him to public school where he also struggled. We had gotten him a tutor that used to come to the house, just as when I was going through menopause. I could not continue the studying with him every single night.

After high school, our younger son went to film editing school in Chicago. The first year was okay, but then the school changed the curriculum the second year, so he moved back home and started to take classes on-line. He could not handle the requirements for the second year of school. I found out the school was sold to someone else, thus the change in the curriculum.

My younger son came home early one morning after my husband went to work. He was falling all over the place and was definitely high on something. I called work and told them I had a family emergency and could not come in. My son had keys to the car in his pocket. The car had a flat tire and he drove off down the block. I called the police and told them to go get him as he was high on something and driving on a flat tire and could hurt himself, someone else or both.

The police brought him in front of our house in a squad car. He had handcuffs on. I went out to the squad car and said to my son, "Nice going." The officer proceeded to reach in my son's back pocket of his jeans and found a pipe, but there was nothing in it. He was taken to the police station and then to the hospital for a drug test. He tested positive for marijuana. Now I believe he has quit.

We were able to bail him out of jail. We brought him back home and I remember my husband, younger son and oldest son arguing at the top of the stairs. The younger one was out of control. I was afraid one of them would fall down the stairs if someone lost their balance or lost control of their temper.

Our younger son ran down the stairs, outside and over the deck rails, and I told my oldest son to, "Go get him." He tackled his younger brother and it was not a pretty picture. I called the police back and told them we needed their help and explained what transpired that day. They came, but there was nothing they could do.

My youngest son ran away to a friend's house. I called him on his cell phone and he said he was going to stay at his friend's for a number of days.

I talked to him the next day and he was crying. He admitted to me that he was gay. I begged and pleaded with him to come home. I told him that his father and I loved him and didn't care if he was gay. He didn't come home for days. My husband had suspected maybe our son was gay, something he saw on the computer, but he never told me. Good communication. My cousin's wife's brother was gay. I didn't tell my son this at the time, but I have two lesbian friends who I love dearly. Is that why God brought my friends into my life? That was the beginning of his gay relationships. I had asked him how he knew he was gay because I knew he had sex with a girl he was dating some time back.

The sad part with my younger son is that my husband didn't think it was a bad thing for our son to be smoking marijuana. I had that going against me.

I remember my cousin and his wife gave my younger son an old van for free. They wanted to dump it. My son used it for a little while and then it pooped out. I believe it had over 200,000 miles on it. He and his friends used to call it, "The Fagon Wagon." Get it?

His one gay friend moved in with us for three-months. After that, my son and his friend got an apartment in the city. They both loved the city. His friend moved out and left without paying his share of the rent for the remainder of the lease. I wanted to go after him for the rent (he owed us around $2,500.00), but my husband told me to forget it. How stupid he was. His friend also took some things of my son's that he got from his grandmother. I had heard from his friend a while later and asked for the stuff back. We never got it, or the rent. So, I dropped it. His friend came over some time later, and I didn't say anything about this to him. He came by again and he had the same lime green sunglasses as I did. We laughed. I always liked him and we had a lot of laughs. Yes, he stole stuff from my son and owed us money, but I forgave his friend. They had a big fight and do not talk any more, but I still see his friend occasionally as his grandparent's live a few blocks away. A few years ago he moved to Florida and I really miss him. We do keep in touch on Facebook which is nice.

Our son's second boyfriend was pretty much the same thing. He lived with me for a while as my husband had already moved out and asked me for a divorce.

I came home from work one day and my son and his boyfriend were having a drinking party by the pool. I was upset, but I went along with it. One girl was so drunk, she was exposing private areas to me that were pierced. No details there. She proceeded to take off her top and swim with her boyfriend. I insisted that my son's friends stay overnight as they were all drunk. I don't know why I did this, but I let the female and her boyfriend sleep in my bed as my husband had moved out and I could not sleep in the bed we had once shared together. At around one a.m., I heard this loud screaming. They were having sex in my house, in my bed. I kicked them out.

I had problems with my son and his boyfriend drinking and carrying on. One night they came home drunk. I was leaving to go out-of-town early the next morning. I had just gotten home from work. My son was outside in the middle of the street screaming at the top of his lungs, "F U." Get my drift? He staggered down the street. His friend told me HE had not been drinking. I called the police as I was afraid my son would get hit by a car if he stumbled into the street and a car came around the corner. I did not want either of them in my house. I told them to call a friend to come pick them up. The police gave both of the boys a breathalyzer test and they were both drunk.

My son's boyfriend went inside the house while the police were there. My son followed him. My son came out and told the police that I hit his boyfriend. What a lie. The police didn't believe it as the boyfriend never said anything to them prior to that.

My son was supposed to take care of my birds while I was out-of-town. He came home before I left for out-of-town and I had gotten a friend to come and watch over my babies. She was my friend, neighbor and cleaning lady. I told my son he was not taking care of my babies, that he could not be trusted. He left the house

That morning I was to leave for Starved Rock with a friend. Starved Rock State Park is in Illinois, known for its many canyons, waterfalls, wildflowers, plants, wildlife, birds and reptiles within its 2,630 acres. I went to my money pouch, where I had some money set aside in case I needed it. My younger son and his boyfriend knew it was there. I know; I know. How stupid of me. Money was missing. I was furious. When I talked to my son about it later on, he had taken the money to stay at a hotel the night I kicked them out. As Carol Burnett said On The View, "Don't be afraid to let your children hate you." How true that is. My son stole from me; my own son. I have forgiven him. He was high. He was angry at me for calling the police.

While I was out-of-town, my son and his boyfriend moved out of the house and got an apartment. My neighbor was watching the house and birds for me and I called her and was told they were in the process of moving out. My son's boyfriend ended up moving out of their apartment and again, my son was left to pay the rent. He was not paying much for rent as it was not a good area of town. So, I worried about that too. I have a friend who is a mail carrier and there were always drug busts going on around the corner from where my son lived. I found out later my son's boyfriend was in jail for drug possession and my son never had anything more to do with him, to my knowledge.

How did I get through these difficult times? My faith that you give everything to God and everything is in His hands. And the power of prayer of family and friends.

Psalm 9:10—And those who know Your Name put their trust in You, for You, O Lord, have not forsaken those who seek You.

My youngest son and I have had numerous conversations about AIDS. I will worry about that until the day I die.

Both of my son's gay friend's parents wanted nothing to do with them. How sad.

Here we go again!

I was at a friend's overnight and came home Saturday morning. I freshened up and went to pick up some prescriptions. When I got home, I noticed that there were voice mail messages. Two were from a suburb of Chicago my oldest son had called, but did not leave a message. I called the town but could not get a "live" person, as they were closed. I called my oldest son's cell phone and had to leave a message. My youngest son wasn't home and a light went off in my head.

I called my youngest son's cell phone and I asked him if everything was alright. He told me his brother had been in jail and would be home in around a half-hour. I was shaking. I decided to call my ex-husband. At first he was nice. He told me not to worry, that everything was alright and I should talk to our son. My ex-husband said he had to go. I heard kids in the background and asked where he was. He was at a park and said he was busy. I told him that nothing was more important than our sons. He then proceeded to tell me that I would have to pay one half of the lawyer's fees and court costs. I was taken aback. I told him I was not going to give him one-half of the $2,000 bond money because I had helped our son with other bills that amounted to $2,000-$3,000.

My ex proceeded to tell me that he wanted to use his divorce lawyer for our son and I told him if I was paying half, there was no way. I did not like his divorce lawyer. He was arrogant and delayed our divorce, I believe, to make more money.

I told him I would get some referrals for lawyers from two of my lawyer friends and would be in contact with him.

He told me he didn't want to talk to me, before we were done with our conversation, and hung up on me. Same ole "shit" from dealing with him throughout the divorce process. I tried calling him back on his cell phone and he did not pick up. Needless to say, I left him a snotty message and sent him a nasty e-mail.

My son got home. He proceeded to tell me that he did not want his grandmother, my mother, to know what happened and I promised to keep it and secret, and I did.

He had been drinking, so his friend was driving his car. She forgot to put the headlights on; only had the parking lights on. She was pulled over and the police officer also noticed that the car didn't have an updated city sticker on the license plate. My younger son was in the process of buying the car from my older son and I guess my older son did not mention to him that the sticker had expired. We were waiting for a copy of the car title as the original had been misplaced. The police ran everyone's ID and the officer asked my son to get out of the car. He was handcuffed and brought to the police station. He was put in a holding cell with some other guys. My son was the one that called from the "Town," but the messages were muffled. It was 5:00 in the morning and he needed $2,000 for bail. He was never read his rights and he was told if he didn't get the money, he would be sent to the Cook County Jail, in Chicago. He asked if they could hold off because banks were not open that early on a Saturday.

My son proceeded to tell me that an ex-friend of his, around 8 years before, had used my son's name to get out of being arrested. Going forward, every time this young man got into trouble, he used my son's name. So, my son and this punk's name were linked.

Unbeknownst to my son, there were two warrants out for his arrest from 2011 and 2012. But, he didn't do it. It was identity theft.

My son was scared in the holding cell with these other guys and made eye contact with one of the officers who moved him to a private cell. He had to sleep on a concrete floor with no blanket or pillow, like he was a criminal.

His older brother came to bail him out, only when he got there to pick up his brother, he was told that the bail was $7,000, not $2,000. So, back to the bank. When he got back to the jail, he was told it was only $2,000 and who told him it was $7,000?

What a nightmare.

After my son got home and told me the whole story, I was very upset and he was very upset.

To make a long story short, we had a meeting with my ex-husband's lawyer and his associate. That was fun seeing my ex-husband, who looked terrible. He looked anorexic. My son was impressed with the associate and hired him.

We did consult a local criminal lawyer who was a former police officer, but my son was not impressed with him.

Now we were waiting to go to court and see what happened to clear my son's name once and for all, as my son was pulled over throughout the years for speeding and when he explained to the officers that his name was linked to this ex-friend, the police let him go. Why was he arrested this time?

When we met with my ex's lawyer and associate, they asked our son if he had been arrested for anything else, that they wanted the truth and no surprises. So, he had to tell them he had been arrested for a DUI when he was younger, which I mentioned earlier in this chapter. Great. We knew about this, but I guess you never get it off your record.

There were two court dates for my son in two different counties. I went with him for the first court date for the first warrant. The good news is that a Dismissal Order was entered and we would be getting back our bail bond money. My son had to keep a copy of the Dismissal Order in his wallet and in his glove compartment.

On the second court date, which was the next day, my ex-husband went with our son. Again. . . a Dismissal Order was entered for the second warrant and our son would also have to carry that Dismissal Order with him at all times.

Our lawyer got our son's name expunged from all of this mess.

He was going to continue his film editing, but decided it wasn't for him. He was offered a full-time position in retail after working at a store for more than two-years. He got health insurance, which is fantastic as once he turned 26, he could not be covered under my health plan any longer. He also got dental insurance. Since then he has received three promotions and I am proud of him. He is currently a floor manager. All on his own.

He was the only one chosen from his retail store to go help open a new store in Kentucky. He was gone for two weeks; his flight, hotel room and food were all paid for. He borrowed my new purple luggage that I hadn't even used yet. He also headed up a breast cancer walk. We have family members that had breast cancer and died. A few weeks before my son left for Kentucky, I got home from work one evening and he vacuumed his room, brought down the dirty dishes, did his laundry, organized. If you knew my son, his room always has looked like a tornado hit it, literally. He also got rid of one huge garbage bag full of junk. I peeked in his room while he was at work one day. It actually looked good. I couldn't believe it. While my son was out of town in Kentucky, he left a voice mail message while I was at work. He sounded great. He had been busy. He apologized for not calling me sooner. And . . . he told me he loved me and missed me and he hoped I had a good week.

Another night I got home from work and was totally exhausted and he cleaned out the garage and reorganized everything so I could get my car in without breaking my side-view mirror. What a pleasant surprise.

A year after being chosen to go to Kentucky to help open a new store, he was chosen to go help open another store in San Antonio. He was excited and, again, was gone for two weeks. I really missed him.

I truly believe my son that lived with me has matured a lot. He left the townhouse a mess one night when I got home from work and I was really tired. He'd left beer bottles around and the TV was loud. When I confronted him about it, he actually apologized.

My son lived with me for five years. It was time for him to move out. He moved into the City of Chicago where he shared an apartment with two of his friends. I went to visit him with my honey. It was a very nice apartment. We loved it and were very happy for him.

He is a floor manager at a retail store not far from his apartment. Then, he moved out to a studio apartment. Something happened and I finally found out. His lease was up and he had mice and had to move. I kept asking him what his address was and he kept avoiding me. I finally met up with him in Chicago for breakfast and he told me he was living in a boarding house until he could find a permanent place to live. He paid for breakfast and walked me to my girlfriend's house in Lincoln Park where my friend and I spent the day together. We had a glorious time together. She is my friend I bird sit for. At 6 p.m. that night I received an e-mail from my Mother wondering why I was not home!!!

My son and his friend started a cologne business. They got a company to manufacture the cologne. They had to form a business name.

I sold a few bottles for them. They had to hire a lawyer. They had a few open houses at lounges and gave out free samples. We are hoping and praying for a successful business! Things have been put on hold due to the covid and tax issues.

Raising children is one of the greatest things. It has its challenges, yes, but the good times far outweigh the bad. When they are growing up . . . seeing their little smiling faces in their crib; learning to talk; growing into their own personalities. It is the best.

While our oldest son was in high school, he was working on his Eagle Scout project which is the highest ranking award you can receive in Boy Scouts. Unfortunately, after his father and I tried to talk to him about continuing with the project, he decided to quit. We tried to explain to him that it would be a great thing to put on his resume, but he was done.

As parents, we were very disappointed, especially his father after all of the years of being involved in scouts. I thank God that my youngest son got through his problems with drugs. I found out recently that he had tried every kind of drug except heroine. God was watching over him. It could have been a nightmare.

CHAPTER 10

My Marriage Starts to Fall Apart

and

Losing A Job after 25 Years

One evening my husband and I were sitting on our deck, on our new patio furniture we picked out together, by our lit-up lap pool and our hot tub that had colorful, flashing lights. It was a beautiful summer night. My husband proceeded to tell me that, he wasn't "attracted" to me anymore. It cut me like a knife. I was crying.

I had gained weight and become diabetic. My mom is diabetic and my grandfather was diabetic. I have type II diabetes and the doctor put me on Metformin to control my high blood sugar. All my husband said was, "That's too bad." He did pay a few times for me to go to Jenny Craig, but there was no longer anything sexual with him. Did he think he was God's gift to women?

My neighbors mentioned to me that when my husband used to walk in the neighborhood, he would have his head down, like he was intense in his thinking. Then, a woman from church, who my husband and I know, knew, mentioned to me that he'd made some comment to her one day that he had to make some changes in his life. Nice that he never talked to me about it

About a year before my husband asked me for a divorce, we went to visit some dear friends for dinner. My husband checked out their new TV and how everything was plugged in. I didn't think about it at the time. My girlfriend told me she thought it was odd him asking about details of a TV. That was the beginning of him moving forward. She mentioned this to me months later after she found out that he asked me for a divorce.

Sometime later I lost weight. We'd attend weddings, parties, and so on and I looked great, but he said absolutely nothing. I was complimented by a lot of people on how I looked.

My husband's cousin's husband even called me and wanted to get together after a family wedding when I told him about my husband's feelings towards me. Thank goodness my girlfriend answered the phone at work when he called. I don't know why I ever gave him my phone number at work. I had a few drinks and I guess I was lonely. There was no way I wanted any kind of an affair as he was married and so was I. I believe in the commandment, "Do not commit adultery."

Throughout our marriage, a few of my friends' husbands showed interest in me, but I wasn't interested. I remember when we bought our first house and got new kitchen cabinets, the salesman was adorably cute and showed interest. It was tempting, but I was married and always faithful. I had seen him at a local burger place with my girlfriend. Was he hot.

My husband slept upstairs and watched TV, and I slept downstairs. How could I be intimate with a man who wasn't attracted to me anymore, even after I lost weight? I thought to myself, if I tried to get intimate with him, I'd just be rejected anyway and how would that make me feel? We lived like this for approximately four years. I remember saying something to him one day, "You never touch me," and his response was cold and he said, "Deal with it." We fought. Things weren't good. We would go out with friends, go to family functions, and acted like everything was fine, but it wasn't.

Here was the beginning. In January 2010, two months before being asked for a divorce, I was in the emergency room. I had a cyst on my ovary and was put on pain medication and sent home. My husband told me he was going to the health club, as he always did. I woke up at midnight and he wasn't home. I tried calling him on his cell phone, but there was no answer. I called the boys and was told they didn't know where he was. I knew that the health club closed at 10:00 p.m.

I called the police and told them the story. I was asked if this was normal for him. I replied, "No." I waited and waited and called my husband again. He answered this time. I asked him where he was and he told me he was at a strip club. What a pig. I told him the police were looking for him. He asked me why I called them. He told me to call them back and tell them he was at a friend's house. I was thinking to myself, you don't have any friends. He was worried he would be pulled over for a DUI. So, I called the police and told them he was at a friend's house.

He eventually came home safe and sound early that morning. I told him if he ever did that to me again, I would change the locks on the door.

Two months later, on a Friday night, I got home from work and he told me he wanted a divorce, and said, "I don't love you anymore." I cried. I told him that he made a vow in front of God, family and friends, and that we should try counseling. He agreed.

I needed some help, so I called the doctor and got in to see him. Our boys, my husband, my mother-in-law; we all went to the same doctor and we all adored him. Anyway, he gave me sleeping pills and some anxiety medication. I was going through a tough time and there were tougher times ahead of me. But . . . this is where my Christian faith comes in. I prayed to God for his help and guidance and put it in his hands.

Isaiah 41:10—Fear not, for I am with you; be not dismayed, for I am your God; I will strengthen you, I will help you, I will uphold you with my righteous right hand.

After I found out my husband was at a strip club, I went for my annual physical at the OB/GYNY. I told him what was happening in my life; divorce and the strip club incident. He insisted on testing me to make sure I didn't have some kind of sexually transmitted disease. It cut me like a knife. Thank goodness it came back negative.

My husband had it all planned out. He had bought $10,000 worth of furniture and rented a townhouse and moved out the next day after asking me for a divorce. The killer was, he told our older son about asking me for the divorce before me. Our son had to help him put his new bed together on a Thursday night. He asked me for the divorce the next night; Friday. My soon-to-be ex-husband asked our son to stay with me at the house, which he did, but eventually he moved out and went to live with his father. My husband didn't want me to be alone. How sleazy my husband was. Here I was working full time and he was planning all of this behind my back.

I started counseling and my husband went to a separate counselor, whom he told me he didn't think much of! Then it was suggested that we start counseling together for six months, along with dating. I know that sounds weird, but I was trying to save our marriage. I know now he was going to counseling just to make himself look good. He didn't want to try. We would meet at counseling and he would put his head down. Was he depressed? The look on his face. It was very scary. I had never seen a look like that on anyone's face before.

Dating was awkward. He would pick me up at our house, drop me off and kiss me on the cheek. We would go to a comedy club often and get some laughs. One nice fall day we went to a beautiful place called Morton Arboretum where there was shopping, flowers, beautiful trees, and a restaurant. We went for a nice walk and he held my hand. We also had lunch together. One night, after a date, he knocked on the front door. I don't remember if he forgot something, but I said, kiddingly, "What? Do you want sex?" He just looked at me.

While my husband and I were in counseling together, our counselor wanted us to write down ten things we loved about our spouse. I had ten items, but he only had three. Boy did that hurt my feelings. One of his was a compliment on how I dealt with this crazy boss of mine. My boss told me, and I quote. . . "You are getting dumber and dumber." He was an ex-teacher and started a very successful real estate company with three other teachers. They are all very rich. Going into work every day with my head held up high was very tough.

After we separated, he had an accident in his BMW company car. I'd had a feeling that was going to happen, though I can't explain it. When I asked him what happened, he told me he looked down. It caused $10,000 in damage.

We went to a family wedding with his mother while we were separated. I bought a new dress and his mother, who hardly ever complimented anyone, told me I looked great. Nothing from him. He didn't even get me a drink at the bar; I had to go get it myself. He got drunk and we danced. That seems to be the only time he was the life of the party; when he drank. He drove home drunk. His mother and I were in the car. The next morning he called me to tell me I looked very nice. It didn't mean anything to me anymore. His mother probably told him to call me.

One day in counseling, he said, "I am worth a lot of money. You will be well taken care of." I responded by saying, "You're not worth a lot of money, we are. I've been with you since I was 16 years old. You have a lot of nerve." I knew then it was over.

I remember my husband used to tell me that "money doesn't matter." I wonder if he still feels that way today.

I found out somehow, and I don't remember how, that my husband borrowed $25,000 from his mother. I wondered why he would borrow such an amount. Later on I found out through the grapevine that it was for taxes. His sister had come into town to take care of it, legally, for his repaying their mother.

I sold my wedding ring. That was tough. It was not my original wedding ring. My original ring was made into a necklace and my husband bought me a bigger diamond around our 20th anniversary. My counselor told me that it was a great start to moving forward and she was very proud of me. It was a healthy move. Having no wedding ring on your finger after so many years is hard and a big adjustment. You are constantly feeling for it. I also donated my wedding gown.

I remember going to his family's party. My husband was acting mean to me and made some comment about, "I'm calling a lawyer." I cried and walked away. His sister followed me. She was in town from Texas. I was embarrassed.

My husband had told me I would be served with divorce papers. No one ever came. He filed for divorce and I responded, "Yes." I hired a female lawyer, who came highly recommended by my sister's ex-husband. My husband never started the divorce, so it was in my hands. I can't believe he originally wanted to use the same lawyer for the divorce. He went to the Yellow Pages for his lawyer. I did not like his lawyer. He was very arrogant. My gentleman friend and neighbor's daughter went to him for a divorce, but didn't hire him. What does that tell you?

My Mother went with me on the first visit to the lawyer. I was a mess. Confused, devastated, heartbroken... I looked terrible as I had been crying. I could not think. My lawyer was great and we have remained friends.

She was the best. I referred friends to her and they adored her.

I was living in the house. The house was paid for. He was paying all of the bills.

Six months after my husband asked me for a divorce, I lost my job after 25 years. What a nightmare working with unemployment was. You never want to go through that. It was terrible being let go from a job. You have to pack up all of your personal belongings and then you are walked out by a security guard past your co-workers. It's humiliating and embarrassing. I had gone from being a legal assistant to an administrative assistant and he wanted me to do all of this fancy stuff on the computer. I took classes, but unless you put it into practice, it is tough. I heard from a friend who still works there that the company is cleaning house right now. I'm so glad I'm out of there. Now they are getting busier and overworking and stressing out their employees.

I was one of the fortunate people who received a good severance package and my insurance covered my family for four months, but then we had to pay for COBRA, which was very expensive.

There is an old movie with Jim Carey called <u>Dumb and Dumber</u>, It was a really silly movie. When I saw the name of the movie, my boss's taunt came back to haunt me.

I found a brochure at church by CareNotes titled, "Pulling Together as a Family After a Job Loss." I did not have my husband to talk to about my job loss. I handled it on my own through prayer.

Jeremiah 29:11—For I know the plans I have for you, declares the Lord, plans for welfare and not for evil, to give you a future and a hope.

The brochure brought out a lot of the feelings that I was having.

"The person who has been laid off is suffering from the loss and needs some time to readjust," it said. "Jobs provide a working person with a sense of identity, accomplishment, and purpose, as well as a paycheck and, sometimes, medical benefits. Jobs provide structure time and provide friendships. Adjusting to life without these measures is not easy."

Per Ann Kaiser Stearns' *Living Through Job Loss*: "Promise yourself that you will discover how job loss can lead to better things. It is important to decide now that you are going to be a wiser and stronger person. Commit yourself to making a better life for yourself and your loved ones."

I was confident that something good was going to come out of this job loss and that God would provide, and he did.

I was struggling with a "grief process."

At the unemployment office, I met a man who I dated on and off. He was a nice Christian man who had lost his wife to cancer. When I met my new gentleman friend, I had to be honest with the first guy. I felt like a teenager; like I was dumping him, but he understood.

My sister-in law lost her job as a lawyer and a good friend of mine lost her job and later went to home-staging classes and helped me home-stage the house. My sister-in-law ended up working at Kohl's during the holiday season. She eventually found another job, but it took a long, long time. I also got a part-time job at Kohl's and collected some unemployment. I hated it. The crazy hours. No set schedule. I remember having to work on Black Friday. I got so disgusted. One night I told the manager I was walking out. I was diabetic and my body was all messed up. It wasn't worth my health. The unemployment workers asked me about why I left; I told them and everything was fine.

I looked for a job. It was close to the holidays and there was nothing out there. I didn't want to do office work anymore. The fancy computer stuff; I just wasn't good at it and didn't enjoy it. I loved typing and shorthand, but there was no call for that anymore. As I mentioned, I took classes for the computer, which the company paid for, but if you don't use it, you lose it.

My husband kept telling me to keep pursuing a job in an office. He wasn't the one who was going to make that decision for me. I was going to do what I wanted to do.

I prayed hard and, one day, I was on the computer. I always wanted to be a nurse and wanted to get back into something in the healthcare field as a medical transcriber, CNA (certified nursing assistant). Something! Jobs were out there for this kind of work. My older son's girlfriend told me about a friend of hers who went to a local school for CNA. I called. I took a test and got in.

Philippians 4:13—I can do all things through him who strengthens me.

During the time my husband and I were separated, he called me one day and asked if he could come over to the house. I told him that it was alright. He proceeded to ask me if we could put a home-equity loan on the house that was paid for, because he wanted to buy a fancy 2-door BMW sports car. I told him to get out of the house. I told him that I always wanted to go to Hawaii, but never did. I told him if he defaulted on the loan, I did not have a job. No way. He proceeded to go to the company business and buy the car anyway. It was still considered marital property. I typed up a Promissory Note that he owed me half of what he paid for his sports car. We both signed it and I got it notarized. At the closing of the house, it was figured in that he owed me one-half of what he spent on the car!

JOKE: What is the difference between a BMW and a porcupine?

The porcupine has pricks on the outside.

My eye doctor told me this joke and I laughed a long time.
Was this a joke from a movie??????

After being out of high school for more than 30 years, I was back in school. It was a three-month class; two times a week and clinicals once a week. I would work out in the mornings at the health club and do homework and study for hours a day. I made straight A's. I had students ask me for the answers to the homework, as I was always ahead on my homework. I told them I was going to charge them for the answers. It was a lot of work, but I did it and I actually enjoyed it. I loved my teacher. I studied hard for the state board. I was nervous about the results. It came in the mail. I passed, first time around! I screamed for joy. I got a job as a CNA (aka a Certified Nursing Assistant) within four days! My dear aunt, who since then passed away, gave me a party for my success. It's a tough, physical job, but I love my residents, though some of the co-workers are pills.

So, at 55 years old, I changed careers. God answered my prayer.

1 John 1:5—This is the message we have heard from him and proclaim to you, that God is light, and in him is no darkness at all.

I remember my husband was at the health club one day and we walked on the track together. He had the nerve to tell me his favorite piece of furniture was his bed. We were separated at the time and he paid for me to get a personal trainer.

One day I showed up at his office. He had converted all of his retirement money into cash. I was mad and he knew it. I asked him what he was doing. We weren't divorced yet and he had no business doing anything with our investments at this point. He was shocked I showed up.

He confronted me about my gentleman friend, who I had met through our local auto mechanic when I was separated. We started dating. I knew my marriage was going to be over. My husband had found out I went out-of-town with my friend. My husband told me he knew I was seeing someone and went away for a weekend. He asked me personal questions and I told him it was none of his business. He didn't want me. I told him to never in his lifetime come and tell me that he'd made a mistake. It was OVER.

I'm sure my son told him about my dating. At first I felt bad dating before I was divorced, that it was a sin. I prayed hard about it and my marriage was over. Now it was just legalizing it.

I went to the bank one day and was told that my husband closed out an account of ours that had $1,200.00 in it. I called him and confronted him about it and told him he had no right to do that behind my back. He owed me $600.00. Well, I never got it. What a sneak. It was not worth having a lawyer handle this.

I started off my CNA job as part time and it eventually became full time. My medical insurance through work was effective the day after my COBRA insurance ran out. My soon to be ex-husband had to get private medical insurance. Oh well. It is expensive.

I spent a whole year cleaning out our house that we lived in for twenty-five years. What a job. No help from my husband. He had a bad back and I didn't want him around anyway. I did it all myself. Our boys didn't offer to help me either. One good thing; I found a printer in the basement for my laptop. I don't know whose it was, nor did I care. It was mine now!

My dear friend was hired to home-stage the house. My husband approved it as we had to pay for her services. We had her business cards in a holder by the front door when prospective buyers would walk through and we were hoping that my friend would get some job offers, but nothing came of it. I hired a broker friend of my sister-in-law's to list the house for sale which was also approved by my husband. I used to party with her and a bunch of other girls years ago. She brought in some staging accessories; furniture, plants, etc.

The house went on the market. Then the sign went up in the front yard. I was devastated, hurt; I cried my eyes out. I was going to have to say good-bye to my beautiful home that we raised our boys in.

I loved my neighbors. How long was this going to take to sell? My husband wanted to list the asking price too high, but the broker and I gave in. After four weeks, 15 showings and no offers and having to be at everyone's beck and call, I phoned my husband and told him we were lowering the price. At first he said no, but then he gave in. Within ten days, we had a contract. I felt like telling my husband, "I told you so." I hired an old boss of mine to be our lawyer, which my husband agreed to as well.

I remember the day our broker and my husband met at the house to sign the sales contract. He came early and walked through the house. He had not been there for a long time and his first comment to me was, "It looks like a model home." I wanted to tell him off at this point, but I bit my tongue.

During the separation, I had gotten my husband to agree to not come over to the house unless he called me first. He didn't have to legally agree to this, because it was our home, but he agreed.

I remember him asking if he could come over and sunbathe and use the pool and I agreed. He used the toilet and he left the seat up. I went out and tapped him on the shoulder and said, "Honey, next time you use the toilet, can you please put the toilet seat back down. After all, my ass is smaller now that I lost weight and I almost fell in the water." Yes, I did call him honey because I was still trying to save my marriage. It came out in counseling later that he didn't think my comment was funny. I thought it was hilarious. Everyone else I told thought it was funny. He has no sense of humor. But, he thinks his humor is funny, which it is not. Both of our sons have told him that he is not funny. The only humor I recall being funny of his were:

- He called Neiman Marcus (an expensive store), "Needless Markup." and
- He has, "Sometimezers All the Timezers."

I thought about the positive things that came out of our marriage, besides our sons and the fact that I walked away with some money. The answer to that question is that my husband had talked me into investing a good amount of money into a 401K during the time I worked as a legal assistant, which was 25 years. So, I had that chunk of money after the divorce.

We did fight about money; I admit that. I don't know why because that was not an issue. Heads up ladies. Don't let the man control how you spend your money. For example: my husband would buy whatever he wanted, without my permission; i.e. a great surround sound system for our TV; a pool and deck instead of what I wanted which was to refinish the basement. But, he got what he wanted. Our master bathroom had a steam shower installed and a raised sink as he had a bad back and did not want to lean over. I did not have a say in any of this.

One day he was supposed to be at the house at 3:00 p.m. to take care of the pool and the lawn. I came home from my gentleman friend's at 5:00 p.m. and he was still there. He asked me if I was hungry and I told him, "Yes." He asked me if I wanted to go for a bite to eat. I told him it was weird wanting to take out his soon to be ex-wife to dinner, but I went.

I had a few glasses of wine. We talked about our differences we had in raising the boys. We went back to the house and sat on the deck and talked. He had a few beers. He told me he would not agree to pay me maintenance for 10 years, but agreed to seven years. I told him no. He eventually caved in. He drove me to the restaurant in his new, bright-blue BMW sports car. He already had a company car which he leased that was a BMW. He asked me if I liked his car and I told him no. He loved it. He told me it was better than having sex with someone half his age. I replied, "How do you even remember what sex is?"

I tried to get more that 50/50 on the sale of the house for all of my hard work for a year in cleaning it up (wasn't that worth something?), but he didn't agree and after all, I thought, he did pay for me to live in the house. My mother-in-law was worth a lot of money. I tried to get something for myself, but after a divorce, you do not have any rights. Damn it!

During this hard time in my life, I tried to quit smoking. I talked to my doctor and got it approved by my insurance company to try Chantix which helps you quit smoking. It is used together with a support program that includes counseling and educational materials.

You can't try and quit smoking when you are stressed out to the max. My goal is to try again soon. It is a hard thing to do. At least I smoke mild cigarettes, but I know that is no excuse.

My husband used to come over to the house and check the scale while I was working. He confronted me why I didn't weigh myself every day. He looked to see if the scale, that was in our bathroom, had been moved so that he could see whether or not I was weighing myself since the last time he was over. That was freaky. I told him that my personal trainer, who he hired for me when we separated, told me you are supposed to only weigh yourself once a week. He told me he weighed himself every day and looked at himself in the mirror.

THE NEXT FEW PARAGRAPHS LEAD UP TO . . . .

I had a bridal shower with my cousin for her brother's oldest daughter. It cost quite a bit of money and it was a lot of work, but it was fun and turned out great. I remember my husband asking me to bring a book he had on sex. It was not my idea, but his. It was not accepted well and her thank you note to him told him so. He deserved it. It was a graphic book with pictures. Catch my drift? My cousin's wife and I were close for many years. They used to come over with their five children every July 4th to swim in our pool and have a cook-out. My husband used to make these special burgers that were delicious of his own creation and everyone loved them. The name of our deck with the lap pool, hot tub and deck was called "Club C" and we used to call the burgers, "Club C burgers." It was cute.

I don't remember all of the details, but one year my cousin's daughter and my youngest son (who were born a week apart), were goofing around and running around outside during one of our get-togethers. Something happened and my cousin swore at my son and bruised his arm when he grabbed him. I was outside by the pool at the time. My son came to me and was crying and told me what had happened. I asked my cousin and his family to leave. We got an apology the next day. If he did that to my son, what does he do to his own kids? I know that there was an episode with his nephew years ago where his nephew was afraid of him.

After a fun-filled day by the pool, we would walk down to the park and enjoy the fireworks. It was a half mile walk and we used to take the wagon and drinks and snacks. I received an invitation at the house for their daughter's wedding, which included a guest. I was told all along by my cousin's wife that I could bring my husband (we were in marriage counseling at the time; he had moved out) to the wedding, even though we were separated. I had mentioned something to my husband right after I received the invitation, but he didn't seem interested.

LED UP TO...

The night before the wedding, my husband, older son and I were in the garage. Our son used the garage as an entertainment area where he set up a TV, couch, etc. My husband asked me if I was bringing anyone to the wedding and I replied, "No." He didn't realize the wedding was the next day. I asked him if he wanted to go, and he replied, "Yes." I was excited and thrilled, as we were trying to save our marriage and I thought maybe this was a good sign.

This was on a Friday night and my cousin and his wife were on their way to their daughter's rehearsal dinner. I tried calling my cousin's wife and left a message on her cell phone and also called them at their house. My cousin's wife called me back on her cell phone and before I could even tell her why I was calling, she handed the phone over to my cousin (who I was also close to my whole life) and told him I would like to bring my husband to the wedding. They were not having a sit-down dinner; just drinks and finger foods and desserts and a cake. Well, he flat out refused for me to bring him, even though his wife all along told me I could bring my husband. I was floored; shocked; upset. How could he tell me no? I didn't understand. I was so upset, I kicked one of the cabinets in the garage and I swore. My husband had gone home to the townhouse he had rented and I had to call him and tell him he couldn't go. I apologized later to my neighbor across the street whose two boys saw me and heard me lose my cool in the garage.

It was the day of the wedding, I saw my cousin at the back of the church before the wedding and he kissed me and told me that he was sorry. I told him we would talk about it later. His wife avoided me at the wedding like the plague. What had I done to deserve this kind of behavior? They go to church every Sunday. And then at the reception she also ignored me. Good Christian right?

My younger son was asked to videotape the wedding and reception. It took my son almost a year to complete editing the videotape. He was busy with school. I remember having to drive him to the city to pick up the video equipment and then return it back to the school; all on my time and gas. My son never got a retainer fee of any kind from my cousin, as promised, for videotaping the wedding and reception, nor did he ever get paid for the job. I brought the videotape to my cousin's family party. Ironically, the bride and groom were there from Pennsylvania. It was a surprise. My cousin runs a hugely successful business and has put his five children through college. Why couldn't he pay my son?

I met my cousin a month after the wedding to discuss why I was not allowed to bring my husband to his daughter's wedding and he told me he didn't want a scene. I told him we were mature adults and his wife told me all along that I could bring him if I wanted to. I saw them at his mother's wake (the morning I got divorced!) and funeral, but it'll never be the same. It's sad. This is family. No wonder there are wars. You can pick your friends, but you can't pick your family.

My soon to be ex-husband told me he signed up for dating services; but no hits. Oh . . . poor baby.

Before getting divorced, I went by my husband's townhouse and I thought he had a lady over. I had his neighbor look through the garage window as I was too short to see. My husband was out on a walk. His neighbor told him about me asking him to look in the garage. My husband called me. "I don't have a girlfriend." I thought to myself, yeah, right. Why did I do this? Curiosity kills the cat. On a Saturday morning I could not sleep. So, I drove by his townhouse on my way to 7-11. It was 6:30 a.m. and his sports car was gone. Why do I do this? I don't know. A form of spying because I suspected he had a woman. I have to accept whatever happens, but it is tough. Things happen for a reason.

I ran into an old friend of my husband's. His father was a resident at the facility I was working at. He told me my husband was, "Having a hard time." I thought to myself, oh well. He made his bed; now he has to lie in it.

Listen to each other, we didn't. He used to have me on the speakerphone, when we were separated, unbeknownst to me, when talking confidentially about our sons. They were listening. What a jerk.

My husband never wanted the guy that worked for him to know he asked me for a divorce. My husband was afraid that if one of the companies that they represented found out, it would jeopardize his accounts. I told my husband that couples got divorced all of the time. He never told the guy that worked for him that we were getting divorced. He used to talk about me and the boys and the house to him like everything was fine. I thought that was strange. I used to talk to this guy at the office when my husband wasn't around. I told him what was going on. He was shocked. He told me my husband was acting fine; like everything was alright. My husband used to be nasty to this guy when he first started working for him, but then my husband mellowed out. HE NEVER TOLD HIM. Even after the divorce was final and the house sold, he never said anything to him.

This gentleman did tell me that he suspected something was wrong. The bills were being paid late. He was acting differently. This was so unlike him. You cannot hide things like this.

CHAPTER 11

Finding a Place to Live, House Sale and Divorce

The divorce took two and a half years, and it was nasty. It cost, between his lawyer and mine, over $45,000. It was a nightmare. Negotiating, seeing him and our lawyers together for meetings; it was awful. I had to fill out a financial statement for my lawyer of what it would cost to live. I was making under half of what I was making before at my office job. I had my gentleman friend help me figure out part of the financial statement, as I paid bills for 25-years before I handed it over to my husband to handle. At the time I handed over the paying of the bills to my husband, I had my hands full with the boys, their activities and homework, and working full time. So, I was pretty much clueless how to fill out this financial statement. I did go look at a few places; apartments and townhomes, to see how much it would cost to rent once I was ready. Rent prices sure had gone up over the years. I needed a garage for my car as I got home late from work at 11:30 p.m. with my new job and new career.

I don't believe there is such a thing as an amicable divorce and to think that my husband wanted to use the same lawyer. I told him, "No way." I thought to myself, whose interest would the lawyer be interested in, mine or his?

My husband owns two businesses and I figured out what he made, what I made, and what would be fair. We finally, after much battling it out, agreed on an amount for maintenance/alimony. As I mentioned, he was to pay me for one-third of the number of years we were married up to ten years; we were married 35, but I was with him a total of 40 years with dating and engagement.

The closing date was set on the house. I had to find a place to live. It was hard because I have birds.

One day my broker called me and told me she had the perfect place for me. But, there was quite a drawback. It was in the same complex where my husband was living. At first I told her, "No," but then I went to see the townhouse and fell in love with it. I signed a one-year lease. About 10 days before my move-in-date, there was a fire in the townhouse. Was it ever going to end?

I had spent a lot of time looking for a place to live and now this.

I was afraid I would have to look again for another place to live due to the fire and I was stressed out. My mom offered to help, and a friend, but I had the problem of my birds. My mom is allergic to them. I would have had to store my stuff for a while. The house was scheduled to close in three weeks. I was a mess.

It all worked out. My broker brought me to see the damage from the fire and it was on the carpet, an area 3 ft. x 3 ft. There was soot all over everything. I felt sorry for my landlord. She had to put new carpeting in all of the rooms and have everything painted. Her prior tenant did a lot of damage to the townhouse that needed to be fixed. As far as I know, the fire was due to painters leaving combustible rags around. It was hot outside at the time.

I moved into the townhouse and after four months of workmen and painters coming for two bathrooms that had peeling border paper in them that needed to be taken down (the prior tenant put the border paper up and did not know what she was doing), and then twice having men come to clean the air vent out due to the smell of smoke from the fire (which each time took them four hours and they would show up at my door without having an appointment), a new kitchen floor installed and blinds . . . my problem getting internet and cable set up with one company and after many, many phone calls to them, I could not use that company because, as they explained it, there was no room for me (the analogy they used was—you go somewhere to sit down and all the seats are occupied, so you have to go to another room, but there are no available seats in there either) and so I had to call another company. I finally got all set up with my land line, computer and TV/cable. That was a long nightmare. Moving is a lot of work: Changing addresses on everything, getting everything set up.

Part of the fun with my move was I took my valance from our living room at the house that matched the fabric of our rattan coach and chairs that I got in the divorce. I found someone who came to the townhouse and fixed them and hung them on the patio door. It looked beautiful.

I finally enjoyed the townhouse. It was a long haul, but it's a great feeling. My landlord and I signed another two-year lease. Yeah. It feels like home and I did everything in purples. My ex-husband hates the color. Hah, hah, hah. I also went crazy and bought purple pots and pans, dishes, silverware. I love it.

At the townhouse, there are five lilac bushes (in purple) that bloomed. I had planted one at the house that we sold. I missed it. A pleasant sign. Where I live it is called, The Lilac Village. I also have a gorgeous red rose bush in the front. I really miss my purple irises at the house. They were gorgeous. Life goes on.

I bought a waterfall for inside the townhouse to help me with my high anxiety.

I finally got divorced after a long, "nasty" time; September, 2012. My husband asked me for a divorce in March, 2010. I lost my job in October, 2010. The morning I got divorced, I thanked my lawyer and her associate and walked out. I could not face my ex-husband. I believe to this day that my ex's attorney was procrastinating due to wanting more money; he was being greedy; like he needed to make more money. He took forever to get work done. It was ridiculous. Even my lawyer was frustrated with him. There were quite a few court hearings before the actual divorce. I remember one day all of the lawyers, his lawyer and my lawyer and her associate, and my husband and I were waiting to get into the courtroom. My husband said, in front of everyone, that he was taking sleeping pills and drinking. Smart to say in front of everyone, right?

I forgot to mention that dividing your furniture is another tough thing to go through. I got the china cabinet and all of the china and crystal. He got the kitchen table; the new, gorgeous patio set and our new "big" grill.

The afternoon I got divorced, I had to go to my aunt's wake. After a year of her being sick with MG, an auto-immune disease, aka Myasthenia Gravis, which caused many complications with her diabetes and many, many infections, she passed away. We prayed for her to pass on, but it's still tough. She was my favorite aunt and I miss her terribly. I miss her Christmas letters, her laugh. She had a small party for me when I passed the state board for CNA (Certified Nursing Assistant). She was a giving, caring, wonderful, fun-loving person, and she liked to drink wine as much as I did.

My mother used to go to MG meetings with my aunt before she got really sick, to learn more about the disease. I went with them once. We also went to a fundraising luncheon with my cousin, my aunt's only daughter. My aunt couldn't make it because she was sick. It was nice to get away at this time when my aunt was so sick. I bought MG license plate covers and had my mechanic put them on for me. My mom and I also participated in a 3-mile MG walk. We walked the 3-miles in 50 minutes. My 79-year old mom and I walked at the same pace. My friend from work asked me if we were going to still walk due to the recent bombing that occurred at the Boston Marathon. My response was, "You can't stop living and be afraid. If God is ready for me, there is nothing I can do." We walk in the 3-mile MG walk every year and I am proud to have the license plate on my lime-green convertible Volkswagen Beetle!

It is rewarding walking for a good cause.

It was tough on my mother. She had lost her older sister three years before, her niece (my cousin) and now her younger sister. My mom said, "I am the Matriarch of the family." That makes me the next in line.

Then, after the divorce, we had to meet up to get our checks from the settlement. When I walked out, my ex-husband said, "Don't go shopping!" What a jerk.

My older son, who had moved in with his father, was barely communicating with me. He told me he was afraid of me while he was growing up. I feel like I was a good mother, but my husband didn't support me on the disciplining. I never beat our son. Did I spank him a few times? Yes. So, I was also dealing with that. He came to my aunt's wake and funeral with his girlfriend and was one of the pallbearers. We talked about what was going on with him and his girlfriend. Things had gotten better between us. My mom surprised me for my birthday dinner at a restaurant and my son showed up. What a great surprise. Then my oldest son also joined us for my mom's birthday dinner along with his long-time girlfriend. It was nice. He even offered to help pay and I appreciated it, but I told him, "No."

My mom had a bird-day (misspelled intentionally, I love birds) celebration for my oldest son/her oldest grandson, in December and he brought his girlfriend. We hugged for a picture. I love him so. My mom also had a Christmas Day celebration and he came.

There is a movie called, Come Dance at My Wedding. Watch it. It is good. It made me cry . . . . . . everything about a wedding; flowers, bridesmaids' dresses were in purple/lilac, my favorite color. It brought back memories of our wedding day.

My father-in-law died a number of years before my husband asked me for a divorce and losing him was a big loss. He was a great man. He is probably rolling around in his grave. I wonder what he would say if he was still alive about his son asking me for a divorce. Oh well, that is life. He'd be proud to know his oldest grandson is now working in the "Family Business" which grandpa started, my ex-husband owns/runs, and now our oldest son is working in the business.

According to my divorce decree, if I got married, I would lose my maintenance/alimony. Also, I can't cohabitate with a male or female or I would also lose my maintenance.

But, read on in a later chapter where I meet the love of my life!!!

In my old neighborhood at the house, I had a male neighbor that used to come and talk to me. He would see me sitting outside crying over everything that was happening; the divorce, selling the house, etc. and we talked. He knew that I had a gentleman friend. He made sexual advances towards me and I would push him away, but never said anything to him. When I moved, I told my immediate neighbors not to give him my address.

Well, I am sitting outside one day, this was the Summer of 2013, I had been in the townhouse for almost a year, and there was a van that drove in front of the townhouse. He waved. I knew who it was. He parked in a parking space and got out of his car. I was nasty. I told him that I had to get ready for work and he kept walking towards me. I asked him what he was doing there and his response was that he was, "At the local shopping center and was in the area." I asked him how he got my address two times. There was no answer.

I told my youngest son that was living with me about this and he knows the guy and was scared. While I was at work that night, my son drove by his house and got his address and license plate number of his van. Sweet huh?

I went to the police department and reported this ex-neighbor coming to my townhouse; told them about the sexual advances, how he looks into neighbors' windows. The police tried calling him. There was no answer. They went to his house and told him under no circumstances should he have any contact with me. I also reported the tire slash (see later chapter).

My dearest old neighbor told me that her son and this neighborhood man had exchanged words a few months back. The guy swore at her son. The police asked me why the neighbor didn't report it. My response was, "How am I supposed to know?"

My cleaning lady, also a friend from my old neighborhood, told me this guy constantly walks in neighbors' yards (front and back) when they aren't around. Creepy.

I talked to my old neighbor again, and this "weird" neighbor and my neighbor's son then got into a shouting match and started swearing. The guy was still looking in neighbors' windows and trying to see if a vacant house is unlocked. The neighbor threatened my neighbor's son with mace. They reported this incident to the police. The police told them next time call them immediately. This guy was very strange.

CHAPTER 12

The Grand Canyon/Rolling Stone's Concert

My mom and I were out for dinner for my birthday while I was separated. She had a proposition for me. She wanted to take me to Arizona for the college graduation of her grandson (my nephew). I replied, "Only if we can go see the Grand Canyon." She had been there before, but that was on my bucket list (like in the movie called *The Bucket List*).

The Bucket List is a 2007 American comedy-drama that starred Jack Nicholson and Morgan Freeman. It is about two terminally ill men who escape from a cancer ward and head off on a road trip with a wish list of to-dos before they die. They were roommates and I believe Jack Nicholson was rich.

My other bucket list item was Invisalign braces, which I got, and hopefully someday I can go to Hawaii. I found out that an ex-choir member at my church, who retired from teaching math, got a two-year contract to teach in Hawaii. Wow. What a lucky dog. My ex-husband never wanted to go to the Grand Canyon. He said, "It's just a hole in the ground." Well, it's the most gorgeous, awesome, breathe taking, huge, beautiful place I have ever seen. Words cannot describe it. It is more. It is God's country and His creation. We went on a tour, which was fantastic.

When my husband found out I went on a four-day trip to Arizona with my mom in May, 2011, over a year after he asked me for a divorce, he asked me why I didn't tell him. My response to him was, "What for?" I was still in the house and not divorced yet, but it was none of his business.

My mom and I had such a great time in Arizona. My nephew's graduation was wonderful and I got to visit with my sister and her husband and saw their beautiful house in Sedona, Arizona that overlooks the red-rock formations; Coffeepot Rock; Snoopy Rock; Sugar Loaf. . . It's awesome, just gorgeous . . .

Another completed item on my Bucket List—I went to see the Rolling Stones with my youngest son . . . in a limo. We had cocktails. It would have been my 36th wedding anniversary; it just happened that way . . . When I called up to confirm my reservation, I told the woman I was going to hear the Rolling Stones, on what would have been my 36th wedding anniversary; but I got divorced. She proceeded to tell me that she and her husband had three small children and he wanted to still be married and see his children, but wanted to live with his girlfriend. It took their divorce three years before it was all over and cost her $95,000. She had to sell her house; the divorce took everything she had. We talked at length. It was nice. As I was talking to her, I was sitting outside, and my ex-husband walked by the townhouse I rented (he lived four blocks away), but on the other side of the street. She told me it takes about two years after a divorce to be at peace with the whole thing. Wow, I wondered, what would my ex-husband say if he knew I had gone to the Rolling Stones concert with our youngest son on what would have been our 36th wedding anniversary? And, I wonder what he was thinking on that particular day.

When we got to the United Center in Chicago for the concert, I had brought a pair of binoculars as we were sitting way in the back. I did this up the right way. I deserved it. The Rolling Stones were fantastic. I bought a purple T-shirt and a memory book and my son and I had a great time. This was the first time I was at the arena, which is huge.

My son held my hand that night of the concert so we wouldn't get separated from one another. He's so sweet. He left me a note the next day while I was at work that he had a great time. It touched my heart. It was great spending time with my baby.

This is funny. My son and I were sitting in our seats. We had sipped a few glasses of wine in the limo and started drinking beers at the concert. I was standing up dancing and singing and all of a sudden I started to fall forward. My son pushed his arm out to me and pushed me in my seat and told me to, "Sit down!" I then asked him how a skunk could get into the United Center. He looked at me and said, "Seriously, Mom. That is high-grade marijuana!" I had no idea.

Later on during the concert, I smelled it again and got sick and had to go downstairs to the bathroom. It was almost the end of the concert, but I did not have the strength to walk back to our seats, so my son asked a woman if we could just stand and listen to the end of the concert as I was sick. This was on the main level. Lucky us, there were empty seats and we got to sit down and enjoy the whole concert.

What a fantastic night.

CHAPTER 13

E-mails Between Me and My Son During my Separation

Here is some correspondence to and from my oldest son:

To my son,

I wanted to tell you something. I have a medical condition that has caused me to take a leave from work. I just found this out yesterday and can't even do "light duty" at work. It's a long story. Hopefully things will work out in two weeks. I just have to pray hard. I wanted you to know.

Second of all, I want you to know that I apologize from deep down in my heart and hopefully you can someday forgive me. I know that you were afraid of me growing up and for that I am truly sorry. I have prayed to God that you will find it in your heart to forgive me. I love you very much and you are my son.

So that's that.

Love,

Mom

Response from son:

Sorry to hear you are sick. What's wrong?

As for the rest of it, it's not something that can be instantly better with and I'm sorry. It will take time. I don't think you fully understand why I was scared. I think that might be you just repeating what you heard me say and that's fine because at least you heard it.

I know the divorce was a big change, but whoever was at the house was the one that took the brunt of it. I was the one sitting with you while you cried and you made it so miserable to be around you and the way things played out made it seem like it was so you could have what's-his-nuts [he was referring to my gentleman friend] at the house. You wouldn't ever talk to me. You would email dad and it was his job to tell me to do something. It was a bad situation.

The more recent things, paired with the stuff from growing up made it easy to give you minimal contact, but at the end of the day that isn't really fair to you or to my future. I know you drive past the house regularly and e-mail and call dad regularly. Don't deny it. I've seen it. That's not a healthy process for moving on. You both need to get in a right place because you will have to see each other again and it can't be a shit show every time. I will get married. I will have kids. I refuse to do 43 holidays a year because my parents can't fake it for a few hours, or at the very least be in the same room and ignore each other. I don't care. Just need to learn to make it work.

I get super high anxiety when I know I'm seeing you. I will make it through it but because of it I probably won't be actively seeking face to face time with you soon. You're just going to have to deal with that. It will change in time.

But the best advice on how to proceed from here is to take it slow. You can't be calling or emailing all the time. It will be one step forward, three steps back situation.

Your son.

My response:

Thank you so much for your email and your honesty. I'll give you space. I can be decent to your Father and am moving on. Hope he can do the same.

As for my health, I really didn't want your father to know because I don't want to hear "I told you so," (meaning not to go into CNA aka Certified Nursing Assistant work).

But, I am on medical leave due to herniated disks in my neck. I worked on Sunday and the following morning I woke up in extreme pain in my left neck. Went to a doctor and neurosurgeon and there is no proof that I got hurt on the job. This could be something that has been brewing over the years.

Anyway, since there is no proof I got hurt on the job, I can't work light duty. So the medical leave is without pay.

The fortunate thing is that work can hold my job for twelve weeks and I am hoping and praying for healing. I have a cortisone injection scheduled for this Friday and Grandma is taking me because I have to be totally put under. I am also having an evaluation with a physical therapist on Wednesday and for six weeks on a Monday and Wednesday, physical therapy. If I respond well, it could be 3x a week. 6 weeks.

So, there is the story. Thanks for asking. Just not feeling well.

Take care my dear son.

Love,

Mom

I e-mailed my oldest son to see if he and his girlfriend could join my mom and me for an early Mother's Day dinner, as I had to work on Mother's Day. Never got a response. Boy, does that hurt. My youngest son had to work.

Surprise, surprise: The day before Mother's Day, my oldest son sent me flowers with a tall purple vase and pink tulips and purple irises. I cried my eyes out. He did remember. It made my day . . . . week . . . month . . . . year. I sent him an e-mail thanking him. Then I found out he also sent my mother roses and a vase.

I called my ex-mother-in-law on Mother's Day. She invited me to brunch with her and my ex. I had to work. I told her that even if I didn't have to work, that I didn't want to see him and she understood.

Church bulletin on Mother's Day: "Thanksgiving pray . . . For your Mom, a gift from God. May the Lord who chose your Mother especially for you, guide her as she continues to nurture and influence your life and lead you to know Him."

I also sent my niece an e-mail to wish her a happy first Mother's Day and my cousin, who lost her mother last year, an e-mail telling her that I was thinking about her. She and her mother used to plant flowers on Mother's Day if it was nice outside. This was my favorite aunt.

And, my good friend at work gave me a gorgeous Mother's Day card. It touched my heart.

The continuing saga:

Somehow my oldest son found out about me writing a book. I never wanted him to know, nor did I want my ex-husband to know. But, somehow my son found out and here are the e-mails that were going back and forth one Saturday morning for three hours.

I knew he was going to Texas for 10 days and I saw his car, so I e-mailed him.

> Me: Hi! You back? Did ya have fun? Love, Mom

> Son: Yep, came back Sunday night. Had tons of fun. All over Texas.

> Me: Cool. Glad you had a ton of fun and are safe. Love, Mom.

I had e-mailed my ex-husband to check and see if he heard from our son while he was in Texas. No response. Surprise, surprise.

Then the horrible day:

I received an e-mail from my son:

> Son: I heard through the grapevine that you are writing a book. Is this true:

> Me: Who the heck did you hear that from?

> Son: Grapevine.

> Me: That's okay. I can figure it out. True. The book is written, just in the "editing" stages. It's going to be a long haul. Love, Mom.

> Son: Probably I don't have an option in being in this or not do I?

> Me: What makes you think you are in this? You don't even know what this book is about. Love, Mom.

> Son: Grapevine says divorce and divorce involves family. I'm related. I can only assume.

> Me: Grapevine is right to a point. You assume correctly. It is a memoir and there are no names in it and the author name will be a fictitious name I have thought of. FYI . . . It is going to be a Christian based book that involves a lot of things such as losing a job after your father asked me for a divorce, divorce, family, sermons, life, a new career, etc. I was not going to say anything to you until I knew whether or not it would go somewhere. I'm not using a publisher. It will be a self-published book or something called I-Book. I have a lot of work ahead of me. Will have to have a website, etc. So, there you go. I've been working on it

for approximately two years and it'll probably be another two years, if it goes somewhere. I am working with someone in New York that came highly recommended by a friend. I hope that answers your question! Love, Mom

Son: I'm pretty sure that I would like to be edited out of it or at the very least see what parts are about me as I know you remember things differently than they happened. Fake name or no fake name, you will tell people that we know to be ready if it does go somewhere and it is easy for anyone who knows me to figure out that it is me.

Me: I'm trying very hard to understand your feelings about this. Truly I am. I can only tell you that your feelings that you voiced/e-mailed me awhile back are included in the book and I will make it known that you feel that, "I remember things differently than they actually happened." I totally understand where you are coming from, but this is my book and my feelings of the way I felt. If you want to meet for lunch or something to discuss this, I would be more than happy to do that. Your brother has already asked me to take out something and I abided by his wishes. All for now. Love, Mom

Son: You remember it your way and then there is what really happened. You will be telling half truths which will make them whole lies. IF you will tell the whole story it would be fine, but you have a way of painting things in a way where you are an innocent victim. Shitty things have happened. I won't discredit that, but the idea that you are completely innocent is where the issue is. We have had an issue for as long as I can remember, and I prefer to block things out for my sake. I heard you many times shit talk on the phone after pops left the house, so I have a strong feeling that is what this is about. It may not be intentional, but if this does go somewhere, I don't want you passing this book around to friends and family so they can go, "Wow, that kid is a _____ (I can't use the word that he used) when there is a huge backstory that is being left out.

Me: Okay. Then give me the "Huge back story," then I will include that in the book. What do you want me to do? Not continue with my book? I know I'm not innocent and have prayed for forgiveness and asked you for the same. I do not expect you to ever understand how I feel. That's fine. You are a young adult and I'm a parent and we would not have the same opinions. The divorce was the best thing for me and your father. And, I'm moving on. The book talks about our marriage problems. I'm trying very hard to get this down on paper in a good way so that you are not looked at as a, "Wow, the kid is a _____." And no one would think that. I'm trying to take your feelings into consideration and am giving you a chance, so take it. If you feel traumatized by our relationship, then go and talk to someone. Everyone needs help at some point in their lives. FYI . . . I have tried to be a friend to your father regarding the last e-mail that I sent him when you were in Texas. He doesn't respond and that is fine. There are always two sides to every story. P.S. Half truths, as you call them, would not equal whole lies Your choice. Mom

Son: I was forced into therapy for a year by you before I was legally an adult and could drop the quack. You have forgotten the beatings (see definitions 2 pages from here!) that you doled out on the countless nights we could not fall asleep listening to you and dad screaming about money or when you made him sit us down when we were around 14 or 15 to explain what divorce was and that it was something that would happen to you guys. You leave those details out of the story. It makes a lie because that is some key information. As I said before, I am willing to look at the parts that I am in. If this isn't something that you want to do, I would like to be left out of it altogether. That doesn't mean to stop your book. If it makes you feel better, than do it.

Me: I have to think about this and ponder over it. You have expressed some of your feelings, and I understand and can include that if that is YOUR huge back story. Key information . . . Being left out altogether is not an option. We have to come to some kind of an agreement. I am willing to do that. I could say so much more, but what's the point? Love, Mom

Son: Say so much more about what? There is nothing you can say because you are clueless to that there is or ever were any issues. You just think I stopped talking to you one day.

Me: Then give me the issues. Let it out. I'm not going to say what I would really like to say as it wouldn't matter.

Son: I have told you many times before. No point in continuing wasting my breathe.

Me: So our e-mails today have hit on everything or not?

Son: Not even a little. Past conversations have touched on everything throughout the years and nothing changed, so I don't expect them to now, that is why I have made the request that I have made.

My younger son thinks his brother was being difficult. I asked him if I was a terrible mother. He told me when I was going through menopause, I was crazy and took a plastic toilet seat cover and spanked his brother. I don't remember.

I never beat up my son. I spanked his butt when he misbehaved, but never beat him and I told him that. I asked him if he ever had to go to the hospital or was anyone else called?

My first gentleman friend was beaten by both of his parents with a barber shop belt and his father was an alcoholic. I hear a lot of stories about what parents did to their children and I feel he needs a little maturity.

I remember years ago, my ex-husband took all of the money out of my checking account. I went to write a check at Kohl's and I couldn't. I went to the bank and found out he moved the money. I was embarrassed and pissed off. I remember going to his parents' house and telling them what he had done and was going to ask for a divorce...

I know my husband and I used to fight a lot, especially over money, but I don't remember the boys being 14 or 15 and talking to them about divorce.

My oldest son thinks that I was a terrible mother, and maybe I was to him in his eyes. I was always there for our boys. I have talked to people about raising kids. They have taken brooms, bats, etc. to their kids. I never did that. I spanked on the butt and screamed, but never hurt them physically. Were the police ever called? No. Were they ever sent out away from us? No.

The love of my life, I call him "Man" in a later chapter, told me that his Mother used to hit him behind the knee with a strap. It was brutal.

Definition of beating: to hit (someone) repeatedly in order to cause pain or injury.

Another definition: to strike with or as if with a series of violent blows; dash or pound repeatedly (against).

I thought about my husband and oldest son and questioned: Do they hold back so long and not discuss things and then explode?

My oldest came over one day to pick-up his car that his brother borrowed to clean it out to make some extra money, but never finished cleaning it, because of the weather. He needed his car because of the flooding down by where he and his father live. I asked him if he wanted to come in. He told me, "Yes." It was great. We talked; he helped me put a bird floor lamp together with the UV bulb specially made for birds. It helps birds produce vitamin D. He also hung a rod by my front door so I could hang a purple valance and he also hung a heavy picture in my kitchen. He has carpentry background and it was great. I gave him some money for helping me and told him to go to lunch with his girlfriend. I thanked him. It was great seeing him. We kissed one another and I asked him to call me, so that he and his girlfriend could come over for dinner. I haven't cooked in a long time. I am working on that. My youngest son and I love casseroles. I finally cooked a casserole and we ate together. It was nice. He made a comment, "The pecans are a special touch, mom."

One of my dear friends and I met for a long, fun-filled breakfast one day. I told her about my e-mails between me and my son. She has a friend from high-school that was adopted and wanted to find her biological mother.

My friend asked me if maybe I thought my son was having a problem with being adopted. I will never know. We were always honest with our boys that they were adopted and told them that if they ever wanted to find their biological mother, that we would help them.

I pray that someday time will heal. At least he responded to my e-mail that, he can "Make it to Thanksgiving."

I sent him an e-mail to see if he and pops would like a loaf of pumpkin bread I baked. He responded, "Yea, that sounds good." I put it in his mail box and a few days later, he sent me an e-mail, "Thanks for the pumpkin bread."

God answers prayer:

My relationship with my oldest son is much, much better. We got together at Christmas time and exchanged gifts. A week before Christmas he sent me a beautiful floral arrangement in an adorable stocking holder/vase. It touched my heart. We got together for my birthday and he gave me a dozen gorgeous roses.

He moved into his own apartment. It was his first one and he was 28 years old. I was happy for him. At my birthday celebration, I gave him his gift for his new apartment, a pressure cooker, and I believe he loved it.

My mom, two sons and I went out to dinner to celebrate my birthday at a restaurant that my oldest son recommended and it was great. He also brought me a dozen, gorgeous pink roses.

I do love my sons very much and would do anything for them and hope that my relationship with them gets closer as time goes by.

For my birthday my youngest son gave me a card that read:

"Love You, Mom"—on the front He inserted a picture of the two of us when we went to the Rolling Stones concert together.

"You don't hear this often enough . . . But thanks for everything.

Happy Birthday."

He drew a smiley face and signed it Love.

That also touched my heart.

My oldest son, bless his heart, came up with an idea to celebrate my great-nephew's first birthday and my mom's (his grandmother's) 80th birthday as they have the same birthdays. We had a great family celebration at my niece's new house and fun was had by all. The "kids" had a puzzle made, 1008 pieces (my mom loves to do puzzles) for their grandmother of a photograph that was from 1999, of family and friends, which covered all generations. My aunt has since died and my mom's gentleman friend has since died. It touched my mom's heart and mine . . . I cried. What a sweet gift. My son's idea!

He got engaged after dating his fiancé for almost seven years. The whole family was excited when they got engaged. They posted pictures on Facebook which I printed and I made a cool shadow box of their engagement with pictures, 3-D pictures of a wedding ring, champagne glasses; all kinds of neat things.

When they opened it, his fiancé told him that they were going to put it in a special place.

They are now happily married and I have a grandson.

Things are a lot better between my oldest son and me. Thank you God.

CHAPTER 14

After The Divorce—"Kinks"

After the divorce, I had to spend an additional $7,000 on my lawyer on various personal issues, plus hire an accountant to do my taxes, in addition to hiring an attorney to draw up my will. The money I went through was appalling. A few months after I moved, my younger son moved in with me.

I had to go to the bank and get a safe deposit box for all of my important documents. My boys had to go to the bank and sign papers for the safe deposit box in case of my death. I did periodically check the box to make sure that they didn't try to look at the will, which they have not. They will be all set when I die and their father dies.

So, after the divorce, my ex-husband and I had to split our assets. We split one asset with no problem. The other investment split got very complicated. I had a retirement fund; he was to get all of one of the other investments to equal my retirement fund value. Everything had to be split 50/50. We were ready to go. Then I found out that one of the investment companies wanted everything recalculated due to my increase in my retirement fund value. So, my ex asked me to compose a letter to the investment company as I was a, "fast typist," so I did. I left it in his mailbox with my calculations. I had gotten his permission to drop it in his mailbox. I waited and waited for his response. Throughout all of this, I definitely had to learn patience.

He contacted me and told me my calculations were wrong, but he didn't explain why he thought this. I called my lawyer and she told me I was on target. After leaving my ex various voicemail messages and sending him e-mails, and being frustrated as I wanted my money so I could figure out investments with my financial advisor, I finally got ahold of my ex. He swore at me and told me to, "F___-off," and hung up on me. The next time I talked to him, he said to me, "You have a way of sending me over the edge." What did he think he was doing to me? It must be part of his mid-life crisis. . . . or whatever. Did he feel he missed out on something because I was the only woman in his life?

Anyway, he finally settled down and focused on my calculations and agreed to everything. This took weeks and weeks. Again, it was all up to me to handle.

He was known to hang up on me a lot. Real mature, right? He wanted the divorce and I had to do and start everything: The divorce proceeding, clean out the house. I had to do it all while he sat back.

It's all over. It is still hard to see his two fancy BMW's. Occasionally I saw him walking on the opposite side of the street in front of my townhouse. It was difficult. Or I see him go by me in one of his cars when I'm in my car and nothing. It is hard not to see his family anymore. One day I was out in the car and I saw his cousin, who works at the Kohl's close to my townhouse, in her car. You never know who you'll run into. We talked for a minute.

After the divorce and the investments were divided, I e-mailed my lawyer and her associate and told them instead of getting a "boob job," I treated myself to Invisalign braces. They laughed.

I was a real smart-ass to my ex-husband on our six-month anniversary from getting divorced and sent him an e-mail congratulating him. This sounds so un-Christian like, but I wanted to get back at him and hurt him for all of the pain he had put me through.

One and a half years after the divorce, I had not received a bill from Triple A for any emergency assistance on my car. For some reason, I checked my card and it had expired two weeks prior to my checking into it. So, I called them and found out that they did send me two bills, only to my ex-husband's address. I had them correct the address, making sure my name was the only one on their records, paid the bill with my credit card and was all set. I was furious. The woman I talked to said when someone moves, my ex-husband, my name follows him to that same address.

I e-mailed my ex-husband and told him going forward, that I wanted all my mail and not to throw anything out. I also told him that I drove home at 11:00 p.m. at night from work, the weather had been awful, and that if I needed car assistance in that two-week period that the bill had not been paid, I would have been in deep trouble. I received no response.

Around a week before I sent him this e-mail, I had to send him another e-mail that I needed some information from him for my taxes. I had to give him a two-week deadline, or he would procrastinate.

Again, no e-mail response from him after the two-week deadline was up.

Almost two-years after our divorce, I was still getting calls for him on my land line phone at the house for one of his side businesses. It aggravated me so that he still had not given his cell phone number out. It finally got settled.

According to my lawyer, in 50% of divorces, there are "**kinks**" after a divorce.

Well, leave it to me. I had a kink. Of course.

When I went to my accountant with the 2011 tax returns, she noticed that page two was missing from the 1040 and the Illinois 1040. She thought it was strange. So, I called my ex-husband on his cell phone, but he did not answer. I wanted to do this in front of someone as proof.

He did send me a copy of the second page. I sent this to my accountant, who called me. There was a tax credit of $5,200. I was working at the time, making pretty good money which brought us into another tax credit. She believed that $2,600 should have been an asset to me at the time of the divorce.

So, to make a long story short, my accountant said I had two options: Get a tax credit; or have a check cut for $2,600. It would be better to have my ex-husband send me a check for the $2,600 so that the IRS didn't question this and he would receive correspondence.

I talked to my lawyer and had them send a letter to my ex-husband's lawyer. We explained the situation regarding the taxes. Were marital funds used or business funds?

Meanwhile, maintenance was late because my ex-husband said he had more important things on his mind. I told him that there was nothing more important than a legal, binding contract unless someone was dying or there was an emergency. Our son could not afford to reimburse me for his medical insurance as he didn't have a full time job anymore. My ex-husband swore in front of the judge the day of our divorce that he wanted to pay for our younger son's medical insurance. I found out a few days before the divorce that our younger son was paying for his medical insurance out of money that had been gifted to him through the years from his grandparents. So, my ex-husband lied to me.

The lawyer for my ex-husband made me wait for a response to the letter regarding the $2,600.00 tax credit. When I sent my ex-husband an e-mail, he told me that he had responded to his lawyer seven days ago and he was going to contact him.

My ex sent me a response to the tax issue via e-mail: "The business was not part of assets split and says so in the divorce decree document. My taxes are paid as an estimate. The government wants me to overpay. The refund was carried over to the next quarter estimated tax." So, this $2,600 tax credit was dropped.

I don't trust anymore. I can't. I wanted proof. My lawyer was going to send a letter asking for proof if the money was used to pay the business taxes from the business or were they paid by marital funds.

We didn't have to send the letter. My lawyer's associate saw my ex's lawyer at court one day. We found out that my ex-husband borrowed $25,000 from his Mom (which I knew about and wondered why he borrowed that kind of money).

My ex paid the maintenance check and medical insurance premium early the next month. But, the next month on the 25th, there was no deposit. So, I e-mailed him. "Yesterday was the 25th and as of this morning, there is no deposit. Please advise when this will be done and confirm." I blind-copied my lawyer's office.

His response: "Sorry. I don't know what day it is. It will be done." He also sent it to my lawyer's office.

Unbelievable. He doesn't know what day it is? That's scary. And he is running a business. He has been complaining for years he has had trouble with his memory. To date, he is actually depositing the maintenance/alimony check early and sending me an e-mail confirming it.

Up until around five years ago, the maintenance check was automatically deposited into a certain account. Then the bank informed us that it could no longer be handled that way. So, he had to send me a check by the 25th, then I had to drive to the bank and make a deposit. Then I had to wait until the check cleared. What a big hassle, again.

After being divorced one and a half years, I went to my accountant to get my taxes done. Again, I needed some information from my ex-husband on purchase dates and the number of stocks that he purchased many years ago and sold before the divorce, as to whether there were any capital gains or losses. I gave him two-weeks, then when the two-weeks were up, he told me that he would have the information "soon." Three weeks went by; four weeks went by. Finally, I received it and it just brought back bad memories.

Alleluia, thank you God. My ex-husband moved out of his townhouse right before we were divorced for four years. This was such a blessing. It was hard seeing him driving his two fancy BMW cars.

Memories of the past dealing with him.

CHAPTER 15

What Does the Bible say about Divorce?

The Bible is the Word of Life!

God never planned on couples getting divorced.

In the New Testament

Matthew Chapter 19, vs. 3-9 reads:

vs. 3—Some Pharisees came to him, and to test him they asked, "Is it lawful for a man to divorce his wife for any cause?"

vs. 4—He answered, "Have you not read that the one who made them at the beginning made them male and female?"

vs. 5—And said, "For this reason a man shall leave his father and mother and be joined to his wife, and the two shall become one flesh?"

vs. 6—So they are no longer two, but one flesh. "Therefore what God has joined together, let no one separate."

vs. 7—They said to him, "Why then did Moses command us to give a certificate of dismissal and to divorce her?"

vs. 8—He said to them, "It was because you were so hard-hearted that Moses allowed you to divorce your wives, but from the beginning it was not so."

vs. 9—"And I say to you, whoever divorces his wife, except for unchastity, and marries another commits adultery."

God and Moses knew divorce would happen.

vs. 10—His disciples said to him, "If such is the case of a man with his wife, it is better not to marry."

vs. 11—But he said to them, "Not everyone can accept this teaching, but only those to whom it is given.

In 2014 I heard on the news that a lot of couples are deciding not to get married.

I met with my Pastor and I asked him the question, "If God created all things and knows all things, why would divorce be possible?" There is no answer to this. It is called free will. God never wanted anyone to get divorced, but He knew it was going to happen.

I mentioned to him that my ex-husband told a member of our church a year or two before he asked me for a divorce, that he had to "change some things" in his life. Being a Christian man, or so I thought, he should have gone to God and me, but he did not. He made the decision to reject me. I felt humiliated and betrayed. What were people going to think of me? I tried to save our marriage with counseling, but when someone falls out of love for you and wants a divorce, there is nothing you can do. It's over. This is failing to, "Love your neighbor as yourself." This is the second commandment, Mark 12 vs. 31.

Like my Pastor first said to me, "A divorce is worse than a death." Your ex-spouse is still around. It's not like a death where it is final and they are gone.

1 Corinthians 7—vs. 10-16—The Holy Spirit speaking through St. Paul… reads as follows:

vs. 10—To the married I give this command—not I but the Lord—that the wife should not separate from her husband vs. 11—(but if she does separate, let her remain unmarried or else be reconciled to her husband), and that the husband should not divorce his wife.

vs. 12—To the rest I say—I and not the Lord—that if any believer has a wife who is an unbeliever, and she consents to live with him, he should not divorce her. (Paul can cite no remembered saying of Jesus as authority for what he now writes).

vs. 13—And if any woman has a husband who is an unbeliever, and he consents to live with her, she should not divorce him.

vs. 14—For the unbelieving husband is made holy through his wife, and the unbelieving wife is holy through her husband. (is made holy is brought in some sense within the sphere of salvation). Otherwise, your children would be unclean, but as it is, they are holy. (They are holy—regarded as Christian children).

vs. 15—But if the unbelieving partner separates, let it be so; in such a case the brother or sister is not bound. It is to peace that God has called you.

vs. 16—Wife, for all you know, you might save your husband. Husband, for all you know, you might save your wife.

In the Old Testament

Malachi Chapter 2, vs. 15-16 reads

vs. 15—Did not one God make her? Both flesh and spirit are his. And what does the one God desire? Godly offspring. So look to yourselves, and do not let anyone be faithless to the wife of his youth.

vs. 16—For I hate divorce, says the Lord, the God of Israel, and covering one's garment with violence, says the Lord of hosts. So take heed to yourselves and do not be faithless."

God hates divorce and demands marital fidelity. Marriage is a sacred covenant, honored by members of the community covenant. "Covering one's garment with violence" refers to a spouse breaking the union of oneness—marriage.

Deuteronomy 21—vs. 10–14

vs. 10—When you go out to war against your enemies, and the Lord your God hands them over to you and you take them captive,

vs. 11—suppose you see among the captives a beautiful woman whom you desire and want to marry,

vs. 12—and so you bring her home to your house; she shall shave her head, pare her nails,

vs. 13—discard her captive's garb, and shall remain in your house a full month, mourning (grieving) for her father and mother; after that you may go in to her and be her husband, and she shall be your wife,

vs. 14—But if you are not satisfied with her, you shall let her go free and not sell her for money. You must not treat her as a slave, since you have dishonored her.

It is implied in this verse that to, "Let her go free," meant through divorce and implied giving her material things.

These verses are a supplement to the law on holy war against a non-Palestinian city that deals with treatment of female captives.

Exodus 21—vs. 7-11 reads:

vs. 7—When a man sells his daughter as a slave, she shall not go out as the male slaves do.

vs. 8—If she does not please her master, who designated her for himself, then he shall let her be redeemed; he shall have no right to sell her to a foreign people, since he has dealt unfairly with her.

vs. 9—If he designates her for his son, he shall deal with her as with a daughter.

vs. 10—If he takes another wife to himself, <u>he shall not diminish the food, clothing, or marital rights of the first wife</u>.

vs. 11—And if he does not do these three things for her, she shall go out without debt, without payment of money.

she has right to say marriage is over and he does not have the right to sell her to slavery.

> *"The Bible is a love story that begins with a divorce. Everything from the third chapter of Genesis through the end of Revelation is the story of a betrayed lover wooing us back into <u>His</u> arms so we can enjoy the love of family forever."* Dr. Larry Crabb, 66 Love Letters

God placed Adam and Eve in a perfect garden . . . no sickness, stress, death or sadness. Imagine being perfectly made, in a perfect environment with a perfect spouse and getting to talk to God each evening.

God couldn't have given them anything more.

But they believed a ridiculous lie about Him and betrayed Him for a piece of fruit. And every time you and I sin, we follow in their footsteps.

But we have a God who continues to woo us back into His arms so we can enjoy Him in eternity.

"How great is the love the Father has lavished on us" 1 John 3:1

Let's ponder God's love today and every day.

I found a brochure that caught my eyes entitled, "God Loves Marriage." I found out that there is a website: GodLovesMarriage.org.

Whether you're newly married—or have been married for decades—good communication is the key to keeping your love relationship vibrant and strong! And only the right communication tools can help your relationship be all that it can be. It can help them continue to grow closer. They have marriage encounter weekends which help them builder richer lives together.

"In Christ, he chose us before the world was made. He chose us in love to be his holy people-people who could stand before him without any fault. And before the world was made, God decided to make us his own children through Jesus Christ. This was what God wanted, and it pleased him to do it."
Ephesians 1:4-5

"Single or married, our mission in life is the same-to build stronger relationships with God and with other people.
All of life is about connections, relationships. We have a natural longing to be closer to God. (Often expressed in phrases like, "One with nature," "Inner peace," "Higher power.") And we desire to connect with other people (How many phone numbers and e-mail addresses do you have?")
When we ignore or forget either of these connections, we find ourselves unsatisfied.
Single or married, what's your mission in life?" Get connected.
I found a brochure at "church entitled, "Never Alone, Never Alone, Never Alone, Conncting to God as a single adult," from Bible League International.
"Staying single can be a good and satisfying way to live, it says. "It's a lifestyle choice that the Bible supports. Jesus was single. At some point, you just have to smile and get on with your mission in life."

"My brothers and sisters, God chose you to be free. But don't use your freedom as an excuse to do what pleases your sinful selves. Instead, serve each other with love.
Galatians 5:13

"Jesus answered, "Love the Lord your God with all your heart, all your soul, and all your mind. This is the first and most important command. And the second command is like the first: "Love your neighbor the same as you love yourself."
Matthew 22: 37-39

"Lord, I decided that my duty is to obey your commandments. I beg you with all my heart, be kind to me, as you promised."
Psalm 119: 57-58

Connecting with God:

"All relationships are developed through talking and listening. Your closest friends and those you talk and listen to every day.

A relationship with God is no different. We need to talk and listen to Him; He wants to talk and listen to us. Every day.

Talking, Listening, Repeatedly.
Talking, Listening, Repeatedly.
That's the mantra of growing relationships.
Talking, Listening, Repeatedly.
You talk to God whenever you pray.

"You will search for me, and when you search for me with all your heart, you will find me. I will let you find me. This message is from the Lord . . . .

Jeremiah 29: 13-14

. . . Whoever comes to God must believe that he is real and that he rewards those who sincerely try and find him.

Hebrews 11:6

The Lord is near to everyone who sincerely calls to him for help.

Psalm 145: 18

Connecting with others:

Your connection with God is your most important relationship. You need to keep caring for that daily. But, other connections are important, too-family, friends, church and neighbors.

Your connection with God should not be kept apart from your other relationships. All of your relationships support each other!

"This is my prayer for you that your love will grow more and more; that you will have knowledge and understanding with your love; that you will see the difference between what is important and what is not and choose what is important; that you will be pure and blameless for the coming of Christ; that your life will be full of many good works that are produced by Jesus Christ to bring glory and praise to God.

Philippians 1: 9-11

Lonely:

"All people—married or single-
  Face loneliness from time to time.
  A husband or wife is not necessarily a cure for loneliness.
  Loneliness is normal, and sometimes we can't escape it. But it doesn't have to be without a purpose.
  And you don't have to go through loneliness alone.
  Share your feelings with others and with God.
  This God, whose closest friends denied knowing Him, knows the pain of loneliness.
  And in a world of "all alone," He builds a bridge from His heart to yours."

God provides homes for those who are lonely. He frees people from prison and makes them happy . . .
  Psalm: 68:6

You will teach me the right way to live. Just being with you will bring complete happiness. Being at your right side will make me happy forever.
  Psalm 16:11

Turn to the Lord for help in everything you do, and you will be successful.
  Proverbs 16:3

The Gospel lesson one Sunday was from 1 Corinthians 7: 1-16; 25-40
  7. Now concerning the matters about which you wrote: "It is good for a man not to have sexual relations with a woman." 2 But because of the temptation to sexual immorality, each man should have his own wife and each woman her own husband. 3 The husband should give to his wife her conjugal rights, and likewise the wife to her husband. 4 For the wife does not have authority over her own body, but the husband does. Likewise the husband does have authority over his own body, but the wife does. 5 Do not deprive one another, except perhaps by agreement for a limited time, that you may devote yourselves to prayer, but then come together again, so that Satan may not tempt you because of your lack of self-control.
  6. Now as a concession, not a command, I say this, 7 I wish that all were as I myself am. But each has his own gift from God, one of one kind and one of another.

8 To the unmarried and the widows I say that it is good for them to remain single, as I am. 9 But if they cannot exercise self-control, they should marry. For it is better to marry than to burn with passion.

10 To the married I give this charge (not I, but the Lord); the wife should not separate from her husband 11 (but if she does, she should remain unmarried or else be reconciled to her husband), and the husband not divorce his wife.

12 To the rest I say (I, not the Lord) that if any brother has a wife who is an unbeliever, and she consents to live with him, he should not divorce her. 13 If any woman has a husband who is an unbeliever, and he consents to live with her, she should not divorce him. 14 For the unbelieving husband is made holy because of his wife, and the unbelieving wife is made holy because of her husband. Otherwise your children would be unclean, but as it is, they are holy. 15 But if the unbelieving partner separates, let it be so. In such cases the brother or sister is not enslaved. God has called you to peace. 16 For how do you know, wife, whether you will save your husband? Or how do you know, husband, whether you will safe your wife?

25 Now concerning the betrothed, I have no comment from the Lord, but I give you my judgment as one who by the Lord's mercy is trustworthy. 26 I think that in view of the present distress it is good for a person to remain as he is. 27 Are you bound to a wife? Do not seek to be free. Are you free from your wife? Do not seek a wife. 28 But if you do marry, you have not sinned, and if a betrothed woman marries, she has not sinned. Yet those who marry will have worldly troubles, and I would spare you that. 29 This is what I mean, brothers; the appointed time has grown very short. From now on, let those who have wives live as though they had none, 30 and those who mourn as though they were not mourning, and those who rejoice as though they were not rejoicing, and those who buy as though they had no goods, 31 and those who deal with the world as though they had no dealings with nit. For the present form of this world is passing away.

32 I want you to be free from anxieties. The unmarried man is anxious about things of the Lord, how to please the Lord. 33 But the married man is anxious about worldly things, how to please his wife, 34 and his interests are divided. And the unmarried or betrothed woman is anxious about the things of the Lord, how to be holy in body and spirit. But the married woman is anxious about worldly things, how to please her husband. 35 I say this for your benefit, not to lay any restraint upon you, but to promote good order and to secure your undivided devotion to the Lord.

36 If anyone thinks that he is not behaving properly toward his betrothed, if his passions are strong, and it has to be, let him do as he wishes; let them marry—it is no sin. 37 But whoever is firmly established in his

heart, being under no necessity but having his desire under control, and has determined this in his heart, to keep her as his betrothed, he will do well. 38 So that he who marries his betrothed does well; and he who refrains from marriage will do better.

39 A wife is bound to her husband, as long as he lives. IF the husband dies, she is free to be married to whom she wishes, only in the Lord. 40 But in my judgment she is happier if she remains as she is. And I think that I have the spirit of God.

You have a devotion to Christ in a marriage. You have children. That is God's plan. You grow together in faith. Faith should be first. Sexuality is God's pleasing way.

You cannot make someone love you. If they want out of the marriage and you gave it your best shot, it's over and you need to move forward. It is very painful, but time will help you to heal.

There are still some days when I look back and still cannot believe I got divorced. We made our vows to God, but my husband broke them, not me.

CHAPTER 16

CNA (Certified Nursing Assistant) —A New Career

While I was dating my ex-husband trying to make my marriage work, I went back to school for Certified Nursing Assistant (CNA). I studied a lot. Before we got divorced, I got a job as a CNA (certified nursing assistant) four days after passing my state board. Not a legal secretary/administrative assistant anymore, but a new career and a lot less money. But I had a job and changed careers in my late 50's.

There is a poem entitled, **_"Tribute to a CNA"_**

It touched my heart so much after I became a CNA, that my Mom cross-stitched it for me. It is beautiful; a keepsake I will always treasure! She is the best.

It talks about caring for the sick and there was a reason that we were made by God. It talks about helping to comfort hearts, being at their side, imparting God's love. It is truly beautiful.

My Mom has cross-stitched and crocheted so many absolutely beautiful gifts for her family, it is hard to believe. I tried to convince her to sell some of her work, but she is not interested. The time she puts into her work; she could not make enough money for the time spent. She loves doing it for her family.

My favorite gifts; a crocheted manger scene of Mary, Joseph, Baby Jesus, the three Kings, angel and animals. Just gorgeous. Another favorite is a cross-stitch of a cockatiel, one of my male birds. And, a crocheted koala bear.

Her work is the best. Better than what you see at craft shows!

I had some orientation on my first CNA job, but then I was on my own. I had never put wheelchair leg rests on a wheelchair before. Each task was somewhat different. Everything was new to me.

The DON (Director of Nursing) called me into his office one day and told me that the employees and residents were complaining that I was too slow. No kidding. I had only been working as a CNA for around a month. It was all new to me and I was doing my best. The DON even made a comment to me about maybe I should reconsider being a CNA. I don't remember his exact words, but I was upset.

Well, I proved him wrong. My yearly review by the DON said that the nurses that I worked with praised me for my efforts, that I was a hard-worker, caring, and always completed my tasks.

I had a resident's daughter tell me, "You're a saint." I asked her how she could come to that conclusion as she just met me.. Her response was, "I can tell." I thanked her and it made me feel good. I was happy at my job, but it was tough and physical, and you need to have a lot of patience when you work with dementia and Alzheimer's patients.

I got my own group of residents that I had every day and everything was going along well until one day, the DON called me up to the nurse's station. There, right in front of residents and my co-workers, he told me two CNAs and a nurse reported that I went into a resident's file and talked to a family member about the resident's condition. It was a lie. I was upset and started to cry. I told the DON that I didn't do that; I would never do something like that. I told him that it's not my job to give family members information on a resident; that was the nurse's responsibility. I also told him I was an honest person, and I would swear on the Holy Bible that it was a lie. I didn't understand, and I don't understand to this day, why three co-workers would lie about me. I suspected who did it, but was never told because there was no proof either way. I was not written up for this incident. I wanted them to pay the consequences, but it was their word versus mine. I was also told that one particular CNA thinks the Administrator showed me favoritism. What does she know? We don't socialize together; just talk about the two birds I gave her before I moved out of the house.

That night, after work, I drove my girlfriend to the train station and heard a weird sound; humming, rubbing. I didn't think much about it at the time. The next day I ran errands and met my mom, cousin and her husband for lunch. The sound got louder. I got home and parked my car in the driveway. I went through the Arby's drive-through to get something to eat before going to choir. I had a flat tire. I was only a mile from home. I know you are not supposed to drive on a flat tire, but I was only a mile away. So, I drove with my flashers on at 10 mph.

When I got home, my son came out. I had called him on my cell phone to tell him about my flat tire.

There was a slit in my tire.

The next day, I had my car towed, got a new tire, and got an oil change. My mechanic came to pick me up and told me it was a knife slit.

I called work and told them I would like someone to look at the videotape of that night from the parking lot. I suspected this neighbor from my old neighborhood or someone from work who maybe had asked someone to do it, as there is a lot of prejudice and hatred toward me. I was asked to save the tire.

Well, the videotape came back with nothing. Maybe it was a random thing, but I find the timing was ironic. I was told the videotape would pick up if someone was crawling along the ground or stooped down. I had permission to view the videotape. Forget it.

This could have been worse. At least it was a slow leak, otherwise I could have lost control of my car. Is someone out to get me?

I went out to buy some mace and pepper spray at a local sporting goods store. My oldest son let me borrow his car because I was scared. A few weeks after someone slit my tire, I was driving home from taking my friend, Violet, to the train station. I hit some kind of animal. It broke my right front grill and right indicator light, so I had to get them fixed. Thank goodness it just cost me for the parts, which was not expensive. I went to Larry Roesch to pick-up the parts. I found myself a lime green pair of sunglasses that match my car with Volkswagens on the side. My auto mechanic didn't even charge me for putting the parts in. I bought him a chocolate shake, as he mentioned to me that my gentleman friend, who the mechanic fixed me up with, always buys his post office friend a chocolate shake from Burger King. A few nights later, again, driving home from the train station, I almost hit a raccoon.

Again, my car went back to the mechanic. I was told my brake light wasn't working. The bulb cracked due to water build-up behind the plastic light cover.

A friend of mine asked me about my car. I told her, "Don't ask, you'll jinx me." She knew about the slit in the tire, etc. She helped me out when I first moved into the townhouse because my mail and my ex's mail were constantly getting messed up since we live in the same complex and on the same street.

I found out that a nurse at work had a problem in the parking lot. Someone took off the spare tire from her CRV and it cost her money. She hugged me because she knew what happened to my car. Well, I found out they have been having problems in the parking lot for a few years.

Again, I got another flat tire. I was very suspicious. I had to have the car towed, again. My mechanic told me I probably either hit a curb or a pot hole. Again, my older son let me borrow his car.

I was pulled from my permanent group after that happened with the terrible lies and worked on a different floor, as a floating staff member. That was tough because I did not know the residents there. But I would ask the nurses questions and I kept at it for an entire month. A few more CNA's had to do the same thing and work on that same floor, so my conclusion was, I knew who did this to me. The facility does not pull you off of your permanent group like that unless there is a problem. I never said anything. Fair or not, I did what I was told. Months later a CNA (who was eventually fired) made a nasty comment to me that, "You were being punished." I thought to myself, what for? She was referring to the fact that I was pulled off of my permanent group for a month. I've never in my life had to deal with something of this sort. I'm a hard worker and maybe they are envious. I do a good job and I care. People are nasty.

I went back to my permanent group a month later and my sweethearts missed me and I missed them. That was a great day. I lost quite a few of my residents to death. It's tough, but as bad as this sounds, it gets easier. God takes and God gives.

Whenever I lost a resident, I tried to attend the wake or I went on-line and said a few personal, kind words in the Guest Book.

I was called down to meet with Human Resources (HR) and the administrator. More bull shit (sorry for the bad language!) regarding someone lying about me. What is it?

The new administrator at work had just lost one of her birds. I was looking for a home for two of mine, because I couldn't move with all the birds I had as I was getting divorced and had to move. I had eight birds at the time; I gave two to the pet store (a parakeet and love bird) I went to for years and gave the administrator two of my birds (cockatiels). She loved them dearly. She spent a lot of time with them and bought them a "castle of a cage." She spoiled them rotten. I have adorable pictures of my sweethearts that she sent me and I thank God they had a good home. My friend brought the original cage I gave her with the birds to my pet store that is now closed. I had bought the cage from the owner of the pet store many years ago. I got $100.00 for it. It was nice of her to bring the big cage in as I had no room in my Volkswagon Beetle.

My friend who took two of my birds was telling me one day that her neighbor bought a "stroller" for her three dogs so that she could take them for a walk to the park. My friend found a stroller for the birds on the internet and was taking them for walks in the park. I told her she would probably get some strange looks. She wants them to get fresh air and doesn't have a small cage to put them in and takes them outside like I've done.

Three things happened since I became a CNA:

A month or so after I started, I had to have an emergency laparoscopy.

A laparoscopy is a surgery that uses a thin, lighted tube put through an incision in the belly to look at the abdominal organs or the female pelvic organs. The tube is known as a laparoscope. There are also two other small incisions made and you are blown up with gas so that the surgeon can see.

I called my youngest son and he rushed me to the emergency room. I was off of work for almost two weeks and felt horrible. I had a cyst that wrapped around my ovary. The doctor had been watching the cyst for a while, but it happened. I was put on morphine while waiting for my surgery. My youngest son stayed with me during the night and my mom came the next morning. I knew it wasn't real, but I was seeing big bugs crawling on the wall. I freaked my mom out. Oh yes, my husband—we were separated at the time—came to see me in the hospital along with our oldest son. My husband leaned over and kissed me on the cheek. What was that for?!

Then around a year later, I got hurt on the job with a moderate hand sprain. I could work on light duty at work. With physical therapy at work, I got better.

Then I had to go on medical leave; I could not relate it to work. I have had three herniated disks in my neck. I got a cortisone injection in the neck. Good ole' mom was by my side, as always. I went to physical therapy two times a week for six weeks and returned to work after a month. I prayed hard along with my family and friends. My job could hold my position for me for twelve weeks. I received no salary and had to pay with a check for my medical insurance and my son's. Thank goodness I had money from the sale of the house. I had no income while on medical leave. I did have a couple of personal time off days, which I used. I had to do exercises every day, which I was faithful about doing.

I did have a mild set-back and got another cortisone injection (you can get three in one-year) and I had to start physical therapy, again. The injection caused "severe discomfort." The cortisone went directly to the inflamed nerve in my neck and I had to be given Vicodin, a painkiller. It was horrible. Then my blood sugar spiked up (I am diabetic) pretty high due to the cortisone injection, which I knew would happen. I had my oldest son, mother, and gentleman friend ready to take me to the emergency room for an insulin shot. One of my friends at church said to me, "Does it ever end for you?" I just kept praying and hoped I don't didn't need surgery. I couldn't even go to the movie theater as my neck went crazy. The only comfortable position was my high-back recliner with a heating pad. I have learned what I can and cannot do, that's for sure. At least while I was on medical leave for a month, I planned a baby shower for my niece. I was talking to my one neighbor who is young and is going to school to become a doctor. She asked me how I was doing and I told her about my neck. She proceeded to tell me that her 19-year-old sister had to have emergency back surgery for herniated disks. She lost a lot of feeling in her leg one day. She used to ride

CNA (CERTIFIED NURSING ASSISTANT)—A NEW CAREER

horses professionally. Back disk problems run in their family. It could have been worse for me.

After returning to work, I got a terrible cold. I ended up having to go to the doctor, who diagnosed me with bronchitis. Again, I was off of work for a couple of days. Then, another day off with another viral infection.

I prayed to God. Please, enough is enough.

I got a shingles vaccination and developed an allergic reaction. One-half of my arm was pink and there was a big hive and it was hard by the injection site, and warm to the touch. I had a headache for hours and then itching began. It was also painful. I called the pharmacist and bought some topical Benedryl and oral Benedryl and that helped a lot. Leave it to me. I was able to go to work, thank goodness.

Then, I got my finger squeezed between some metal on a wheelchair leg rest, cutting the skin. I waited two days to report it at work, as I didn't think much of it, until my good friend at work told me I needed a tetanus shot. What a big deal at work: You have to report any injury of any kind.

My friend at work (a CNA), let's call her Violet, and I hit it off from the start. She was a single mom, struggling, who lived in the city and worked in the suburbs. To help her save money on taxis and buses, I would pick her up about a mile and a half from work so she didn't have to walk. Then I used to drive her after work to the train station, which took half an hour, and then half an hour to drive back home. I had to stop taking her to the train station as I was so tired after work. I had received two red-light violations. It was too dangerous, driving when you are that tired, and my friend totally understood. She had to fend for herself when I was on medical leave. She is a doll and a good friend. She is my confidant. She knows everything about my life. Love you, Violet, even though sometimes you are a pain in my buttock!

A funny thing happened when I walked into work one day. There was a nice looking, older gentleman at the front and he asked me if I knew what CNA stood for. I told him, "Yes, I am a CNA, see?" He said, "It stands for "Cleaning nasty asses." It was hilarious. I also had a different gentleman, who saw my CNA name tag, told me it stands for, "Can't know anything."

I had to occasionally teach, shadow/orientate new CNAs.

We had a CNA walk out on us on July 4th. Wow. She was a big woman; used to drive a truck. One of the dementia patients slapped her twice in the face. When you work with these kinds of residents, you always have to have your guard up. They do not know what they are doing. They called her back into work. She came in and then got fired. I was told by one CNA that, "You overdo it on your job." I never sit down. I told her, "That's me. I care." Am I making them look bad? I don't care. I am who I am.

One night I had around six residents to put to bed at the same time. Sorry . . . no can do. I decided to write numbers on small pieces of paper numbered one through six. I put them in a bowl and had each resident pick a number. That was the order I was putting them to bed. They loved it.

One night the floor that I worked on was short two CNAs. The nurse called down to the first floor to ask that a CNA be brought up to help. The nurse proceeded to call the Assistant Director of Nursing (ADON) and she advised that a CNA should come up and help. All of the CNAs on the first floor refused to come up to help us and said if they had to come up and help us, they would walk out. Then one of the CNAs on the first floor paged all of the CNAs on the second floor and came up to the nurse's station. I wasn't there. I was in with one of my residents. She told them that no one was coming up to help or they would walk out. All of us CNAs were livid. How can that CNA get away with that?

Someone at work borrowed money from me—$350.00. She paid me back. She asked to borrow from me again, only this time $500.00. After I left the job and sent her a text, she said she would start paying me. I found out from a friend that still worked there that she went out gambling, so I sent her a text message:

"When are you going to start paying me back?"

Her nasty reply: I couldn't believe it. Via text:

"Do you think that I am not going to pay? I told you I will. What is the problem?" Another one: "Anyway, I told you when I get my income tax I was going to give it all to you so what happened to what I told you? If I knew you were going to be on me like this, I wouldn't have asked you for help, but I will pay you. Don't worry. I am not like that. I paid you before didn't I?" Next text: "I told you when I get paid I will give you something

My response: "Well, I 4-got. No problem."

If she told me February, I would have written it down. Then she tells me when she gets paid she'll pay me something. Well, six-weeks went by, and nothing.

My response:

"I didn't know when you expected the income tax; that's all. Chill out!"

Wow, you help someone and get treated like this. I'm done.

Well, she left me a message on my cell phone, which I only used for emergencies, but I did check it occasionally. She met up with me to give me some money. I apologized to her and she told me we were cool and that everyone at work missed my jokes and silliness. That made me feel good. There are supposed to be seven CNAs working on the floor; she said they usually only have four CNAs. Crazy. I'm so glad I'm gone from that job. They are cleaning house. She just sits down at work and cries, it's so BAD.

She called me on my landline one day and we met up and she paid me back in full.

One day I was at Target and a young woman in front of me had swiped her card to pay for her merchandise. She had made some comment like she was dizzy and I thought she was tired and forgot her PIN number. A few minutes later, she complained of being dizzy again. So, as a CNA, I came to her rescue. She was a petite woman. I came behind her to hold her with my weight and strength. There was a bench close by, but I did not want her to walk. I asked for a chair, had her put her head down, and took her pulse and respirations. I asked her if she could possibly be pregnant, if she was diabetic and whether or not she had eaten breakfast. She had eaten a yogurt with granola, she said. She told me there was one occasion where she was hypoglycemic; which is low blood sugar. Someone from Target got her an orange juice. I spent around 45 minutes with her and she got some snacks. She said she was going to medical school and thanked me for helping her. It was cool and I was not nervous. It was great helping someone. She had just gotten engaged two days before. I think she was stressed out. I gave her a hug, wished her well and told her that I would pray for her.

I used to run into residents that I knew at the facility. My ex-husband's parent's old neighbors. Two members from my church. Friends of my ex-in-laws. That was interesting. They told me that my ex's father told them that it made him sad that his own son didn't come to visit him when he was sick. A number of years before I worked at the facility where my ex-mother-in-law was living in assisted living, I worked across in the other building as a CNA. When I went to visit her a few times, the lady at the front desk told me it was sad that no family member ever came to visit her.

I had a resident who lived at the assisted living facility. She knows my ex-mother-in-law and my resident told me she took the divorce real hard.

I also had a resident, older, who had contracted arms. A contracture is an abnormal shortening of muscle tissue, causing the muscle highly resistant to stretching; this can lead to permanent disability. You cannot move it. She was my sweetheart and had the same name as my sister. She really didn't talk, but sometimes it sounded like she was saying, "I need you; I need you." My CNA friend heard her one day and told me it definitely sounded like she was saying that to me.

I saw my doctor where I worked. He was visiting some of the residents who were his patients. He mentioned to me that my ex mother-in-law needed to get in to see him. I told him my hands were washed of that responsibility now. We were divorced and it was up to my ex-husband to take care of.

Awards I received at work: Most Wired and Most Lovable.

We had a resident who sexually abused his daughter and she came to see him every night. He was a real "bastard." (Excuse my French.). He called the female CNAs sluts, says "F/U" and on and on and on. He grabs, kicks, ... I can't go into details, but he was now gone from the facility. Alleluia. He grabbed a CNA so hard on her arm, that she had to have surgery. I found out he passed away. A number of years later I ran into his daughter at another facility I worked at.

One of my residents was in the dining room one evening and I was introduced to him. I recognized him and when I heard his name, and I asked him where he grew up: the same town as I did; we went to the same high school; he graduated with my ex-husband. It's a small world. He was not allowed to visit his mother because he supposedly stole a lot of money from her. I saw his friend one day, before the son was not allowed to visit his mother. His friend used to play sports in high school with my ex-husband. When I told him about the divorce after 35-years, he was surprised.

I had an older resident who I used to take care of. He died. His son used to come and visit me at work occasionally. He was married and his wife had brain cancer and I was going through a nasty divorce. He is a nice man and caring. Too bad he was married. We are just friends. See chapter 24 for the continuing saga! "The Love of my Life!"

I had another resident, I know this sounds sick, who had a terrible bed sore on her back end with a rod in it. I never saw anything like it.

We had a resident at work with Parkinson's Disease. She wanted to talk to me in confidence. Parkinson's patients can get confused by the disease. She told me she thought she was in love with my ex-husband. She didn't even know this guy's name and when she described him to me; it wasn't him.

Interesting things after being a CNA: Families were appreciative and complimented me. One resident got moved into the facility and requested me. You get some men that try to get fresh with you. Dirty ole' men.

CNA (CERTIFIED NURSING ASSISTANT)—A NEW CAREER

I had a resident who was going home on one of my days off and received the following card along with some candy. It touched my heart:

Many Thanks From The Heart

Dear Iris, (my fictitious name)

It's nice to know

that there are still people

who take the time

to do the special things

that make others feel good...

You're someone really special.

Thank You.

Handwritten: For all the help you gave me during my stay at

_____.

Love, SI

Gossip going around at my job: I was living and sleeping with the Administrator. Wow. Where did that story come from? And, I was accused of sleeping with my friend at work. I heard stories all the time. It was getting worse and worse. CNAs getting fired for stealing; one stole a woman's diamond ring when she passed away. At least she got caught. A CNA who I had worked with had put in a good word for me at another facility, a Christian Community. I sent my resume in, had an interview, passed the test with flying colors, went to fill out the employment papers and got hired. The day I went to fill out the paperwork at my new place of employment, I was right around the corner from my job and dropped off copies of my "Letter of Resignation."

The administrator who took two of my birds was very upset that I was going to, "the competition." I told her it was business. When she asked me why I was leaving, I told her we were always short-handed and I was tired of the gossip and the back-stabbing was terrible. I had worked there for 2 1/2 years. I told her to, "Get a clue."

That same day I handed in my letter of resignation, I still had to work. I was immediately asked by a young woman from the corporate office if I could go down to Human Resources with her. Gossip, again: Someone had accused me of living with the administrator. You can imagine how upset I was. I told her that it was not true and that I was sick of the gossip.

I told her if she wanted proof, I would give it to her. I would give her a copy of:

- My Lease for the townhouse I was renting;
- My divorce document; and
- The house papers on the sale.

I was so glad I was getting out of that place. It was not a healthy place to work. You get gossip anywhere you work, but this was BAD.

I gave my two-week notice and the administrator never came to talk to me again. It really hurt. I heard she didn't ever want to talk to me again. I e-mailed her and she was not upset that I left. She was hurt and angry about something and just needed some time. At least we were communicating. I miss her.

I was told I could work at the old job PRN, which means, as needed. They wanted me to work a few days after leaving and I told the scheduler that I needed a break in-between jobs and that I was not going to work until I knew what the hourly wage was (it was supposed to be at a higher pay per hour) and that it had to get approved by higher up.

Upon finally catching up with Human Resources, I was told there was no PRN, that they were fully staffed and that I could work "per diem" which meant every weekend. I told her that was impossible because I had to work at my new job every other weekend. I wanted to keep my foot in the door. That didn't work out. I was getting text messages for a while from the scheduler and I texted her back and told her to talk to Human Resources.

My last day of work, it was supposed to be on a Wednesday, but, a dear friend of ours (me and my ex-husband's) from 30 years ago died in his sleep. Great timing. He was a race horse vet and it was very tough to handle. He was laid out at the same funeral home and in the same parlor room where my dear aunt was laid out. It brought tears to my eyes as the morning of my aunt's wake, I got divorced. My ex-husband showed up for a short time. This was the first time I saw him on a "social" basis since way before we got divorced. It was quite awkward. He walked right by me and I said, "What . . . you don't say hi to me?" I asked him if he wanted me to walk him up to the casket as I needed someone to do it for me. He replied, "No, thanks." While he was standing up front, I asked him how he was feeling. He replied, "It's tough." He asked if I sent flowers and I told him, "Yes, from me and the boys and I made something for the floral arrangement having to do with a race horse vet." He told me, "That was nice." That was it. It was a tough day. I had called him and told him what had happened and where our friend was being laid out. Nice of me, huh? There were videos of the deceased. I looked

CNA (CERTIFIED NURSING ASSISTANT)—A NEW CAREER

up to see one of him lying on our couch at our first house with their baby daughter. Memories.

I decided after working at my current job as a CNA for more than two years, it was getting to be too much for me and my health.

On my week off between my old job and new job, I went with my mother to visit her 95-year-old friend from church who was at a nursing home. My mother e-mailed me and thanked me for going with her. My dear mother told me, "You have always had a way with older people, you know." That really meant a lot to me.

The night before I started my new job, my younger son, who lived with me, took me out for a filet mignon dinner and drinks. I was so happy. We ordered salads with big mushrooms. Neither of us like mushrooms, so I called my oldest son and he came the next day to pick them up and we talked. It was nice. That morning, I got together with a long-time friend, who has been supportive, for a three-mile walk. It felt great. Then I treated her to a nice breakfast. We both love breakfast. It's our favorite meal of the day. It was a place I had never been, so now I have another place to go.

I went on-line one day to see if there were any items to purchase for a certified nursing assistant. I went absolutely crazy. I bought a tank top, shirts, earrings, a necklace and earring box. It's amazing what you can find on the computer.

I started my new job at a Christian facility. I was working on the dementia/Alzheimer's section.

The daughter of another resident at the new job told me about a friend of hers who was getting divorced after 39 years. She came up to me one day and asked me for my phone number, so that when her friend was ready, she could call me and have a shoulder to lean on.

Another resident's daughter and I somehow got on the subject of divorce. We high-fived one another. She was married 35 years and her husband told her that he was leaving on her birthday. What a scum-bag.

I miss my friends and residents at my old jobs, but I had to do what was best for me. I was at a brand new facility and I orientated on each floor; two different shifts. I loved it. Except, the first day of orientation, I was introducing myself to residents on the floor where I was going to be working. This is the dementia/Alzheimer's ward. Anyway, the first resident I talked to and asked what her name was slapped me two times. They have dementia.

At the new job, they celebrated a year of being open and I went to the celebration. We got lunch bags in purple, my favorite color.

My first night on my own at my new job went very well. I typed up a lot of notes to help me.

1. The concierge asked the CNAs if we wanted to work a double. Here we go again; just like at the other job.
2. I had a lot of very confused residents.
3. We had a resident who was moving his dresser down the hallway on wheels.
4. A CNA from the other side was telling the CNAs that she heard of a 50-year-old man who had a tumor on his testicles that weighed 130 lbs. I never heard of that before.
5. I had a resident whose sister was a resident at my old job. Small world. She ended up visiting one night at the new job and it was great to see her and her daughter.

The two-day training I had at their corporate offices was great. I learned a lot. I found out that I had another two-day training class on residents with dementia. You had to take both of these two-day classes once a year. I was impressed by the teacher starting off the training session with prayer and asked if anyone had any special requests. I asked for a prayer for my mom's best friend, who died a few days later. They also prayed before we had lunch.

My gentleman friend drove me to the town where the corporate training was held. He got lost driving there and we almost got into an accident. We got a hotel room and after class, we went out for dinner and drinks and had a great time. It was nice to get away.

The second day of training, we had just discussed dementia residents and how they sometimes yell out and how we needed to figure out why they were yelling. Were they hungry? Did they have to go to the bathroom? During break I told the teacher that I thought about yelling out to see if anyone could figure out what I was doing, but I didn't want to interrupt the class. I had to go to the bathroom. The teacher told me I should have, that it would have been funny. I told her that I would do it next year. The teachers were great.

One day I had a resident who wanted to go for a walk out to the garden. I didn't know that it was even there. It was in the upper 90's that day and I told her that we could only stay out for a short time; that the weather was dangerously hot. She held my arm and walked me around the garden. It was very sweet. There was a section in the garden for the residents. There was a huge sunflower that was as tall as corn. The flowers were very pretty. They also had tomatoes and pumpkins. After we got back, she thanked me and I asked her if she wanted something to drink—good ole apple juice. I really enjoyed taking her outside.

A few months later, her son baked a delicious carrot cake and used fresh carrots from his mom's garden. She enjoyed the compliments!

One of my resident's daughter-in-law's asked me a question about her mother-in-law wandering out of the building as she had been confused and was threatening to do so. I talked with her around 15 minutes and assured her that the CNAs had pagers that go off if someone tries to wander out of the building. She was upset about her mother-in-law's confusion and after we spoke, she gave me a hug and thanked me.

I liked the fact that on the new job, we got to take vitals and accu checks (blood sugar test for diabetics).

One night one of my 90-year-old male residents was streaking down the hallway. He had never done this before. He was laughing.

Quite a few of my residents had good lives. One sailed around the world in a sailboat with his wife. Another was a doctor in the military and did well for himself. He and his wife, deceased at an old age, raised six daughters.

One evening I had to call a hospice nurse for one of my male residents. He had a catheter and there was no output. The hospice nurse came and had to put a new catheter in. The output was 2300 cc (a huge amount); the nurse told me if I had not called her, my resident would have ended up with sepsis.

A catheter is a flexible tube inserted through a narrow opening into a body cavity, particularly the bladder, for removing fluid.

Sepsis is an illness in which the body has a severe response to bacteria or other germs. It can be fatal.

Another evening I noticed that his catheter bag had blood in it. Again, I had to call the hospice nurse and she inserted a new catheter. She told me that this resident was lucky to have me as his CNA. That made me feel good coming from a nurse.

One of my residents was caught in bed with someone of the opposite sex who was married. It is very sad. They do not know what is going on as they have dementia. They just need that human contact!

One night I saw lights on in someone's car and told the concierge the make, color and license plate. When I went out to my car to get something during my break, the lights were still on. Someone was going to have a dead battery. It had been hours. So I went to each floor at work and found the girl that the car belonged to. She thanked me up and down. While I was looking for the owner of the car, I went up to a floor where one of the CNAs from the facility I left was there. We talked. She told me, as she still works at the other facility, that there was word going around that I wasn't allowed back into the building. As you can imagine, I was pretty upset.

I went to pick up some prescriptions at my K-Mart and the female pharmacist, who I have known for quite some time, asked me what was new. When I told her I got a new job and what I was going to be doing, she started to cry. "God bless people that take care of dementia and Alzheimer's residents," she said. Her Mom had advanced dementia and it really touched her heart. I told her that's where God had led me.

The great thing is that my new job gave me Thursday nights off to still be able to attend choir rehearsal. Thank you God.

One of the CNAs at the new job worked at a beautiful, local hospital for 20 years in labor/delivery and got laid off. I totally understand that feeling.

I also worked with someone who had been working as a CNA for years. I asked her why she didn't pursue nursing. I would have had I been younger. She told me her dream and passion is acting and Gospel singing and she wanted to pursue that. Good for her.

Go for your dream!

During orientation at the new job, they wanted us to become involved with the residents' activities. I love doing crafts. I came up with an idea for my residents at work. I talked to the Director of Activities to see if I could do this. It was approved. I love to think of different activities for the resident's as I love being creative. I love to also do scrapbooking.

I found out from each of my resident's families what they did for a living, hobbies, etc. and made them special posters with their names and I signed it with my name and Love. It had pictures on it that I got off of the internet. The families thought it was a great idea and hung them in their family member's room. It really touched them. A nurse I worked with made a comment to me that I must have too much time on my hands. That sure wasn't nice.

I found out one of our nurses got fired and there was a nurse from an agency that was on the floor with me. She was very nice and complimentary to me. She told me that I was very thorough at my job. That made me feel so good.

When I was at Dollar General, I found some items to do activities with the residents. Little smiley faces and peace signs where the residents can glue colorful stems on for their rooms;

And . . . Peace is the name of my church. The day I found the Peace picture, I looked at the calendar for some reason and it was Saturday, 9-21-13 and it was Peace Day; whatever that means. And . . . .

Stencils where they could color their names on something. Some of the residents loved to color!

Also, our choir sang for the residents a few weeks before Christmas. One of my residents has a son and when I told him about our choir singing, he asked me the date and showed up. I loved it and so did the residents.

I loved the fact that they did activities with the residents: Movies, strawberry floats (not root beer), art work for the holiday season that they put up in the dining room windows. Also, this was the first year that they had Family/Friend's Day. They had delicious food, a band, and a red, white and blue jumping castle for the kids. It was really awesome. The ladies get their nails painted. They had bean bag games; games on the computer such as bowling. At the kids' corner, kids came and cut up fruit and made fruit salads for the residents. Each kid gave attendees little cards with crocheted octopuses on the front with sayings inside and printed their names! There was a fashion show where the CNAs modeled shirts the women residents made. They had a red carpet set up. It was very cute and everyone loved it.

The activity assistant did "Story Time" with the residents. She researched actors/actresses and laminated pictures of them and read their life stories to the residents. It was people from their era. They loved it. We sang YMCA and danced for the residents one day and it was a lot of fun.

The new job is advertising the facility on TV. It's a beautiful facility. My ex-mother-in-law was checking the facility out, but it was going to take a couple of years to build, so she had to choose another facility.

I was at my new job for two and half months.

I was diagnosed by my family doctor with Achilles tendon. It's an inflammation of the tendon and I had a very sore heel. He gave me exercises to do until I could get into the podiatrist, just in case it was a bone spur. It was great seeing the doctor again. He did my surgery on that same foot around 10 years prior. Then I ended up getting an infection at the surgery site because I was allergic to the sutures. I had plantar fasciitis, and the biggest bone spur in my heel that he had ever seen. He was surprised when I told him that I got divorced.

Plantar fasciitis is an inflammation of the thick tissue on the bottom of the foot. This tissue is called the plantar fascia. It connects the heel bone to the toes and creates the arch of the foot.

He gave me a cortisone shot and it was extremely painful. I had another cortisone injection six-months later and it was so painful I screamed. The heel was tender to the touch, swollen and inflamed. After the procedure, I could not walk and got a note from the doctor that I could not work the next day. I would eventually have to have surgery. There is a new procedure that has only been used for the past two years. It is called Tenex Health TX. It is similar to zapping a kidney stone; they zap the bone spur and it is non-invasive. Sounds good to me. I really missed wearing closed back shoes.

One night I was throwing away garbage and unbeknownst to me, the janitor had just washed the floor, but did not put a "caution: wet floor" sign up, and I slipped. I didn't fall, but jerked my neck (and had herniated disks, but had been fine). I had to go to the emergency room and sat there for four hours. My son had to come and pick me up, so I had to leave my car at the hospital, because I was put on medications which would not allow me to drive.

I went home and slept and the next morning I had to borrow my son's car and get my prescriptions filled and we went back to pick up my car. Then I was able to take my medications which knocked me out.

The next day I had to go to the doctor to see what he said about me returning back to full duty. I was given a few more days to recuperate.

That afternoon I had another doctor appointment, so again . . . I could not take my medications.

I got home from the doctor's appointment and received a call from my gentleman friend's friend. My friend was in the emergency room. He called for an ambulance that morning. It was ironic, because I was at the medical building around the corner from the emergency room, but I didn't know he was there. I called him and he told me I could come and visit him.

They tried to do a CT scan on my friend, but he wouldn't do it. They needed to do a CT scan to determine what was going on with him. I talked him into it and was right there by his side, but I had to cancel my doctor's appointment for the afternoon.

A CT scan uses a computer that takes data from several X-ray images of structures inside a human's or animal's body and converts them into pictures on a monitor. CT stands for computerized tomography.

The results came back. He had a good-sized kidney stone. They had to do surgery and put a stent in. He was miserable with the pain before the surgery and he kept saying, "Oh my God. I want to die."

A ureteral stent is a thin, flexible tube threaded into the ureter to help urine drain from the kidney to the bladder or to an external collection system.

The surgery went well. I picked him up the next morning and brought him home; that morning I went over to his house and took care of his cat.

A kidney stone is a solid mass made up of tiny crystals. One or more stones can be in the kidney or ureter at the same time.

He had a procedure where they laser the kidney stone and hopefully pass the smaller stones, which he did. The procedure is called lithotripsy

Then a while later I had to take him to the hospital to have the stent removed.

When I went back to work after my slip on the wet floor, the nurse and CNA I worked with the night I slipped never asked me how I was doing. I was really hurt by no reaction. I am the kind of person who cares about others and I want others to treat me in the same way; in the real world, that doesn't happen. Then, after I was back at work for a week, the floor in the dining room was washed and again, no sign. I talked to the woman and asked her to please make sure that she puts up the sign at all times. No one needs to slip. A week later I was shopping and went into the lady's room and there was a sign and another wet floor. I was careful. Wet floors seem to follow me around!

I love working with the LPNs (licensed practical nurses) and CNAs. We try and have fun because of the residents that we work with and try and make them laugh.

I have been told that I am too nice and gullible. That is my personality. I was told by a friend that I am "kind" and "encouraging" and one of the nicest people she knew. Why didn't my ex-husband realize this?

I worked every Friday and was off every other weekend. Our scheduler came up to me one Friday of the weekend I was to be off and she asked me if I could work on my weekend off. If I said "No," she needed a reason why I couldn't work so that she could write the reason why and give it to the higher up. I told her that it was my weekend off, but if she really needed to know, I told her I was "Having sex on Saturday!" She laughed. Then I told her the real reasons why I could not work on my weekend off. I had plans with my family.

St. Patrick's Day was coming up and I found stencils for the residents to color, and earrings and socks for me to wear.

One morning I was picking up a breakfast sandwich and a guy had a small St. Patrick's Day hat on. When I say "small," it was like a decoration for a party. I asked him where he got it at and he said one of the guys he worked with dared him to wear it. I asked him if he could ask his friend where he bought it as I worked with dementia/Alzheimer's residents and they would love for me to wear it. I guess it touched his heart. He insisted on giving it to me. It almost made me cry. There are nice people out there in the world.

On my day off, I was scheduled to go to the corporate office and take a dementia class. I found it interesting. I have to go back for a second day of training. I went to the class with the activity assistant and we had fun.

At the dementia class through work:

"Pleasant words are a honeycomb, sweet to the soul and healing to the bones." Proverbs 16:24

"Speak up for those who cannot speak for themselves . . . " Proverbs 31:8a

"Stand up in the presence of the aged, show respect for the elderly and revere your God. I am the Lord." Leviticus 19:32

Working with dementia/Alzheimer's patients is not an easy job. I compare it to watching a two-year old child. Not anyone can work with them. They sometimes:

Bite

Scratch

Slap

Kick

Hold tightly onto a part of your body—and we can't scream out.

Try to escape out of the facility, a/k/a elopement.

Some try to take off their wander guards which is set off if they try to escape.

Then you have to deal with sundowning.

Sundowning syndrome is defined as the onset of confusion and agitation that generally affects people with dementia/Alzheimer's or cognitive (learning) impairment and usually strikes around sunset.

Dealing with these sorts of residents is hard, sad and requires a lot of prayer and patience. They can't help it.

I went to a local Farmer's Market. If you don't know what that is, it is a place set up in local towns that sell fresh vegetables, fruits, some have jewelry vendors and other vendors set up such as ones that sell fresh bakery goods. I was wearing my scrubs and was buying a cherry catsup item and the woman asked me if I was a nurse. I told her that I was a nursing assistant. She said, "Oh, thank you for taking care of sick people. I think that is great." This touched my heart. I felt that I was definitely in the right career.

There are poems about Alzheimer's that can really make you cry.

Is this ironic?

As I mentioned in an earlier chapter... Years ago, I knew something was happening with my mother-in-law. Her personality was changing. She acted out at my father-in-law's Christmas party one year. She was rude to the waiters and everyone at our table. On the way home I remember telling my husband that this was the worst Christmas party ever. He said nothing.

My father-in-law and mother-in-law were planning a 50th wedding anniversary party. My husband and I went over to their house to talk about the party and offer our help. I don't remember the details, but my mother-in-law got mad at me at slapped me and was verbally abusive. My husband and father-in-law just sat there and said nothing.

I mentioned to my husband that something was going on with his mother.

After my father-in-law died, my mother-in-law had to sell the house. My husband was out of town that day, so I decided to go over and help my sister-in-law pack. Again, my mother-in-law was being nasty.

Then years later she got into a car accident. She said that she got confused at the intersection. I mentioned to her family that maybe it was time to take the car away from her. My father-in-law knew when it was time to give up driving and he did it on his own. God bless him. He was the best Father-in-Law a girl could ever ask for. I miss him terribly.

After my husband and I were separated, I found out through the grapevine that my mother-in-law was driving around for six hours and got lost far away. The family finally took her car keys away from her.

I had seen my ex-sister-in-law since the divorce as she came in every few months to take care of paperwork for her Mom. She was suffering from some sort of dementia. I have seen "Mom" a few times since the divorce and at one point she asked me my name. This is hard to deal with. My ex-sister-in-law had talked to her brother about visiting his mom occasionally.

Conclusion: Did God lead me to take care of dementia patients? Yes.

Dealing with a family member who has this disease is hard. My oldest son doesn't understand why his grandmother mistreated his grandfather and had a hard time dealing with that.

When my older son saw her during the holidays, she asked if he had a brother.

I pray every day before I go to work for patience and understanding. I treat residents like I would want my own mother to be treated.

My most recent client, a lovely 92 year old woman and I were singing together one day. A religious song. I mentioned to her that I loved the song, "On Eagle's Wings" by Michael Joncas. She proceeded to tell me the following story.

Her husband had been in the hospital for quite a while. She would go and visit him every day and was exhausted. She prayed, "Lord, carry me on your eagle's wings like you did the children of Israel." This is from Exodus 19.4. All of a sudden she looked to the right and there was a white van with eagle's wings spread out. What a sign from God.

> Isaiah 40 Verse 31—Those who hope in the Lord will renew their strength. They will soar on wings like eagles; they will run and not grow weary, they will walk and not faint.

It's a lot of work to be a CNA. You have to keep up with your CPR card every two years. We have on-line classes, staff meetings (where we pray!), skilled tests. We also go to corporate for a two-day class once a year; dementia class at corporate for two-days of class once a year. But, I love it. It beats working in an office.

Residents are a big part of my life.

This was God's calling for me.

I recently got a hospice (end-of-life) client. 92 years old. Very sad. I found out that she lived with her daughter for the past five years, but could not handle it any more due to health issues including a bad back. Let's call her Cal. She got a divorce which cost over $350,000 and took 10 years. I could not imagine. Cal said it was the worst. She said, and I quote, "It is worse than a death." Sound familiar? That's what my pastor told me!

I know this may sound strange to some people, but I really do enjoy taking care of hospice patients and their families. There is a certain "peacefulness" to it.

One Sunday morning the family was getting ready to go to church. Cal's daughter saw that her father was receiving and sending e-mails to four different women he was keeping in four different houses. The house the family lived in was a very expensive area in the Midwest. They sold it and also had a summer home which was sold.

He was of Chinese decent and was a well-known emergency doctor. A number of years later he ended up in jail as he was $1 million behind in taxes.

I could not believe it. What a scum!

CHAPTER 17

A Friend in Need

A friend from the old job called me. She had a streak of bad luck. She needs shoulder surgery and had been waiting and waiting and waiting. They can't find the original case worker. It is strange. I let her borrow a good amount of money because she was going to lose her car. She signed a Promissory Note for me. Her boyfriend of two-years left her and he was living with another woman. He was going to help her out financially. She had not talked to her family for six months. The day she called me, she was crying. She told me she was depressed and was calling in sick at work. I asked her if she was taking her medication. She hadn't taken any for a few days. I asked her if she was thinking about doing anything drastic and she said, "No."

I told her in a loving way to call her doctor immediately and get some help. She was at the point where she could not pay her rent. I prayed for her. She never called me to update me. I left her alone, nothing more than a voice mail message.

I finally heard from my friend early one morning. She knows I am an early bird that catches the worm. She had listened to me. She called the doctor immediately and was hospitalized for depression. She was not able to call me because they had told her to relax and took her phone away. They gave her something by intravenous (I.V.) and she told me she felt much better and thanked me. They changed her medication. She told me that I was right and it was good she was hospitalized. She is now back at work and I am so glad. She admitted to me that she was so deep in the well, she was thinking about doing something. I told her not to talk about this to anyone at work. Thank God. She was also going to meetings to help her with her depression and be around others so that they could talk and share their feelings. I told her that she was the one that took the first steps and that I was proud of her.

I was working with our parish nurse to try and help my friend out financially. I met up with her to give her some money for food; I was going to meet up with her right away, but she got a cooked chicken from a neighbor, so she put it off for a few days. I also mentioned to her that our parish nurse would like to talk to her face-to-face. She said, "We'll see." She told me that she is on a painkiller that makes her like in a "trance." I let her borrow money for food and she applied for food stamps. I did not hear back from her about meeting up with our parish nurse.

I heard from this friend after a few months had gone by. She asked me why I wasn't texting her back. She was sending me text messages on my land-line phone, not my cell phone. She told me that she had been in the hospital for two-weeks. Now she was back to work. I was told by a friend that she bought a new car! I never said anything to her about her car, but I did contact her and she started paying me back a little every month. Well . . . the first month. I received a phone call from her that she would be late with her payment the second month. I will never do this again!

It will be almost five years since I let her borrow the money, but she lost a job and had some streaks of bad luck, so I deducted some money from what she owed. To date she has never contacted me or paid me in full. Very sad. I hope and pray that she is well.

CHAPTER 18

Another Job Loss—Termination (PP)

Then, I ran into my ex-husband's cousin's daughter, who was at the facility I was working at recuperating from hip-replacement surgery. She is a few years younger than me and we were surprised and happy to see one another. She updated me on the family and I came to find out that my father-in-law's brother had passed away. This was my family for over 35 years and I was glad I found out, but also upset that my ex-husband could not be nice enough to inform me of his uncle's passing so that I could send his aunt a card.

His cousin's family was there one night and asked if they could say hi to me. One family member, who caught me off guard, called my ex an "a__." That really surprised me. His own family.

I spoke with another cousin of my ex-husband's and he mentioned to me that he did not appreciate his humor. Our sons have tried to explain to their father that his humor is not funny.

Then an old male friend that I saw told me he thought my ex-husband's humor was different!

I also remember being told by my mother-in-law's sister-in-law that she did not like my husband much. I was in shock!

Now I let the boys handle "bugging Pops" if I can't get an answer from him.

I again had high anxiety and gave it to The Lord.

I was working one evening and one of my residents was misbehaving. She was trying to hit me and was interrupting the other residents. I got somewhat aggravated and put my hand on her arm to make her stop hitting me. I also whispered in her ear and said sternly, "Behave yourself; I will take you to bed after dinner and you need to stop aggravating the other residents." She was in the dining room waiting for dinner and had to be watched very closely as she was a "high fall risk" resident. The day before this particular resident had grabbed my breast and twisted it. It didn't feel good.

A head nurse saw the frustration in my face and called me on it and told me to stay away from the resident for a while. Sometimes you need to walk away.

The next day the nurse wrote me up for abuse. I could not believe it. She wrote that if it ever happened again, that I would be terminated. I told her that I did not verbally or physically abuse her. I asked her to make a copy of my write-up.

As you can imagine, I was terribly upset.

I found out that night that the nurse, who was my supervisor on the floor, told me this head nurse checked out the resident the morning after she told me to walk away; she was checking for bruise marks. There weren't any. The supervising nurse told me to watch my back.

The story gets worse.

That evening, unbeknownst to me, a CNA from another department, was spying on me. At 9:00 p.m., two hours before I was supposed to punch out, the head nurse called me and told me to punch out. I asked her why and she responded that she received two phone calls that I had verbally abused residents. I was shocked. I knew which CNA it was and I confronted her. She told me she was the one who made the phone call. I asked her why. She told me that I was verbally abusing the residents, which was so untrue.

I loved my residents and their families and would never do anything to hurt them. I was told by a dear friend from church that, "I'm a very compassionate person." Why was this happening?

The head nurse told me that she would check with someone higher up and call me the next day, which was to be on a Wednesday. The phone rang, my gentleman friend was with me. They waited to call me until 3:30 p.m. I was off that Wednesday and the following day, Thursday.

The head nurse and the woman from Human Resources told me, over the phone mind you, that I was terminated. The head nurse had talked to the head honchos, and there was no changing their minds. I could not even go and plead my case. They were to pay me for my days of working and a few vacation days I accumulated.

I mentioned to the head nurse that two months' prior to this, she told me what a good CNA I was. She said nothing. I asked if this was going to be reported to the State of Illinois, because if it was, I would lose my CNA license. They promised me that they would not do that. I didn't believe them and tried to get this in writing from them; but received nothing.

I was numb, embarrassed, lost and devastated.

I lost my health insurance and then had to go on COBRA, which cost $500.00 per month back then.

That day I got terminated, my gentleman friend was with me. I was crying. Then my younger son came home and hugged me. How was I going to sleep? My gentleman friend told me he was going to have a hard time sleeping that night and when I asked him why, he replied, "Because I am worried about you." How sweet.

The day I was terminated, I realized I had to contact unemployment, which I knew from previously being laid off is a real hassle. The next day I went to the unemployment office, but it was now a call center. The gentleman at the front door gave me unemployment paperwork. What a hassle.

I was back to finding a job; CNA, secretary, receptionist, anything. I was 58 years old. What was going to happen? I worked diligently on updating my resume and sending out applications left and right. I did networking with everyone I could possibly think of, even people at my church. I must have applied for 25 jobs.

During the three weeks of looking for a job, I went through the drive-through at McDonald's and a young man from there mentioned he hadn't seen me for a while. I told him that, "I lost my job." His response was, "People are shitty!"

I have an old-time friend, a lawyer I used to work for. He had just met a woman who specialized in this sort of thing. I told the lawyer what had happened to me. It was a free consultation. The lawyers had to meet and discuss my situation. It took them a few days to get back to me. There was no case. The State of Illinois can fire you on the spot, for no reason.

Oh well, I thought, life goes on.

Then I received a letter from unemployment for a phone interview because my former employer told them I was, "discharged" due to "misconduct." I could not make the phone interview because I already had a job, so I wrote a response to unemployment and faxed it. I couldn't even collect the low unemployment benefit of $150.00. Nice.

A few weeks later, I received something else from unemployment. It stated that I was discharged due to, "inappropriate behavior. The claimant was yelling at residents. She was seen pushing and abusing clients. There was a witness statement provided by the employer."

Again, I was really upset. Did this happen to me? This is not my character.

I e-mailed my mother to tell her what I had received.

Her response: "You have to try and put this aside and be grateful that you are out of that place where you were a workhorse. There is nothing you can do about it anyway. If you were to try, you might be opening up a can of worms making your situation worse. Let's be grateful that it wasn't reported to the State, otherwise you would have to hire a lawyer and fight it. I know it is difficult to hear something so untrue about yourself, but I think you have to put it all behind you. It hurts me to see you hurting, but that's why you have to put it out of your mind."

As always, my mother was right—and there for me, again!

A friend of mine sent me an e-mail after I told her about what happened at my job: "You NEVER would or could do that. They are terribly mistaken. You always have been a caring, giving soul and always will be. I am certain that you did NOTHING wrong and I'm sorry that you were wrongly accused and lost your job because of it. It is their loss. I most certainly will keep you in my prayers."

Another friend's comment: "They lost a good and caring employee. Best of luck on your job search."

A supervising nurse that I worked with called me to tell me one of my residents had died. She also told me that I was wrongly accused and I did not commit any abuse.

When my friend, a cleaning lady, found out about my job loss and new job, she sent me an e-mail that read:

"I wish I could have found someone as loving and caring as you to care for my mom. I am so happy for you. . . such a need for that too. People want to stay in their homes as long as they can. . . can't blame them."

Another friend e-mailed me, "You have so much to offer."

Our Pastor's message during the time I lost my job: "Long Live the King"

There are 2 billion Christians. He has our attention 100% of the time. He does not prioritize our prayers. They are all heard at the same time.

Think of every Sunday as a little celebration of Easter.

Just when I was feeling down a week after losing my job, I received the following from my Pastor:

> ~~Dear Church Family,
>
> Below you will find an email written by a Peace member about his daughter, age 24. Please read through the email with prayer and let the Lord guide you.
>
> In Christ,
>
> Pastor

ANOTHER JOB LOSS—TERMINATION

It is with a sad heart that I write this email. My daughter's tumor is growing again very rapidly. She has elected to stop all treatment and focus on:

- Making memories
- Enjoying life
- Checking things off her bucket list

Creating happy lasting memories with family and friends has become very important to her. We would like to surprise her in the very near future with a memory book, "Why You Are Special to me" so that she can see how special she is to all those who know her. If you would like to add a page, (or more) to her memory book please do so. The memory book will consist of 8 ½ x 11 pages, (the same size as copy paper you use in your printer). We will be laminating and spiral binding the pages, so if you make a page please leave a 1" margin on the left side page so your message doesn't get cut off. The message on the page can be a written thought, a memory, poem, words of inspiration, pictures, drawings, paintings, collages . . . .Please make sure that anything written is printed, no cursive please. The page or pages need to be in our hands by Saturday, April 12th.

She received a blessed financial donation to help her accomplish some of her bucket list. Due to that contribution, a trust had been established to assist her in completing a couple of things on her bucket list. The biggest item was a trip to Disney World with her brothers, sister and their families. I have engaged the Dream Foundation (similar to Make-A-Wish but for adults) for help in making this wish come true. Hopefully they will be able to assist her in completing a portion of this Disney World trip.

So many of you have expressed a desire to help (or already have) her and I through this struggle. If God puts it on your heart to help make her wishes come true, the foundation Information is below.

God's Peace, Blessing and Love,

I can't begin to tell you how the e-mail from the Pastor to our church family touched my heart.

My thoughts and prayers are with her and her family.

I made a small donation to the, "Special Trust Number." I included the following: "I am hoping and praying that your whole family can take your "biggest" trip to Disney World. What a great Bucket List item!

Attached is something I hope you can put in her Memory Book.

I may even know you and your daughter, but we have such a large church.

Prayers and God Bless.

A Church Member.

Signed by me.

What a great feeling I had in helping the family out in just one small way!

MAKING MEMORIES... ENJOYING LIFE...

CHECKING THINGS OFF YOUR BUCKET LIST!

Your Guardian Angel!

My thoughts and are prayers are with you and your family

The week of Easter, on Wednesday, the 24-year old died. She and her family did make it to Disney World, but only for two days, then they had to fly home and the next day she died.

I went to the wake and the line was out the door. A friend of the family's bought each family a t-shirt, in purple, as a dedication to this young, courageous woman.

Before I walked into the funeral home, I saw two women from my church that I hadn't seen for a while. Was I surprised. They had both left the church. One was separated from her husband and did not want to get a divorce because she was the sole bread winner. The other woman, did she have a story, which I am sworn to secrecy, but I thought my divorce situation was bad.

I gave both women my phone number and told them about my book. One woman called me a week later and we talked for two hours. I recommended to her that it was time to get a lawyer and gave her my lawyer's number. I was praying for her.

I believe God gave me this divorce situation to help others.

This is what Christianity is all about.

I received a thank-you note a short time later from the young woman's family which read:

> With Sincere Thanks....
>
> Thank you to our friends and
>
> family for your generosity.
>
> Your overwhelming support
>
> helped (24-year old's name) accomplish
>
> significant aspects of her bucket
>
> list and blessed our family in
>
> the days that followed her death.
>
> (24-year old's name)'s special needs
> trust will continue to support
>
> (and there were various names listed,
> including our church)

The entire family attended the late service on Easter. Some tears were shed and afterwards, I went and hugged all of them.

I received a lot of cards during this job loss. My reason for including this in my book is that I have a lot of family and friends that helped me get through another tough time in my life. Christians.

CHAPTER 19

Worked at 2 Other Facilities

A and LP

I have talked in length about my CNA career.

I got a job at "**A**," another facility, as I needed medical insurance. I was paying $1,170.00 per month and could not afford it anymore.

I still had one client at the home health care company just in case this job did not work out.

I liked my job at A. I liked my co-workers and the residents.

Well . . . I hurt my back pulling a heavy resident in bed. I was off for 2-months. It was a terrible time for me. I was in extreme pain, having to drive to specialists, etc. I was on a muscle relaxant and pain pill. All I did was go to the dr, eat, sleep, go to the bathroom and pray. I was also going to physical thereapy.

In the meantime, I hired a lawyer for my workman's comp claim.

I went back to work and hurt my back again. I was in a resident's room and my foot got caught in a chord under her bed. The resident's daughter saw what happened.

I reported my back injury to the nurse on duty and then reported it to the DON (Director of Nursing). The DON never asked me to fill out an incident report. I immediately hand wrote an incident report and had the resident's daughter sign it. I went to work the next day and gave my hand written incident to Human Resources. I left. The next day I got terminated due to all lies. They just didn't want me working there because I was a risk. I could not even collect unemployment.

The great news is a year later, my lawyer settled with my workman's comp claim. I got enough money to pay my medical bills, pay the lawyer, and have some extra money. I felt good. I got them real good!

What a cold, cruel world.

Last facility I worked at, "LP." I was there for a year. I got physically sick from this job.

Overworked
Underpaid
Crazy residents throwing furniture, yelling, screaming, taking off their bottoms and pooping in the hallways on furniture and the workers having to clean it up, urinating in the main tv room, cleaning up the dining room and loading the dishwasher for 25 residents, sweeping the floors and wiping down the tables
Had residents that should have been in a psychiatric ward
Turnover of employees was bad
No supervision

I was done. I gave my 2-week notice, but only stayed for a week. I could not do it any longer.

I did not go to school to become a CNA to do kitchen duty jobs, etc. I went back to school to take care of people!

One interesting resident we had at LP was a gentleman whose brother was in the movie, "The Wizard of Oz." He had very nice memorabilia in his room.

I am back to home health care and I love it.

I had a special client, 92-year old, who has touched my heart.

This is where I belong.

CHAPTER 20

Finding My Perfect Job

Home Health Care

Surprise. . . three weeks after I lost my job I heard from a company that wanted to interview me for doing CNA home health care, which was becoming popular. I went in for an interview to provide them with the necessary paperwork. But I needed a physical and TB test. I had to take care of that before finishing the interview.

I got my physical, TB test and was called in on a Wednesday night for an interview and then was to attend a three-hour orientation. In between the interview and the orientation, the scheduler asked me if I wanted to start work the next day at a home that was 20-minutes from my house. I was to have every weekend off. I replied, "Yes, yes, yes." I almost cried, but I held back the happy tears.

Let me mention that the woman who interviewed me, a recruiter, told me that she had helped a nurse find a job that I used to work with. It's a very small world.

God had a plan for me, and I love home health care. I even make a little more money than I made at the facilities and only had two residents to take care of in their homes.

I heard on the news that Illinois is rated the worst state for nursing home facilities. I found that interesting.

I went in one Friday to give the office my time-sheets and the scheduler told me that everyone adored me. My patients, my co-workers, everyone. I felt wonderful. I found where I belonged! One of the nurses made a comment, "Where has she been/She is good!"

My first patient was a sweetheart. She was 84-years old and I took care of her for six months. She was like a second mom to me. We used to have "mother-daughter conversations." We played a game called Yatzee which we both loved. When she would sit on her butt for a long time, she would call it, "Fannie Fatigue" which I thought was cute. Her mother used to tell her if something went down the wrong pipe, her mom called it, "Going down the red path!" I used to bring her long-john donuts to fatten her up; made milk shakes for her every day; and loved her dearly. I adored her husband and the rest of her family.

She ended up in the hospital. I called her and told her I was praying for her, missed her and loved her. She told me that she loved me too.

My patient was supposed to go home in hospice care and I was asked by the case manager nurse, who was very sweet, if I would be okay with taking care of her because when you go into hospice care, that usually means you have less than six months to live. I wanted to be there for my sweetheart, but she never did go home from the hospital.

I truly miss her and her husband and family. I talked to her less than a week before she died.

I remember right before she went into the hospital I was singing, "How Great Thou Art." She asked me if I could sing it at her funeral.

I did keep in touch with her husband and daughters for awhile.

After I lost my sweetheart, I would have a few different at home care patients here and there, but then I finally got a regular schedule.

Then I had two patients that I took care of and I loved them both and their families. I loved the fact that I was on my own taking time to care for, "My girls" the way that they deserved. If I have any questions, all I needed to do was contact the case manager nurse and ask them what I should do.

I also love to go above and beyond my job. I will go early or stay late and don't charge the patient. I will pick up miscellaneous items for the families to help them out as I can get a discount on items that they need and they paid me back. I got discounts on some medical supplies as I am a CNA. Sometimes I would buy a sandwich or something yummy for my girls and they loved it.

It is a perfect job for me.

The staff that I work with is awesome too.

I have been working at my current job for over eight years and have missed some time due to: hurting my back on the job, having the flu, a subcutaneous cyst under my breast that had to be removed after numerous infections, and a Baker's cyst behind my knee that was so painful I could not walk. It was always something!

My afternoon client went on vacation for a month; no income. A week after she went on vacation, my morning client went into hospice; no income. I was on call for a job(s), and I had received an ongoing client on Saturdays and an ongoing client on Mondays. The bad part was only working ten hours a week. How did I do it? I leave it in God's hands.

I received something in the mail from St. Jude Children's Research Hospital,

There was a note inside and it was signed:

"For the children,"

Marlo Thomas

"Butterflies symbolize hope for a second chance at life."

I donated a small amount of money. I received some note pads with butterflies and a statement that support has helped St. Jude triple the overall survival for childhood cancer since opening their doors in 1962, even though they still have a long way to go."—This touched my heart.

I received a card from a friend in choir that read:

"Thinking of You . . ."

"You're on my mind today.

I hope these scriptures lift your spirits a little."

"He will not break off a bent reed, nor put out a flickering lamp. He will persist until he causes justice to triumph." Matthew 12:20

"All who are oppressed may come to him. He is a refuge for them in their times of trouble." Psalm 9:9

"The good man (woman!) does not escape all troubles—he has them too. But the Lord helps him in each and every one." Psalm 34:19

"Rise up, O Lord my God; vindicate me. Declare me not guilty, for you are just. Don't let my enemies rejoice over me in my troubles." Psalm 35:23

The card inside read:

"Wishing you all the patience and strength you need to see you through."

Handwritten: "Lifting you up in prayer to our awesome God. You have what it takes to get through this. In Christ . . . signed

This really touched my heart.

My sister and husband sent me the following note:

"Sending You Sunshine to brighten your day."

Handwritten: "It's going to be fine. You're being proactive. Good job!"

They also sent me a beautifully engraved, with my name—in purple, daily devotional book, also in purple.

This also touched my heart.

The first day I read from the devotional book: "He never loses patience. You no more need a holiday from spiritual concentration than your heart makes a holiday from beating. You cannot have a moral holiday and remain moral, nor can you have a spiritual holiday and remain spiritual. God wants you to be entirely His, and this means that you have to watch to keep yourself fit."

I also found out from an old friend that one of my old neighbors had their house foreclosed on. It was very sad. I also found out that the woman's brother had serious problems with alcoholism and my old neighbors would have the brother come over and get him so drunk. He ended up in an assisted living facility and the couple moved into his house. Unbelievable.

Another devotion the next day:

John 12:36

"While ye have light, believe in the light."

Shake off your laziness. Laziness is always seen in cravings for the higher hour. Work up to a time on the mount! We have to learn to live in the grey day according to what we saw on the mount.

The essential message is, "Don't wait."

Don't cave in because you have been baffled once, get at it again. Burn your bridges behind you, and stand committed to God by your own act. Never revise your decisions, but see that you make your decisions in the light of the high hour.

Right before I was told that my book was going to be published, I lost two clients.

Here is what my quadriplegic's wife told me (I took care of her husband three times a week for five years): She loves my energy, my humor, my heart and my honesty.

We have remained friends. Her nighttime caregiver found her husband not breathing. She called up to his wife who came down immediately. He was gone.

I found out that morning while I was with my other client. I was sad, but happy for him. He was out of his misery. Now he could move, dance, sing, talk and enjoy Heaven.

His wonderful wife, an angel, took care of him for 17 years. What does it mean to be a quadriplegic? In his case, he could not move anything. He could not talk. The only response he could make was blink once for yes and two times for no. It was very sad.

He had this awesome bed which I called a Lambergini. It did everything. It even weighed him. Amazing.

What a special family. Their daughter, son and his Mother.

The first time I met him, I did not think I would be able to continue caring for him, but I did and I am glad I did.

I remember telling his wife that she was an angel and there was a special place for her in Heaven. She did not agree with me. She told me, "There are no special places in Heaven." I believe there are.

The love she had for him to take care of him all of those years. What a PRECIOUS thing to witness.

After he died, because of the covid, the memorial service was delayed. It was at a local country club, outside under a tent, on a very hot, humid day. She hired a string quartet, food, videos. It was very nice.

She got up and talked about her wonderful husband and his beautiful blue eyes. I lost it. . . I got tears in my eyes. Every time I took care of him, before I left, I had to pull him up in bed. I talked to him all of the time I cared for him and told him what beautiful blue eyes he had.

I took care of a 92 year old patient in hospice just for a few months. I got to know her daughter pretty well. One night, before I left, the daughter asked me how long I thought it would be before her Mom passed away. I told her I thought it would be early the next morning.

I received a call from work that her Mom passed away early the next morning.

I received the following text. "I was glad you could be here with my mother and me just before her passing. Thanks for the reminiscing about (the town I grew up in! She lived there for awhile!) You were right about the time being between 12 and 4 a.m. My son woke up just as Mom was passing away! I probably should have stayed awake for the night, but I sang her some hymns, said the Our Father, told her I LOVED HER AND THAT SHE WAS KNOWN BY God.

This really touched my heart. My client is 86 years old and when he was 16, he had cancer of the colon and had to have surgery to remove it. He has had a colostomy bag since then. A colonoscopy is where they remove the entire colon and the feces comes through the lower abdomen through something called a stoma. The entire rectum is closed off and rerouted through the abdomen. The patient needs to wear a colostomy bag to collect the waste.

His family adores me, and so does he. They trust me with his life. I would do anything for him.

I pick up his special newspaper on Tuesday mornings which he loves. He is an avid reader and has taught me alot.

I also have an 82 year old woman that I take care of privately through my small business I have tried to start. I have $3.5 million of liability insurance. My "Man" introduced me to my client's daughter a number of years ago and she was looking for someone to take care of her Mom a few days a week for a few hours. I love this client and her family and would do anything for them.

My "Man" also referred me to another friend of his, a 77 year old woman, who I cared for for around six months. I loved her and her husband too. Unfortunately she passed away from a liver disease. I miss her.

Word of mouth and business cards and friends have helped me, but I still work for the home health care agency which I love.

Currently I have two clients. One is a retired doctor who I have had for almost two years. I adore him. He is like a Dad to me. He has great kids. He has traveled all over the world and is a real character.

The Life of a CNA

Caregivers go through more than they will tell you.

They give up a lot and rarely have a social life.

They get sick and emotionally worn out.

It's a lot for one person.

We never really know until we walk the path of a caregiver ourself.

Kelly's Tree House.

Words to describe a CNA

Caring, dedicated, patient, a role model, supportive, professional, understanding, compassionate, inspiring, observant, hardworking, empathetic, a friend, devoted, nurturing, helpful, reliable, encouraging, respectable, passionate and knowledgeable.

CHAPTER 21

Choir/Church

When I first started my job as a certified nursing assistant, I had to bow out of church choir for a while. I really missed it. But now my schedule at work allowed me to return back to singing, which I truly love.

In 2021, because of the covid, we were not rehearsing. At the beginning of the pandemic, we rehearsed virtually, but that changed.

We are hoping and praying that some time in 2022, we can get our choir back singing. Our choir director bought us special masks to wear, but we have not met yet for rehearsals. Every time we plan to meet, the weather here in the Midwest is too dangerous.

God has a plan for us.

Hopefully we can sing this Easter, 2022!

At Easter and Christmas, our 35 choir members sing a lot of music along with a small band and orchestra. It is very uplifting for me to sing to the Lord. It is a passion of mine. Friends of mine have come to hear us sing at Easter and they love it. My gentleman friend, the love of my life, has come to hear us sing on Easter and Christmas and he really enjoys it.

Our church used to rent a chapel where we held our Easter service. It was perfect. We had 1,000 people attend the service and it was amazing: Banners where young adults would walk down the aisle with a tall cross, a big Bible, the pastors walking together, our choir, band, and orchestra. It was fantastic. We held the service at the chapel for a few years, and then we were told we could not hold it there anymore because the people who had to work on Easter Sunday didn't want to work on the holiday anymore. We understood their feelings, but were disappointed. So now, because our sanctuary is relatively small, we hold three services on Easter. It is a long day, but well worth it.

A prayer in our bulletin before Easter: "For our music director, the choir and musicians as they prepare to sing beautiful Easter music."

There was a note posted in our choir room regarding what we call, "Lessons and Carols," which is performed a few weeks before Christmas.

The note read: "The service was outstanding. We brought six guests that thought the music was beautiful, uplifting and a wonderful way to start the Christmas season." Their friends said, "The music and song are so beautiful. It was the highest standard performance that he had ever heard of for Christmas. You have very talented singers and musicians." When I read the note, it made me feel so good inside. Our choir reaches out to a lot of people and is thoroughly enjoyed.

An interesting fact. One of our choir members was is a retired TWA pilot. He and his wife are one of the nicest couples I have ever met.During the pandemic he passed away quickly from prostrate cancer. I went to his wake and it was great seeing my friends from choir. I will truly miss him.

We also lost another choir member right before the pandemic. He passed away from lung cancer.

I saw a sticker on a car that read:

"Pilots are just plane people with a special AIR about them." I thought that was adorable.

As I mentioned, a few weeks before Christmas, our choir sings for all three services. It is called Lessons and Carols. The choir sings and then there are Bible readings in between singing. It is a very tiring day. We all love to be there.

We found out one Sunday that our choir director was celebrating 20 years of faithful service. I planned a little party for him on a Thursday night during choir rehearsal. I ordered a cake with our Peace logo, music notes and, underneath, "Singing." One of the members got a piece of cake that just had "sin" on it from the word "singing." I had also found paper products with crosses on them. I found the choir director a t-shirt that read, "My choir rocks!" I also found him a card on-line that read, Music Director with a treble cleft. Thank goodness for the internet. He wore the t-shirt that Sunday under a sports coat. It made me laugh and it touched my heart. It was so cute.

Crosses were the in thing in clothing. I had found an adorable blouse on sale with small crosses on them. I didn't try it on. I gave it to my petite mom, but it didn't fit her either. I gave it to a choir member at rehearsal and she wore it the Sunday our choir director wore his T-shirt!

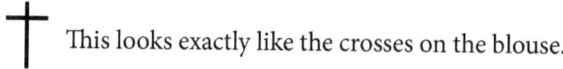 This looks exactly like the crosses on the blouse.

Our church has set goals each year for what we call the, "Diaper Derby." The church members donate diapers, wipes and formula. We met our goals for a few years in a row for an organization called CareNet, for young women who get pregnant. We went way over our goals for the previous year. I found out that out of 15 churches that participated in the Diaper Derby, our church took 1st place for the fifth year in a row with the highest number of donations.

Care Net is an evangelical Christian pregnancy center operating primarily in the United States. As a pro-life organization, its centers seek to educate and inform pregnant women about all of their legal options

Our church also supports and donates food to Feed My Starving Children, a non-profit Christian organization committed to feeding God's children hungry in body and spirit. The approach is simple: children and adults hand-pack meals specifically formulated for malnourished children, and we ship the meals to nearly 70 countries around the world.

One of our choir members lost her husband. He was 64 years-old. He had dementia and a bad heart. The wake and funeral were held at our church. I gave her a sympathy card and a check.

My will states that I want my service to be held at my church.

She sent me a card that read: "God Bless You for your Expression of Sympathy."—

Handwritten: "We want to thank you so very much for coming to my husband's/father's 'visitation,' and for the card and money. You have been so very kind, loving and generous—showing the love of Christ. I pray that the Lord will touch your heart in a special way—that He will give you a sense of His presence and peace. Thank you again! Love . . . "

My ex-husband and I used to go to church together. I would sing in choir and he would either usher or sexton. Sexton is when you help serve the bread and wine for Communion.

A couple who used to sing in choir were sitting in church together and the husband was hugging the wife and rubbing her back. She was just sitting there and I was thinking to myself, "Why was she not giving him back some kind of affection?" It touched my heart. I wanted to cry. I was envious I wasn't married any more. This couple actually became members of our church and came from the church that my sister and her ex-husband attended. They made comments to me about being surprised that my sister and husband got divorced.

It is a small world.

Our church bulletin has prayer requests where your name is typed and members can pray for you. My name was in the bulletin for prayers during my divorce and health issues and then a personal family matter. I love my church family.

It was unbelievable the tons of cards I received from friends at work and my church before, during and after the divorce.

I mentioned in my Dedication about my dear friend from church who sang in choir with me and was my Stewardship Minister. One morning she had a cross bracelet on that I loved and I asked her where she bought it. She had it for so long, but she didn't remember where it came from. She mentioned that she tried to find it recently, but did not have any luck.

The next Sunday morning, she surprised me with two of her cross bracelet watches. One in gold, that worked, and the other one in silver, that didn't work, but you can still wear as a bracelet. She had the watches in a Thanksgiving card and when she gave it to me and I opened it, I was so touched that I started to cry. It really touched my heart. She always says to me that, "I am a dear person and I thank God for our friendship."

I sent her a thank you e-mail for the watches and part of her response e-mail was as follows:

"May you be blessed with health, happiness, and peace in heart and mind, especially during the forthcoming holidays. You have touched my heart many times being a very special friend."

Unfortunately, my Stewardship friend has advanced Alzheimer's. It is so sad. I have gone to visit her a few times and she still remembers who I am and we sing choir songs together. She is happy and so am I!

After I got divorced, they still had "Mrs." on my church mail box. I had asked months before to have it changed. I was upset. A choir member said to me, "Don't sweat the small stuff." Wasn't that the name of a book? My mom told me that after a divorce, you are still considered Mrs. I don't agree and don't like it.

I received a card in the mail from a couple from church. I used to sing in choir with him. The card read, "Just to let you know someone is remembering you in prayer, (it had a bird on the front of the card as they know that I love birds!) Be joyful in hope, patient in affliction, faithful in prayer (Romans 12:12 (NIV)) and trusting in God to touch your life with warmth and loving care. Praying for your overall healing. Love to you, J & K." How sweet and touching.

I sing with choir members that still work at the office where I lost my job. It used to bother me when they would talk about the office, but now I'm cool with it.

I met up with a friend that I used to sing with in choir and took a Bible study class with years ago. We went for a walk and then out for breakfast. She and her husband lived half-block down from me. He used to perform some acting at the church services. After our get-together, she sent me an adorable card with two parrots; the one was cleaning his/her tail feathers and the other was watching. It was colorful and perfect for me. The card read as follows:

"My dear friend,

Thank you so much for the yummy breakfast. Better than the food was your company. I'm glad we got to spend some time together. I know I've told you before, but it bears saying again that you are an amazing woman who cares deeply and you are an inspiration to me. I know you will always succeed because in spite of everything, your head and heart are always in the right place. Love you lots."

It really touched my heart. She has an "adopted" granddaughter. I love that word, "Adoption."

"The aim and final reason for music should be none else but the glory of God."
J. S. Bach

From Psalm 104:
"[33] I will sing unto the LORD as long as I live: I will sing praise to my God while I have my being.

Our church is all saying prayers for our Associate Pastor as he gets ready to go on a 10-day trip to Ethiopia, Africa. We pray that we as a congregation can help raise $4,000 for his trip. The latest figure was $1,350. My heart was touched by this and I gave a small donation.

God keep him safe and bring him back to his family and his church.

CHAPTER 22

Family Relationships

Every family has some kind of broken relationships. Some last only a short period of time and others last a long time. Forgiveness, time, prayer and love help mend those relationships. I can say for me, I can forgive... but sometimes I just can't forget. I keep praying for strength.

My sister got divorced ten years ago and married her old-time friend, who played guitar at her wedding. He was divorced two times. He's a nice guy and used to live and teach in Japan. We all adore him.

My sister and I were not close for ten years. She asked her husband for a divorce after 24 years of marriage. They have three children. She wanted me to take her to the airport to fly out and visit her future husband, but told our mother that she was going to Arizona to visit a girlfriend. I wasn't going to be a part of that. I told her she was still married and her emotions would get the better of her and she would end up sleeping with him. She asked me if I would still love her. I replied, "Yes."

I remember this day like it was yesterday. She was leaving her family. We both just happened to be at our mom's house at the same time. I let her have it. I told her how I felt, that she was lying to our mother and I wasn't going to be a part of it. I had just had foot surgery. She got mad at me and pushed me. I pushed her a few feet back into our mom's back door, told her off, and told her not to touch me. I held her against the door with my knee. We exchanged some bad words.

She didn't invite me to her wedding, but at the last minute, we did talk and she did invite me. I didn't accept. I had just had foot surgery and there was no time to make travel arrangements and I was not about to travel after my surgery. It would have been too much for me.

It was not a good time. My younger niece lived with her father after the divorce because he didn't know my sister's husband and didn't want her living with this man that he didn't know. He was in a two-person band and played "weird" music. I can't describe it. He wanted to keep his daughter safe.

After six months of my niece living with her father, she stood at the top of the stairs with a suitcase and cried and told her father that mom was coming to get her. He gave in and let her move in with her mother and step-father. My sister accused me of not letting her daughter move out to Arizona and I told her I had nothing to do with any of that. When I was asked my opinion by her father, I could understand why he did not want his daughter to move to Arizona. He did not know her step-father and it's a crazy world we live in. She was young and shy.

After all of this, my mother didn't speak to me for three months. It was horrible. Then the love of her life and dance partner ended up with prostate cancer and my mom took care of him until he died. I remember trying to explain things to my mom and she would hand the phone over to him and they'd both hang up on me. It wasn't pretty.

Now, ten plus years later, my sister and I are getting along great. I went out to Arizona with my mom for her 80th birthday and we stayed with my sister and brother-in-law. It was a great trip. We shopped, talked, walked. My sister e-mails me her opinions on different life experiences and I listen and think about it. Family is the best.

My mom has had a hard life. She divorced my father, raised two girls by herself, married my step-father, who died of a heart attack close to their 24th wedding anniversary. She found found him dead on the floor when she got home from work, and then lost the, "Love of her life." He died of prostrate cancer.

As I mentioned, my sister and I were not close for many years. Actually, we were not speaking to one another. I had seen her throughout the ten years for weddings, showers, graduations, but it was not the same.

She worked at the same office as me as I got her the job. After our falling out, she was totally ignoring me at work. It was uncomfortable. I went up to try and talk to her for our mom's sake and clear the air. She told me, "If you don't get away from me, I am going to report you." I followed her a short distance in the office, but then returned to my work station. There was no talking to her. To this day, my mom will not talk to me about it. It bothers her too much. And what about me and my feelings?

A short time later, a security guard, a cute one I knew, wanted to see me in the conference room. He said my sister reported me. I was to stay away from her or I would get in big trouble. She was crazy then. Going through a divorce (which I now understand). He told me he was serious. I told him, kiddingly, to handcuff me and take me away. Wow, my own sister. How could she do this to me? I tried calling our mother later to explain what had happened and she didn't want to hear my story. I assume to this day that my sister lied to her. To this day, my mom will not talk about it.

This has hurt me for many years and I feel like my mom and I should someday talk about it, but I have decided to leave well enough alone. For whatever reason she had, I have to forgive.

Years later I tried to talk to my mom... no way. She said she is "Too old and can't handle it."

When I went out to Arizona with my mom for the second time for my nephew's college graduation and went to the Grand Canyon, we were sitting, waiting for the graduation to start, and my sister was sitting in front of me. She turned around and said she should have told me this a long time ago, but said, "I'm very proud of you for going back to school." She was referring to my going to school to become a certified nursing assistant. I was shocked and happy.

Now things are great. I had a baby shower for her oldest daughter; my niece/goddaughter. I sent my sister a care package of the favors, menu, etc. from the shower as she couldn't attend. She thanked me from the bottom of her heart via e-mail for having such a wonderful shower for her daughter. We started e-mailing one another. Our mom, my sister and her husband, went to see my niece's (God daughter's) new baby that was born on our mom's 79th birthday. He is now nine years old. What a gift from God. Now my niece has five children and lives in Arizona. We really miss her and her family. Hopefully we can see them sooner rather than later.

I spent a month on the baby shower for my niece trying to make it as perfect as possible for her. I was on medical leave from work at the time. The theme was Noah's Ark and everything tied in perfectly. It was a lot of work and a big expense, but it was well worth it. My friend helped me. I love planning parties. I had special invitations I ordered off of the internet, along with special thank-you notes to match which I gave to my niece as a gift.

I found out that my oldest son sent a nice baby gift from him and his father... That was nice of them.

My sister's daughter (my niece and Ggoddaughter for whom I had the baby shower for) had to have a prenatal procedure done called ECV (external cephalic version) where they externally try to move the baby into position. We were all worried. There is a 60% success rate, and possibly serious complications. The umbilical cord could have wrapped around the baby's neck, or there might have been problems with the placenta. My niece was also a gestational diabetic.

The procedure did not work, so she had to have a C-section. Mom and baby did great. My niece, husband and great-nephew moved from Kalamazoo, Michigan back to Chicago. Her husband got a great job offer that he couldn't refuse. They have moved a number of times. They bought a camper aand boat and go out on the lake. Fun times. They also have two dogs and two cats and home school their five children. Wow are they busy!

<u>Because of God's spirit living in me, I pray that I am able to give life giving words of encouragement to others. When we immerse ourselves in getting to know God, we can have reactions that honor Him and bring life into our relationships.</u>

My sister and husband's dog had to have surgery on tumors. I sent her an e-mail that I was praying for their dog. I told her about the Rolling Stones concert I was going to, and she and her husband were going to a religious concert out in Arizona. She e-mailed me asking how the concert went and vice versa. She also asked me about my neck problems. She has neck problems too so I tried to give her some suggestions as she couldn't afford to have an MRI. So, e-mailing is better and she signed the e-mail, "Love." She included pictures of the dog's surgery, which is something that always interested me.

Our cousin, whose daughter I had a bridal shower for, never invited my sister to the wedding. She sent a gift anyway and never got a thank-you note. Family. . . I think they resented her divorce.

My sister sent me a beautiful card for Thanksgiving of the Red Rock scene from her house and it touched my heart. Sedona, Arizona is beautiful.

She was scheduled for shoulder surgery and we kept e-mailing back and forth and I tried to keep her chin up, that everything would work out with her surgery, which it did. When the surgeon got in there, it wasn't as bad as he had thought. Since her surgery, we have been e-mailing back and forth, signing off, "Love."

Mom and I went out to visit my sister and brother-in-law in Arizona and had a fantastic time. We are e-mailing one another back and forth almost every day it and feels great. She told me that she appreciates me!

Hang in there as time does help heal.

See page "LED UP TO . . . wedding Chapter 10 . . .

As I mentioned in an earlier chapter, my cousin's daughter was pregnant. This ought to be interesting. One of their sons graduated from college, yet we heard nothing. I guess they have written me off. What's wrong with people? I was trying to make my marriage work and I was told all along that I could bring my husband to the wedding. My cousin's wife was invited to my niece's baby shower that I hosted with a friend, but responded, "No" to the other woman that was hosting the shower with me, even though I'm the relative. She never sent a gift.

Now their daughter had a baby and there was an open house at my cousin's house who wasn't speaking to me for a long time. It was right after Christmas time to celebrate the baby's birth and Christmas and their son's engagement. Ironic, Christmas is when we celebrate the birth of Jesus. My mother and I were invited and everything went very well. My mom and I brought gifts for the newly engaged couple and the baby. We brought a gift for the baby, even though the mother's mother never sent a gift for the baby shower I had for my niece.

I mentioned everything at the open house went well. . . .

Except my cousin, remember the videotape situation, pulled me into his office and showed me a DVD that had his daughter and husband's picture on the front with the date of the wedding and he told me that it was sitting inside their door a few days before the open house. He thought my son, who videotaped the wedding, put it there. As I reflect on this, was this a joke or what was going on?

E-Mail from my sister . . .

> How was the open house?????
>
> Secondly, you have asked me in two emails to pray for your book. I have prayed for you, and whatever God sees the outcome to be. We have all been through a lot in our lifetime, and all have a story to share (should there be an appropriate time to share that to help others). I KNOW, that WRITING this book was very therapeutic for you. That's what journaling IS. It helps heal us by writing our experiences down so we can let them go. It is a friend to talk to. Why do you think diaries were so big? Therapeutic. . . . .that's why. . . . . . .I don't know much about your book, except for some things you have let on about it. When we visited you at your condo, you mentioned that you were writing it, and that it was about your married life and how hard it was to get pregnant, adopting two kids, and only to end in divorce. I urge you not to go through with printing this book. I know that you would tell others about your book when it is published, hoping that people would read it. It will be the family and friends reading it FIRST, don't you think? So. . . . .now you have people reading your side of the story about your life with them. How will it impact the ones that are written about IN the book? On that thought, alone, I would not publish it. What do you hope to accomplish in publishing this? Everyone has a story to tell, and if you have a way of helping anyone in the future by offering YOUR advice, from YOUR experiences, then God will PROMPT you to help that person. You don't need to publish a book, possibly hurting the ones written about. Life goes on and it keeps moving whether you are stuck or not in a certain space. The one thing that was SO hard in divorce, is that you have nothing to draw from except all of your experiences and memories

from a married life that you are now not a part of. Time heals by giving you new experiences to draw from. I don't know what, specifically, you have written, but I would ask you.......would it hurt the boys? Would it hurt Mom? I won't ask you about (your ex-husband), because I think you don't care what he thinks, but he is a person that tried to make you happy, and there was conflict from both of you, and between you, so there should be no fingers being pointed......just a place that you come to in your life where you say, "I forgive you," even though it was both sides' fault.....without condemnation...There is a freedom of just saying.....I forgive you....and move on....

Your written book/journaling, served it's purpose in a kind of therapy to write it all down so that you could then release it......let it go.....move on.....

I thought about my sister's e-mail long and hard. But, I decided to move forward with my book. It took me almost a year of thinking about and praying about my book, and God has led me to finish.

I asked my friend who was helping me with my book his opinion on my sister's comment after I decided to pursue my book and he was happy to hear I was continuing with my book.

I e-mailed my oldest son with the chapters he wanted to read from my book. I asked him if we could meet on certain dates with times to meet for lunch to discuss the chapters that talked about him. I did not hear from him until a few weeks later.

He was sorry he had taken so long to get back to me. He had not forgotten. Him and his wife and son had been very busy. I told him if he wanted to talk, to let me know.

I attempted a number of times via text to see if he wanted to talk. I saw him for a brief time one day at his office and nothing was said.

So.... I am moving forward.

There have been a few things since I got divorced that were weighing on me and so, I sent an e-mail to my cousin to get it, "Off of my chest."

(To my cousin and his wife):

Hi,

I don't want you to respond to this e-mail.

I just wanted you to know how I feel.

I was at a wake/funeral close to your home the other day. A good friend died and was laid out at the same funeral home and parlor room as your dear mother (my aunt). Plus, the day of my dear aunt's wake, that morning, I got divorced. It brought back memories and that was the last time I saw everyone. If things were good between us, I could have stopped by.

I don't understand what happened, but I sure know who cares about me during this difficult time in my life.

I have been divorced for almost a year.

I hope all is well at your end and send my love to all.

Note: I think it's terrible that you both never paid my son for videotaping the church/reception for your daughter's wedding. If you had a problem, you should have said something. We had to drive to Chicago a few times for the equipment and never got paid. How do you think that made him feel?

I do understand why my ex-*husband* could not attend the wedding, but... you totally ignored me and I didn't do anything. So much for our friendship and your true character has come out throughout all of this.

I heard your daughter is pregnant. Congrats.

Sometime later, my son received a letter from my cousin. My son didn't want anything to do with this, so he gave me permission to read the letter. The letter read:

RE: Follow-Up on Wedding Video
Payment for Services

I am touching base with you concerning the wedding video you were preparing for our daughter's wedding—and the corresponding payment for your services.

Frankly, until a recent communication from your mother, I had forgotten about the video. However, after discussing it among ourselves, our recollection is that you showed the original video, but then took it back in order to more professionally edit the video before final delivery. At the time of the original video, I did offer to pay you for your services, but, you stated you did not want any payment until you finished the project.

Currently we do not believe the final version of the video was every (he mis-spelled and meant ever) finished and delivered to any of us.

And, I have never received from you any further communication or request for compensation—the timing or the amount—until the accusation from your mother that I had basically stiffed you. I have no such intention—and, usually take the opposite approach—I generously compensate those who provide work and provide services for me.

So—I trust you can deliver the final, edited version of the wedding, and you will provide a request for what you believe is reasonable compensation for your time, services, and any out of pocket costs. And, I do request that you forward this to me.

Finally, if you believe I am in error, I look forward to hearing from you

Thank you.

I thought this was rather weird. A professional letter. This is my cousin. My response:

Thank you for your letter of September 11.th My son gave me permission to read your letter.

FYI . . . he is not pursing this. This was all my idea. I want to set that record straight.

As I recall; mom and I came to a party at your house and to our surprise, your daughter and her husband were there. I had the copy of the video and remember specifically giving it to them. You were with us there in your driveway. I mentioned that it took a long time to get the video to them; he was in school and it was time-consuming to do the first edit. I believe the video I delivered that day was close to their one-year anniversary. I asked that someone get back to us with any changes, comments, etc. I was told somewhere along the line that a few of the kids watched the video, but we never heard anything from you or your family.

I am sending this letter to let you know that this matter is dropped and there will be no more correspondence regarding this matter.

CHAPTER 23

My First Gentleman Friend

I went to my auto mechanic one day. I've been going to him for years. He had a friend, who also was going to him for years. He was divorced for five years and I was asked if he could call me. I was still married, but separated and the divorce was started.

I didn't think much about it at the time. After all, I was still married.

He called me. Our first date was dinner and drinks. I dressed up and I chose the restaurant.

Our second date was dinner and a comedy club; I kissed him! Me—taking the first step. I was lonely.

He was a professional painter when he was younger and I hired him to paint all of the rooms at the house, except for a bathroom that was just wallpapered. He also put up new light fixtures at the house. We went shopping together to pick them out. I got this all okayed by my husband, of course.

We had gone to craft shows together. At the November craft show, my mother and cousin and my cousin's friend were with us and I saw a wall decoration I loved. I asked the vendor to hold it for me for a while as I walked through the craft show. My gentleman friend got separated from us and when I found him, he wanted to bring packages to his car before we had lunch. When I went back to the vendor to get my wall hanging decoration, he told me it was gone. I knew what was going on. My gentleman friend gave it to me as an early Christmas present. How sweet. You should see the wonderful things I found for him for Christmas which he loved. We both loved craft shows. Some unique things can be found. He used to make decorations for Halloween and Christmas. We both loved decorating for the holidays. My ex-husband used to make fun of my decorating, especially a month ahead of time. I told him I wanted to enjoy the decorations.

We went to the movies together, sometimes with my mom. We both enjoyed watching the Christmas shows on Hallmark. He loves science fiction, I don't. And, he loved to watch all kinds of sports on TV. We always seem to have the same opinions regarding movies.

We loved the same kind of fast foods, and oldies but goodies music. My ex-husband loved German march music. Yuck . . . weird. We went to outdoor festivals, carnivals and outdoor band concerts. We had the same kind of cell phones.

We both loved Barbra Streisand's music and Tom Jones!

We had gone gambling—the first time I won $100.00. Beginner's luck. I brought $200.00, but only spent $100.00 and made $100.00. Not bad. The second time we went, I won $70.00 and quit while I was ahead. We went back a few weeks later to listen to an Elvis impersonator. We both loved Elvis, The King of Rock N' Roll. There was a song that I wanted to dance to, but he didn't want to because of the fact that it was a love song. I apologized. That night I ran into his sister in the woman's washroom and talked for a while. I did not say anything to him. When I found him, he was ready to leave and said he lost too much money. We were only there one hour after the Elvis impersonator was done. I knew that he probably saw his sister or brother-in-law, but I didn't say anything. A few weeks later the subject came up and he was nice about it. I told him I didn't say anything to him that I saw his sister because I knew it upset him. They were not close.

Another time we went to the casino and I asked him what he would do with money if he won big-time. He told me he would donate some money to my church and that really touched my heart.

We went to a casino to hear our favorite band, 7th Heaven. I took off from work. What a night. The band started two-hours late; I complained to management. It was Holy Week and I had choir rehearsals. Then, to top it off, he saw his sister and brother-in-law at the casino. He doesn't talk to his family. His sister didn't talk to him; I talked to her, but his brother-in-law went up to him and they shook hands and then he turned his head. Was he being stubborn? His brother-in-law was ready to kill him. His sister told me she loved him and the reason he was mad is because they went to his daughter's wedding. I found out his mom had been in the hospital and was going to a rehab facility eventually. When I talked to him about it on the way home, he got angry; he didn't want to hear about it, so I dropped the subject. He didn't even attend his own daughter's wedding. I know his son was dealing drugs. He didn't really talk about it. I know his uncle and older brother found out where he lived and showed up at his front door. He let them in. At least his older brother was going on a fishing trip with my friend and my gentleman's friends.

We went to Starved Rock for a weekend. After we got back, he sent flowers thanking me for a great weekend. We had a lot of fun.

He always remembered my birthday. He bought me Fannie Mae pixies. For his birthday, even though he doesn't like cards, I found a card at the craft show that had a picture of Wrigley Field. He loved it and was going to keep it. I bought him a "Honker" for his birthday which is what makes the sound at sports events when a team scores. I got free Sports Illustrated magazines and gave them to him. He used to get them. At first he didn't want to look through them because he said he might be tempted to spend money, but he kept them.

On my next birthday he came over as he was in the neighborhood for a doctor's appointment. He brought me a painting of Jesus that he had made and given to his mother when he was young and he knew that I loved it. After his mother died, his nephew gave it to him and now I have it.

Our last year together, he completely missed my birthday.

He was divorced, two grown kids; he doesn't talk to them. He told me his wife was cheating on him. He understood my emotions with the divorce, selling the house, finding a place to live, and so on.

We discussed the night that our spouses asked us for a divorce. Both happened in the kitchen!

He also had a pool at his house while married. He helped me at the house with the lap pool before I sold it. He only lived a few blocks from where I lived while he was married. Ironic. . . My address was 66 and his was 67.

He was funny and I could be myself around him. I didn't hold back. I am who I am. When we were together or talked on the phone, we talk a long time. He was just a friend. We talked almost every day or saw one another on my days off. We told one another our secrets. He offered to drive me to physical therapy when I had a herniated disk. He offered to pick my son up at the airport when he went out of town. He always said to me, "Have a good day at work." The next day I talked to him and he would ask me how work was.

He had some emergencies with his back and I had to run over to his apartment one day and call the paramedics. He had knee replacement surgery. I went to see him every day at the hospital. When he was having his surgery, I went to the hospital gift shop. Those are dangerous. I did some shopping and got a few Christmas presents. I used to take him for doctor visits and physical therapy appointments. It was more than a three-month recuperation. He stayed one week to get physical therapy where I worked, so I saw him every day. We went to see the play, "Xanadu" at a local theatre and had dinner; this was before his knee surgery. It was fun.

I called him one morning; "Is it a beautiful woman?" he asked. "Yes," I said. "My neck is bad." He called me later to see how I was. I was upset and we talked about my older son. Parents that get divorced and kids take sides. He totally understands my feelings. That's why he doesn't talk to his kids.

He eventually bought a house and I went with him to look at all of the houses he was interested in. There was one we both really loved, but it fell through.

He used to give me hickeys on my neck which was embarrassing. Boy, did I get teased at work by my co-workers. My response was, "Are you ever too old for passion?" One day I wore a turtleneck to work to cover them up. A male nurse, who I adored, and a CNA, kind of tackled me while I was standing up. The nurse figured it out and we all laughed.

He is retired from the post office. First he was a mail carrier for many years, then he got promoted to being a supervisor; then he retired from there and worked as a supervisor at a gas station.

On the Saturday nights I did not work, I used to go watch him bowl. He was in a league. This was before he had his knee replacement surgery. Years ago I bowled and my uncle loved to bowl, so I had been around bowling alleys. At my new job, we played a video game of bowling and I got three strikes and jumped and danced around. The residents loved it.

He had a colonoscopy and I took him for the test. Oh boy—shopping at the hospital gift store again. They have the neatest things.

A colonoscopy is a test that allows your doctor to look at the inner lining of your large intestine. He or she uses a thin, flexible tube called a colonoscopy to look at the colon. A colonoscopy helps find ulcers, colon polyps, tumors, and areas of inflammation or bleeding. During a colonoscopy, tissue samples can be collected (biopsy) and abnormal growths can be taken out. Colonoscopy can also be used as a screening test to check for cancer or precancerous growths in the colon or rectum (polyps).

Before the test, you have to clean out your colon (colon prep). You have to stay home during your prep time since you will need to use the bathroom often! The colon prep causes loose, frequent stools and diarrhea so that your colon will be empty for the test.

It's pretty "shitty!"

When I took him for his colonoscopy test at a local hospital and he was asking everyone if the hospital was looking for any CNAs. I had to find a different job as a CNA because my job was, "killing me."

He fought in Vietnam and was in the 1st Cavalry Division and got a tattoo of a shield with a horse. I wanted to get a tattoo of a cockatiel, but will not because I'm diabetic and I don't want an infection. What does the Bible say about tattoos? Leviticus 19:28 says, "You shall not make any cutting in your flesh for the dead, nor tattoo any marks on you." While he was in 'Nam, he got bit by a mosquito and ran a 106-degree fever. They put him in a tub of ice water for two hours. He said it, "Felt great." I cringed. One of my residents was in Vietnam and he is funny, like my friend. Maybe they would get along. Talk about 'Nam maybe? I don't understand why my gentleman friend watches movies about Vietnam that bring back such "terrible, awful memories" and then when I talk to him, he gets all choked up. We can't understand what it must have been like to be over there and lose friends and killed Vietnamese.

When he was in Vietnam, he used to send money home to his mom; when he got home, he found out that his mom had spent it all on various things like custom-made drapes. He asked her to pay him back and she refused. She felt that he owed her.... His mother passed away and he did not attend the wake and funeral. I tried to persuade him to go, but he couldn't. He blamed his mother for his father's death. He was 16 at the time. When his younger sister was born, his mother's water broke and he had to clean it up!

Does he have post-traumatic stress disorder from the war? I believe he does. We can't imagine what our men went through.

I was with him the night before Veterans Day. His cat got loose outside and it seemed like it took us forever to get her. We had the front and back doors open, and she finally walked into the front door. We got on the subject of the animals we had. We both had to have our favorite dogs put to sleep. He had mentioned his dog that he had in Vietnam and brought out his scrapbook that his mom made for him of pictures he sent home from 'Nam. We talked quite a bit about the war.

I called him on Veterans Day and thanked him for serving his country. He thanked me.

It is impossible for our Veterans to come back from a war and not have some type of scars.

I bought a flat-screen TV and a purple (my favorite color, and his) recliner that is awesome. It is electric powered and you can sleep in it, it's so comfortable. My cousin wants me to will it to her. My gentleman friend was looking for couch pillows and I was the one that spent money.

He bought me an AM/FM radio when we first met because I didn't have one and he wanted to listen to music while he was painting.

One day I drove over to his house and his friend told him to ask me if I could drive him to meet another female. He wasn't driving at the time because of his knee replacement surgery. I didn't know quite what to say. We had gone to see a stray cat at his friend's sister's apartment. That was the female! He fell in love with the cat. We went to the pet store to get everything the cat needed.

We went back to pick her up. She was a real sweetheart and he kept him company. She was adorable. I found out she passed away a few years ago from a mutual friend.

I watched his "adorable" cat while he was on his fishing trip. It was weird not talking to him. He left me the vet's business card just in case I had an emergency. I would go over early in the morning, and there she would be looking out the front window. I would walk in and she would start meowing and purring. Then I would give her treats I brought and check on her food and litter box and cuddle with her for a while. I would also check my friend's mailbox and any packages that were delivered. When he got back from his fishing trip, he gave me two thank you gifts. One was a yellow bird figurine with purple flowers (reminded him of my favorite yellow female cockatiel) and the other a black/gray figurine (reminded him of my favorite male cockatiel.) How sweet. He told me that the guys say, "Goodnight **NICKNAME**." "Goodnight **NICKNAME**." "Goodnight **NICKNAME**." "Goodnight **NICKNAME**." There were four guys that went. Get it. Like John Boy on the Waltons. Neither one of us liked that old show, but it was quite funny. Now since he is back from his fishing trip, he is going to go get his will drawn up and talk to his doctor about having surgery on his ankle.

When he got back from his fishing trip, I had written a note inside a beautiful card that had an eagle on it and told him I had missed him. He loved the card. He asked me where I found it. I told him I found it at a gas station along with a card for my mom with a cardinal on it and another card for my dear friend of a butterfly. She loves butterflies.

He bought a beautiful eagle picture while he was on his fishing trip. Lovely. He was like a woman in a clothing store.

I have bought eagle earrings and an eagle shirt as I knew he loved them.

At work one Friday we could wear our favorite baseball t-shirt and a hat. My gentleman friend gave me one of his Cubs' hats; he had two others and I bought a t-shirt of the "Cubbies" with stones. Everyone at work loved it. Too bad I didn't have earrings to match. Another day at work I wore a Bear's t-shirt and he gave me one of his Bear's hats.

In all the time I had known him, we had three disagreements. Not bad.

He finally told me that his family took his ex-wife's side; he never told his family what happened.

He told me his father was a drunk and both his father and mother used to hit the kids with a barber belt. His mother asked for a divorce and my mother asked my father for a divorce. Both fathers were sick. His brother called him one day and left a message on his cell phone that their mother was in the hospital. We discussed why he doesn't care about his mom. The beatings; stealing his money that he sent home while in Vietnam; after high school, charging him a lot of money to live with her because he owed her. He finally got fed up and moved out on his own.

We talked about if we were younger and got divorced, would we ever get married? Both of us agreed that the first marriage was supposed to be "For better or for worse." We wouldn't get married again. I asked him if he had a wife that had a radical mastectomy, like Angelina Jolie did, if he'd stay with his wife and he said, "Yes." IF they were married for quite a while.

As I mentioned, he's retired. He told me when I go to work to think of the Seven Dwarf's song . . . . Hi ho . . . Hi hoh . . . It's off to work I go. Cute. He left a voice mail message one night while I was at work singing this. It made me laugh. One night at work, one of my resident's daughter's sang this for some reason and I cracked up. I told her about how my gentleman friend left a voice mail message singing this song.

We have talked about our marriage counseling with our ex-spouses.

He pulled a good one on me one day. He has a bad back. He was supposedly outside taking care of weeds and ended up in the house flat on his back and could not get upstairs to get his pain pill. After worrying and asking him if he needed me to come over, he told me his landscaper did the work, not him. I told him I was going to, "Kick his ass" and that I would get him back. Not nice. He told me all of the time that I was gullible. Not funny.

We went with another couple to The Broadway Theater next to Water Tower Place in Chicago and saw the show, "Australian Bee Gees." What a fantastic show. We loved it. We clapped, sang and danced. It was a lot of fun. He rented and paid for a limo. It is fun watching the younger generation stand outside bars downtown late at night. Oh, to be young again.

I had to work on July 4th. I went to visit my friend and he said to me, "Are you cheating on me? I thought that you were working on July 4th." I asked him what he was talking about. In the local paper, there was a picture of a woman at the July 4th parade that looked exactly like me. Oh my gosh. She even dressed like I would have if I were going to the parade. He knew it wasn't me because her name was in the paper. When I showed the picture to my co-workers, some of them actually thought it was me. I must have a twin out there. They say everyone has a twin.

After he got back from his trip, we left for my corporate training for work and got a hotel room as I had training for work for two days. It was great. We went out one evening and had a bunch of drinks and a good dinner. His friend called and I answered my friend's cell phone. It was one of his fishing buddies. He told me that my friend had to put a dollar bill in a jar every time he mentioned my name, which was approximately 60 times.

We used to go to a local meat market. While he was on his fishing trip, I went to the meat market. He had told me his son was working there. His son is pretty messed up with drugs and other things and jumps from job to job. I had asked about him and I was told the he had been out sick for two weeks. I told my friend I had gone to the meat market and he asked if I asked about his son and I told him. I felt bad. I thank God that at least my son, who is the same age as his son, works part-time and goes (WHERE?).

He has a female friend from the post office that he trained and she works part-time at a local bar. Usually I worked on the evening she was at the bar. I was off and mentioned to my gentleman friend that we should go visit her. He called her and left a message. She called him back and he answered the phone, "Hi honey." I acted like I was jealous. I wasn't. When we went to see her at the bar, they talked, hugged, kissed. I gave him a dirty look, but it didn't bother me at all. I told him I have a lot of male friends too. I told him, "As a matter of fact, I have a male friend who sent me an e-mail and started by writing, 'Hi girlfriend,' and I replied, 'Hi boyfriend.'" He could be my son. He's just a friend. He is married and has a few kids. He is helping me with details on this book. That night we went back to his house. I inadvertently took all of my night time pills, including my sleeping pill on top of having a few drinks. I will never live that down. He told me the next day when he called me that his friend had accidently called him at 2 a.m. I sure didn't hear it ring. That night at the bar, he told me that my feet stunk. How can my feet stink? I was wearing sandals. The next morning I found a Halloween sign that read, "Trick or Treat . . . Smell my Feet."

I had a large blind fall and break in my bedroom. I e-mailed my landlord the measurements and suggested that we buy two blinds, instead of a big, heavy one. She ordered the wrong sizes. My friend and I went shopping and bought two new blinds and I found purple drapes. My bedspread is white and purple. He told me I didn't need the drapes. Like a husband. He helped me with the blinds and then on a different day, the drapes. Took us a couple of hours for each project. He had a hammer and ice water in his hands walking down my steep flight of stairs. I was on the main floor and I heard the hammer and water fall on the ground. He had fallen down six stairs. Thank goodness he was alright.

He came over and helped me put things together such as a shelf unit for my bathroom and a small stationary bike. We helped one another.

He had a picture in his car of me at 16 years old in a white bikini.

He had a lot of problems in English in grade school. He did not have good English teachers. What is, "I before E except after C?" No one can explain it to him. Two different spellings: DEAR and DEER. He had problems that carried over into high school. He thinks he's dumb. I told him that was not true. He just didn't have good teachers. He grew up in the city.

On one of my days off, I went out with my cousin to look for a dress for her for a wedding. I always bring her good luck and she actually found two dresses. She is so cute. She sent pictures modeling the dresses to her husband to get his opinion. They have been married 30 years. I told her to, "Get a little sexy." The manager of the dress shop offered me a job. I told her I used to work at a boutique and loved it. When we left, the manager gave me her business card, hugged me, and told me that, I was "adorable." It made me feel good. Maybe I could work a seasonal job she said. We met up with my mom for lunch.

Then my cousin and I went to the Shoe Carnival to get two pairs of shoes that were open in the back, for my bone spurs, and for my treat for a pedicure for her birthday. She picked out purple and we had our toes painted the same color. People thought we were sisters. Then we went to Dollar General and went our own ways. We had a lot of laughs.

I got home at 5:00 p.m. and had choir rehearsal that night. My gentleman friend left a message at 2:00. I called him back. He wanted me to drive to his house, pick him up, drop him at a bar with a bunch of his friends to watch the Kansas City football game vs. the Pittsburg Eagles. His "adopted son" was there, our mutual mechanic and his wife and the mechanic's assistant and the mechanic's long-time friend. So, I dropped my friend off at the bar, came back after choir, and went to join them and had a lot of fun. I wore my taxi hat I bought for Halloween inside and it was really funny. My friend didn't want to drive because he was going to be drinking beer. Aren't I nice?

He called me the Sunday of the first Bears game. He was wondering why I wasn't there watching the beginning of the game with him and bringing him barbecue chicken wings, which heloved. I told him to get off his butt and come to my place and pick up chicken wings, as I don't like them. We kept getting disconnected because of his cell phone. I kept calling him back and he would answer the phone, "Don't call when there is a football game." I kept calling him back and I finally caught him. I said that I hoped the Bears lost. Well, I got to work and they were losing by quite a bit; but they came back and won. He told me if they had lost, he wouldn't call me for a week. Wow. I'm so glad that they won. I would have been in a lot of trouble.

I tried to watch the Bears game with him when I was off of work. One day I went over to his house with a blue/orange scarf and Bears earrings which I found at a school craft show. He loved it.

My oldest son helped his younger brother move out of the house and he walked right past my gentleman friend, who was sitting outside on a chair, without saying anything or acknowledging him in any way. I didn't raise him like that. He wouldn't even hug or kiss me. It was awful. He had a hateful look on his face. When he left, he didn't even say goodbye. This was not a good impression on my gentleman friend, who believes to this day my son for some reason didn't like him. I told him that my oldest son has to accept the fact that I have a gentleman friend and that I want him to spend time with me and my boys, especially on special holidays, and that I would like my friend to eventually come and hear our choir.

He always asked for my work schedule so that we could make plans, or just sit around and watch sports, movies on TV, or just cuddle and listen to music. It was great having him in my life. I cherished every day because you don't know what tomorrow brings.

After his mother's death, he has had some communication with his older brother and nephews, which was a good sign. I hope and pray that he continues to communicate with at least some of his family. His brother sent him a late Christmas present—a one-year subscription to Playboy. Oh boy!

It was his birthday month. He called me one day and told me that anything he asks me during that month, I could not say, "No." It was kind of cute.

I met someone, after a nasty divorce. Again, God's plan.

Now telling my gentleman friend that we were over with. I called him and told him that I couldn't be with him anymore, that I found someone else. I had been with him for four years, but I was never in love with him. I cared about him, but I was never in love with him. I had been wanting to break it off even before I started dating the love of my life (see the next chapter).

He always expected me to go over to his house. He only came to visit me a few times. He never thanked me or took me out to dinner for all the times I took care of him after surgeries, drove him to physical therapy appointments, etc. When I told him I was with someone else, he wanted to be together for a weekend and try. I told him no. He only got together with my family once and complained about it to his friends. He never came to church with me to hear me sing. I always did what he wanted; watch sports, go gambling (where I had to pay for my own drinks!) and he would blow $1,000+.

He used to tell me about all of his female friends and about being in Vietnam. He also grew up in the city and got into a gang fight and killed someone. I knew that he had PTSD (Post Traumatic Stress Disorder). He had the signs.

He left numerous messages on my landline and cell phone and wanted to talk. I called him and told him that it was over.

One day when I was at work, he was knocking profusely on my front door and scared my son. He had a key and I asked for it back. He returned all of the gifts that I had ever bought him for Christmas, birthdays and items I had bought when I went on vacation to Arizona. I called the police to tell them about the incident and that he was driving by my home. We changed the locks on the house. The police told him to stay away from my house.

He had pulled this same thing on his daughter when she sent him a gift after he got divorced and never even saw his granddaughter. He also never went to his mother's wake.

It was over and I was done.

As I mentioned earlier in the chapter, he forgot my birthday the last year we were together. Almost a year after I broke it off with him, and I found out from a mutual friend he was not taking our break up very well. He sent me a vase of beautiful flowers for my 60th birthday. There was a card in it that said he didn't miss this birthday. Hah, hah, hah.

If I had known it was from him, I would have sent it back. I sent him a very simple thank you note and a few days later, he called me and left a message. He wanted to make sure that I received the flowers. He was told by our mutual friend that I had received them. Our friend told me that he is always talking about me.

I found out from a mutual friend of ours that he went to the doctor for a physical and told the doctor that he wanted to kill himself. I knew all along there was something wrong with him. I believed he was dangerous and I did not want to get involved. A bunch of police showed up at his front door and he was brought to a psychiatric ward for a few days.

I hope and pray he got the help that he needed.

CHAPTER 24

The Love of My Life

I was working at the first facility after I became a CNA. I was there for about a year and then got a very sweet Italian patient. He was so cute. He could never remember my name and called me, "The blonde blondina!"

His son, let's call him, "N-man," would come and visit his father frequently. We hit it off from the start. Whenever he would come to visit his father, if I was not around, he would ask for me.

We would talk at length about our lives while I was in the dining room watching the residents. He could tell I was going through a tough time and I would tell him about my nasty divorce. He was going through a tough time too. His wife was dying of brain cancer.

The girls at the facility used to tease me that he had the, "hots" for me. I told them we were just friends and that I was going through a nasty divorce and his wife was dying of brain cancer. We were friends; that was all. I was very attracted to him.

Every time we would see one another, we talked a lot.

The N-man and his wife and family had a 95th birthday/Father's Day party for his dad. I was invited and got to meet his family, including his wife, who was in remission at the time. I had a great time. I was invited to assist with his Father.

His father passed away and I attended the memorial service.

Sometime later I saw him at a memorial service for patients who had died during that previous year. We both attended and talked. His brother was also there. His brother died a number of years later.

After that I quit the facility and went to another facility to work.

Some time went by and we did not talk for a while.

I then went to work in home health care. He called me one day and told me his wife was going into hospice and asked me if I knew of anyone that could help. I could not help him as I was very busy with my job, but told him I would pray for him and his wife.

I had a feeling his wife passed away, but I never heard from him. So, I called. She died in June and I had called him some time later. I sent him my condolences and told him that if he ever needed a friend that he should call me. I had a gift certificate to an Italian restaurant called Maggiano's and told him if he wanted to meet, it would be my treat.

He told me he would call me.

Months went by and one day my first gentleman friend was over and we were watching TV. He hardly ever came over to my house. The phone rang and and N-man's name/number showed up on my television. My friend asked me who it was and I never answered him. I proceeded to walk outside and N-man asked me what I was doing on Sunday night. I told him nothing. He told me he wanted to go to Maggiano's, but he first wanted to take me somewhere that I had never been to before. He asked me if I had ever been to Mike Ditka's. I told him I always wanted to go there, but I had never been.

I told my gentleman friend that I was spending the day and evening with a long-time friend. We were going shopping and then to dinner.

I got all dolled up for my first date with him, which was on May 3, 2015. We were going to meet there. I had not seen him for a long time and I was very nervous. I got there early and had a glass of wine to loosen up and chat with the two waitresses there. I told them I was meeting up with a male friend and that I was nervous and felt like a school girl.

I was facing the entrance into the restaurant and there he was. He walked in and came up to me and gave me a big smooch on the lips. That was it. We had a great time. Great dinner; drinks, talked. It turned out he knew one of the waitresses that I was talking to. We walked outside to claim our cars and he kissed me on the lips, again, and told me he would call me.

I got hurt on my job and was off for a while on Workers' Comp. He has Mondays off as he is a barber. He took over his dad's shop. I took a chance and called him and asked if he was busy. He told me to come over. We went to a cigar shop, he loves to smoke cigars, and it was a fancy shop. Then we had lunch at an Italian restaurant. This was our second date.

Our third date was another cigar shop where we sat by an open patio and watched it rain and talked. He smoked a cigar and I smoked my slim cigarette and we talked a lot. After the cigar shop, he grabbed my hand and we ran across the street to an Italian restaurant.

Our fourth date was on Memorial Day. He had a cookout at his house and I got to see his family. I love them all. He has a granddaughter who is a nurse, so we would talk a lot about nursing and my job as a certified nursing assistant. She is a real sweetheart.

Our fifth date was at his house. He cooked for me. There was an attraction, but he was grieving over his wife and wanted to take a year before he got into a relationship. Things were heating up for both of us!

That was the beginning of our great, awesome, fantastic intimacy. Both of us told one another that we loved one another. I never felt anything like it before. We both thanked God for one another. Since he is quite a bit older than me, he thought it would be a problem. No problem for me. I told him that God could take me before him and that we had to enjoy every moment together.

He then told me some interesting stories about when I saw him and his brother at the memorial service for all of the patients that had passed away the year before. His brother told him that, I had the hots for him! He also told me that, after I left the facility and he found out where I worked, he used to look for my car. You can't miss my car. It was a lime green Beetle with a convertible top. He also told me that when I worked at the first facility where I took care of his father, he used to come around my dinner break and try to meet up with me as he knew I used to go sit in my car. Wow!

Our sixth date was at my house. We talked, shopped and held hands, went out to dinner; were intimate. He brought me a dozen yellow roses, Fannie Mae pixies, which are my favorite, two pairs of Victoria's Secret undies he got for a cheap price, a bottle of my favorite wine, and an autograph and coin from a star on "Criminal Minds."

Speaking of yellow roses. . . this is a true story. A number of years after we were together, I walked outside by his rose bush on his wife's birthday and there was one beautiful yellow rose. And, it has happened every year since.

I asked "The man" to come out and see something and he was shocked. We both said it was a sign from her telling us that it was great we are together.

Every day we text, and talk on the phone, sometimes two or more times a day! We talk about our days at work. Talk. That's a key word in a relationship. I did not have that with my ex-husband. He calls me his, "Bella" (means love in Italian!) and I call him my, "Bello." I was looking for perfume one day at Carson Pirie Scotts, who has since closed their doors. I could not find the one I was looking for. The lady behind the perfume counter wanted me to try a perfume. I tried it and liked it. When I asked her what it was called, she replied, "Bella!" I bought it and he loved it.

A year after his wife passed away, he found a bunch of severely tangled necklace chains with charms on them. There were around eight chains. I told my honey that I would work on it and get in untangled so that when the holiday arrived when his family was coming in, his granddaughter from out-of-town and his other granddaughter, who lives in town, could choose which ones they wanted.

After eight hours of working on the tangled up mess, I finally got it all done and his granddaughters picked out the ones that they wanted. I was very happy to have accomplished this and so was my honey.

Every Tuesday night after work I went over to his house and we had dinner together. Every Saturday night I used to go over to his house after he got off of work; I was off on Saturdays, and we also had dinner together. We love to cook together. On Sunday mornings during the summer when our choir didn't sing, as we are on a break, he used to cook me breakfast. It was great. Then I would leave and go home and meet up with him later. Almost every Sunday we would go visit his granddaughter and his son and girlfriend and spend time together and have dinner.

His granddaughter and husband have a great pitbull-dog. He is a real sweetheart and we enjoy playing with him. Since we started dating, she graduated from nursing school, passed the state board and is working as an RN (registered nurse).

They had a beautiful wedding and now have an adorablefour-year old daughter who I love dearly. So my honey is now a great-grandfather. Their wedding was a year after my son and daughter-in-law got married!She is now pregnant with their third child which is going to be a girl!

I love his family very much. We see his granddaughter and great grandchildren once a week. I love it. I have baby sat a number of times and enjoy every minute of it. I have seen the kids all the time since they were born. One year I met them and had an enjoyable day at Brookfield Zoo.

During the holidays we kept very busy with his family and friends and my family. It is like we are married, trying to coordinate seeing everyone, but it is a lot of fun.

He has met my mom and sons and part of my family and they all adore him, as I adore all of his family and friends. He has two sons. One son and family live out of state. My honey has two grandsons and a granddaughter. They are all the best.

His other son lives close by and we see him and his lady friend once a week for dinner to see the kids.

He drove my Mom to an important doctor appointment during a terrible snowstorm as I was unavailable. My Mom had met him before and calls him, "A gem!"

My Mother's doctor appointment was very important as she had a spot on her nose which was skin cancer, called basil cell carcinoma. Thank God it was not the serious cancer. Her surgery had required a skin graft and the dr. appointment was a check up.

All went well, even with the snow storm. They both got home safely and she got a good report from the surgeon.

We have done so many things together that it is hard to remember. One day we went to Oak Street Beach in Chicago. I had never been there and he couldn't believe it. It was a beautiful day. I walked in the sand and water and watched the seagulls. I was like a little kid. Then we sat on the park bench together and held hands and talked and watched all of the people. Then on to shopping at Water Tower Place and to dinner.

We do yard work together at his house, which I love, and it is great just being together. We even planted a vegetable garden!

He is so sweet that he has come to church with me and listened to me sing in choir. That alone means a lot to me.

His cousin owns a cottage a few blocks from a lake in Indiana. We drove out there and had a great day. It was the summer and they own a boat that we went out on for hours. I found out that day, and what a surprise, that his godson was married to someone I used to work with at the office. When we saw one another, we screamed and hugged each other and talked about the company, (she is still there), and our lives. It was a lot of fun. Recently we found out they got divorced.

This is ironic. My mom met the love of her life, who was older than her. Now I am following in her footsteps and in love with the love of my life, who is also older.

My mom was a secretary and I was a secretary

One day we were at his granddaughter's house and my man was talking about a passport. He asked me if I had a passport and I told him no. I did have one at one time, but it expired and I told him I didn't need one as I wasn't planning on going out of the country.

A few days later he suggested that I get a passport. I asked him where he was going with this. He told me that he wanted to go on vacation and he wanted to bring me. I was shocked. I told him that I could not afford to go on vacation and he told me he was bringing me, that he loved me and he didn't want to go alone.

He booked a trip for us to the Dominican Republic, Punta Cana, for one week and I was super excited.

We went on our vacation for one glorious week. It was paradise. The hotel was like a palace. We drank, laid on the beach, walked along the shore every day, shopped, had fantastic meals, had a great room. It was wonderful. It was like a honeymoon. No fights, just fun. We even danced. I love him so much.

He bought me a forever ring on vacation and when we got back, I bought him a forever charm for his gold chain; an Italian horn. He loved it.

My oldest great-nephew, who is three years old, saw my forever ring for the first time and pointed at it and said, "Nice." This touched my heart because he was having some problems in talking, but doing great to this day.

Every time we go on vacation, I have to bring two suitcases. One for clothes and one for shoes. I have to be coordinated with my outfits, shoes and jewelry. I love to do this. My honey's son always teases me. "Two suitcases!"

This is how sweet he is. My mom took the family out to a restaurant for my 60th birthday which is close to Valentine's Day. My honey bought a bouquet of flowers for each of the girls. How nice is that?

Our second vacation was a Caribbean cruise, which was awesome. Then back to Punta Cana, and then to Jamaica. We always have a great time. We both love the sun and the palm trees. We have also gone to Philadelphia to visit his son and family. One year he went to Philly for one of his grandchildren's graduations. I could not go with him. He brought me back a small plunger which was adorable. He knows I love the color purple! Wasn't that the name of a movie? Color Purple. So sweet.

Jamaica. We got home. Unpacked our luggage. He asked me where our coconut oil was. He was referring to our "love oil!" I told him I wiped it off, sealed it and put it in the pocket of his luggage. It was not found. We figured that someone at the airport went through his luggage and stole it! Who would want a used bottle of love oil! We still laugh.

I went back to the store where I bought it and told the sales girl what happened with the first bottle of coconut oil. We laughed.

Months later he did find the coconut oil in his luggage! Woops!

We have visited the lake front on Lake Michigan a few times; Lincoln Park Zoo on the hottest day of the year. We went to the Shedd Aquarium. Fun times. Places I had never visited in my life living near Chicago in the western suburbs!

We laugh. It seems like almost every time we go somewhere, someone compliments me on my outfit, shoes, earrings, etc. It kinda drives him crazy. I can't help it. I am a clothes, shoes, purse and earrings person. I love to match.

The following is a text message I received from my honey's granddaughter.

At first I was devastated, but then after reading it and re-reading it and thinking about it and praying over it, I totally understood.

I signed the Christmas present from us to his great-granddaughter, love Great Grandpa and Great Grandma. I was trying to be funny. Note: My honey's wife died, her Great Grandmother.

OMG. I felt terrible.

Merry Christmas!!

We have been busy and with work I've been catching up on my sleep.

First off I want to thank you for the gifts for both myself and A, and for G. The Mickey Mouse is adorable.

I also wanted to address something and wanted to wait until after Christmas because I didn't want to feel like I was hurting anyone's feelings. I'm not exactly sure why my grandpa said that it was okay to just sign G's (his Great Granddaughter's) as great grandpa and great grandma without talking to me first. I am actually surprised.

We have accepted you as being part of the family, however I am not comfortable nor will I ever be comfortable okay with you being addressed as great grandma. That is just a boundary that I will not let be crossed. It is nothing personal against you, it's just not fair to my grandma & we plan on raising G knowing who she was.

I have accepted that my grandpa has a right to move on in life and I am happy he has found a companion so that he is happy and not alone.

I just hope you can understand where I'm coming from when I say that that's something I'm just not okay with. We know that you'll be a part of her growing up and appreciate the love and support that you have for us and for her, but that's a title that belongs to my grandma whether she is here or not. And just know I'm not trying to hurt your feelings which is why I didn't want to bring it up right away.

PS also hope you got our gift.

I sent her a text message back apologizing from the bottom of my heart and that I never meant anything by it. All is good. My honey's great-granddaughter calls me by my nickname and it is so adorable and touches my heart.

I adore my man's granddaughter. I feel close to her. I have gone over to babysit a few times and I love it. I have fun and she appreciates me.

She had a little boy at the end of 2020. Great year right? She had another C-section. So now they will have a girl and a boy. Purrfect family! And now pregnant with the third baby which is going to be a girl!

While his family was in for the 80th birthday party, The man, his two sons and I went to a Cubs game at Wrigley Field.

We went on the most humid, hot day of the summer. I had never been to a Cubs game or Wrigley Field. I wore a Cubs shirt and hat and felt like a little kid.

After the game, they lost by the way, we were walking out and I saw a stand with kids. I went up there and told the guy that this was my first time at a real, live baseball game and at Wrigley Field. I got a certificate and framed it. When I told my sons, they laughed.

Because I work in health care and I lose clients and have a different schedule, we work around my schedule and his. It works. We grocery shop together, cook together, talk a few times a day, I help him around his house and yard and he helps me at mine. I do my thing and he does his thing.

It is an awesomely wonderful relationship.

His family and I had an 80th birthday party for him at a restaurant. His entire family came from Philly along with other family and friends. It was so much fun. My son and daughter-in-law and grandson attended which meant alot to me. Unfortunately, my Mom was sick and not able to attend.

During the summer his entire family and I went up to Wisconsin for a family wedding. I drove my VW Beetle. I had never driven out of state. We had a great time. I got the car up to 90 mph for a few minutes. I had never done that before either. While in Wisconsin, my honey and I went to a local A&W root beer place to get two large root beer floats. Yum, yum, yum. Boy did my blood sugar spike. My man totally understands. He has his house and I have my house and it is perfect right now.

Isn't love grand?

It sure is!

And love means never having to say you are sorry. I love him and his family dearly and would do anything for them. Every night we spend together, before we go to sleep, we kiss one another and say, "I love you." One night, during a dream, he woke up and called me by his wife's name, then corrected himself. He felt terrible. No big deal.

He calls me his Marilyn Monroe.

I call him my Richard Gere.

CHAPTER 25

My Birds; My Babies

My older son got me interested in cockatiels.

While the boys were in Texas visiting their aunt and family one year when they were younger, I had a bird on my chest and fell asleep. I killed him and felt terrible. I didn't tell the boys until they came home from their trip. I remember feeling something while I was half asleep, like a flutter. I rolled over on him in my sleep. They are my sweethearts. They know my moods and are very loving. I hand-fed one bird at two-and-a-half weeks old. I used to take her to work and hand-feed her there. I remember telling my boss I was going to get a baby bird, and he asked if I wanted to go on maternity leave. I told him no and asked if I could bring her to work to hand feed her there. He said, "Yes. Hurry up before I change my mind." Everyone at work enjoyed watching her change and grow feathers.

I remember a female cockatiel I had years ago. She used to lay eggs and I would set up a nest for her and her mate to sit on the eggs. When I would try and clean the cage, "Daddy" would jump out of the cage, run after me and bite me on my feet. He was very protective of his babies. The eggs never hatched. After the incubation period, 28 days, I would crack open the eggs. I had one that had a small embryo in it. It was so cool. I lost my female, Pearl, suddenly to what the vet felt was a heart attack. I showed the embryo to the boys who found it interesting.

Years ago, my husband turned the lights off in the room where the birds were. I had eight birds. Turning off lights for my cockatiels is a "No, No". They bang, knock blood feathers out and can bleed to death. I came home from work and it looked like a cat got to my babies. Feathers and blood were all over their cages, the rug and the wall. I was so upset. I had the four of them on the floor in the bathroom and didn't know which one to help first. What a nightmare.

My husband came home and saw me crying and went upstairs to get his credit card. I rushed my babies to my wonderful vet and friend. $1,500.00 later, I brought my three babies home; one died. I used to go visit them during my lunch break so that they could hear my voice. Yes, I know it sounds funny, but they are my babies. I was so upset with my husband. He knew better than that. He never did like my birds.

After I lost my job at the office, I bought a male cockatiel; gray-and-white-faced, which is pretty rare.

While I was still living at the house before we sold it, I took one of the birds from work for six weeks and nursed him back to health. He got sick again and I took him back to the vet. He wasn't perching. Poor guy. He has arthritis. He had to have medicine every day in his water for the rest of his life. There were no guarantees at work that someone could give him his medicine every day, so he is mine and I got his cage. He is over 30 years old and is happy. What was ironic is that, years ago, my father-in-law was a patient at the facility and the bird was there, and now I got him! I admired him back then!

I moved after the divorce and now had a loft with a skylight where I keep all of them. They love it. I was worried about the move, but they did great. They are very happy babies.

Yes, I'm crazy. I bought another cockatiel. I missed my white one (Frosty) who I gave to a friend. She told me that a pet store had a gold/white cockatiel. I bought it sight unseen and named her Golden Frosty. Now I have six birds. Hey, I'm the one who has to take care of them, right? I bought a female cockatiel at a local pet store. At the time I bought her, I thought she had pink eye (aka conjunctivitis) because her eye was all full of gook. I did get a small discount when I bought her.

I took her to the vet that day. She was diagnosed as having pink eye and something called psittacosis, a very contagious respiratory disease to birds and humans.

I had to gown up, glove up, mask up (use PPE-personal protective equipment) and keep her separated from my other birds.

I went back to the pet store that I bought her from and complained. They had to move all of the birds in the pet store to the back room. She was very sick. They wanted me to bring her back and I told them NO. After many months of back and forth trips to the vet and $2,200 later, the pet store reimbursed me. What a long haul.

A few months later, she got the pink eye again and a respiratory infection, but it was not psittacosis or another contagious disease.

After a month of treatments, she finally got better.

Golden Frosty has been one of my more difficult female cockatiels. She lays clutches and clutches of eggs. I have had to take her to the vet on numerous occasions. Two times for a hormone shot and two times for antibiotic shots as laying all of these eggs depletes her system. The vet suggested maybe doing surgery on her at $1,000 to stop her egg laying. I don't think so. I told her we needed to try something else.

That's when she suggested that I purchase on-line something called, "Dummy Eggs." They are the size of cockatiel eggs and the principal behind it is to put eggs in their cage so that they see them and it is supposed to send a signal to their brains to stop the egg laying.

I had to give her stress drops in her water, stress powder in her food and in addition to all of that, calcium drops to help increase her calcium from all of her egg laying. Oh me oh my. The calcium powder is for reptiles. When the vet told me that, I was surprised.

An average clutch for a cockatiel is four to seven. My "Fertile Mertile" laid nine eggs. At least it is not painful for them when they lay an egg. They are soft and when they come out of their body, they harden up. I am to leave her alone and let her lay on the eggs until she totally ignores them. Then take all of the eggs out and pray she stops laying eggs.

If she does lay an egg, when she is not looking, I am to take the egg out of her cage. Replace it with a, "Dummy Egg," then each morning put another dummy egg in and that is supposed to send a signal to her brain not to lay another egg in 48 hours. We will see how that goes.

It is going great now. The eight dummy eggs have been in her cage for months and she has stopped laying eggs. Alleluia!

She was laying more eggs. The vet gave her an "implant" and she did not lay an egg for almost a year. Then she started laying more eggs. Clutch after clutch after clutch. I finally got her in to see the vet. She got another Lupron, hormone shot.

The most recent adventure with Golden Frosty was she was laying clutches of eggs from October through February. I had made appointments for her to get a hormone shot, but had to cancel a few because my Mom was sick.

I finally got her in for her appointment. She received a hormone shot. She was acting very funny when I brought her home. She was not moving.

She could not get up on her feet or perch. It was very scary. The next morning I took her out of her cage, set her on the floor and it was as if she was ready to lay another egg. She was in the egg laying position. She was very cuddly and not getting up on her legs. That afternoon I took her to the vet and she was in the hospital for six days.

What a huge bill.

The vet told me she had something called, "Cage layer fatigue." It is an inflammation of the nerves in the legs due to excessive egg laying. They had to give her oxygen, anti-inflammatories, pain meds, and calcium.

I was very worried about her. After she was in the hospital for three days, I was told that she had a 70% chance of recovering. She was moving more, but still not her normal self. She was slowly improving and had less inflammation in her belly. On top of all of that, she had a slight heart murmur. She was well hydrated at this point which was great.

The aviary vets called me every day to give me an update of her progress. I was praying for her along with my family and my honey.

After six days of her being in the hospital, I was finally able to bring her home. Thank you God.

A friend of mine told me about an overhead lamp that would work for my excessive egg laying female. I checked with my vet and he told me to try it. The lamp has something to do with the temperature as they are from Australia where it is tropical. They are very intelligent birds. I did buy the lamp and fixtures, but never put it up. Why? I don't know.

Pets are a lot of work, and can cost a lot of money, but they give you unconditional love.

My birds hear me come home from work and they go crazy until I talk to them and take a few out that love to come out.

I have a male bird who comes out and just sits on the top of his cage for hours and hours. When he needs to go eat or drink, he just lets himself back into his cage. One day I was cleaning on the main floor of my townhouse and I could hear him talking to me at the top of the stairs. I walked up there and he was facing me and talking to me. It was so darn cute. He somehow got down on the floor and wanted to tell me so and I picked him up and put him back in his cage.

Now he is in the same cage with the 30 year old I got from a facility I first worked at as a CNA. I call them Mutt and Jeff! If you see one, you see both of them!

I currently have eight birds. I came home one morning and found my youngest on the bottom of her cage, eyes open and wings spread out. I picked her up to try and give her CPR, but she was cold and already gone. My honey and I buried her in his back yard. Crazy huh?

When you have pets, you have to be ready for things to happen. Yes, illness, but in my case, I had a big problem. A particular kind of moth breeds in birdseed if you do not have it tightly covered.

I had an outbreak of moths in my house. They were numerous. I was getting them on the ceiling along with their larvae. It was disgusting. It took me months to kill them all with special moth traps meant for this particular problem.

My mom made me two crocheted cockatiels as a surprise. She is the best! I bought a flag for my yard that is so appropriate for me.

It has a bird-house with a door closed and a door open and it reads:

ONE DOOR CLOSES

AND

ANOTHER DOOR OPENS

Can you give a cockatiel a shower?

Believe it or not, that moisture is good for their sinuses. In the winter, the air gets dry (ever notice that everything has a bit more static? My hair sure does!) and most pet birds have a lot of sinus problems. They are from tropical habitats and are used to having lots of moisture in the air. So, as you can imagine, that steam from the shower must feel GREAT to their poor noses. Try getting a shower perch and introduce your cockatiel to it over the course of about a week. Take him into the bathroom and set him on it when you get ready in the morning. Any time spent with you is valuable to them. Good luck.

I have tried bathing mine and most of them hate it. I have a spray from my vet to help clean them. I have since then purchased a shower bird bather for the bathroom for trying again.

I never tried the shower bird bather again. I bought a spray birdbath plumage and skin conditioner and they love it. The vet approved it and keeps them clean.

I have a three-year-old white-faced cockatiel who is very rare. One night, when I got home from work, he was singing away like I've never heard. It was music to my ears and I fell asleep listening to his sweet singing. When I had to put the house up for sale, I made a sign that read, "Bird's Room" because my broker mentioned that some people are afraid of birds.

The association at the townhouse was coming to put a new roof on. It was very noisy and I was afraid that my babies would go crazy, so I had to move them from the "loft" to the main floor so that they didn't get scared. They loved the main floor: it was something different for them. They went crazy when the roofers were there. The first day, the roofers replaced the skylight, so it was open for awhile. It was the coldest day we had and it was lightly snowing. It was a strange feeling having guys on your roof being able to look in!

Many years ago I bought, on two separate occasions, two hand-fed cockatiels from a friend of mine. Their parents, who have now passed away, had a number of clutches. Her bird is the sibling to my two! We are very good friends and love our babies. We did lose touch for a number of years, but reconnected. I watch her male bird when she goes on her vacations. He loves it here with all of his friends. It is almost like he knows my two birds are related to him because when he comes for a visit, he goes right to them. He loves the shower the little stinker. I spoil him when he comes for a visit and give him coffee ice cream which he loves. I love him as if he were my own.

Believe what you want, but I truly believe that my birds, and other animals, communicate amongst themselves!

Note: There was a man that owned a cockatiel who woke him up during a fire and saved his life!

I met a young gentleman who had 20 cockatiels. Did we have a lot to talk about. His female has laid two clutches of eggs and all of them hatched. What a wonderful thing.

Any kind of a pet is a real comfort. They may be work, but it is well worth it.

Recently I bought two female guinea pigs. They are so adorable and I love to cuddle with them.

This is funny. One night I was in bed and one of my birds were making the "squeaky" sound like the guinea pigs. I have been trying to train the birds to talk for years, and here we have the guinea pigs for two months and they are imitating them!

CHAPTER 26

Words of Wisdom

What can I say? Life turned around for me; a divorce, I lost my job six months after my husband asked me for a divorce, I sold the house (worked hard cleaning it out for a year with no help from anyone), I sold it in six weeks, moved, had a lot of problems with my car that never seemed to end, took medical leave, had a rocky relationship with my older son. On and on and on.

Sometimes I get down, but my belief in God has gotten me through and I know it could be worse. A friend of mine has a friend whose young daughter has an inoperable brain tumor. I have another friend who has been through hell with her health. She has been dealing with a lot for years. She had back surgery years ago that was botched and she almost died. She tried to sue the doctor, but no luck. Surprise, surprise. She has an auto-immune disease, eye problems, tumors in her feet and has undergone numerous surgeries. The latest problem is her back has a fracture and a tumor in the lower back. She wanted to die because she was told that the tumor was cancer; but . . . our Easter miracle. The doctor was wrong. She did not have cancer. Years later she got cervical cancer. She beat it. Then, a number of years later she got cancer in her lung and liver. She went for treatments for a long time. She then had to have emergency surgery as she had a blocked colon. She just didn't have the strength to survive any more.

On September 11, 2020, she left us and went up to Heaven. She wanted to die on September 11th so that everyone would remember the date! Her best friend was right by her side. Her friend told me that as she was dying, there was a feeling in the air that angels were all around her lifting her to Heaven. Wow. I believe it! Our friend was going up to her, "Secret Garden." She loved planting flowers!

Thank God. So, as you see, I know life can be so much worse.

I was afraid of being by myself, but I was fortunate to get money from the house and investments. I have a financial advisor. I got an accountant highly recommended by my dear ol' Mother.

I hoped and prayed that my ex-husband would move forward, too. I will always care for him. After all, I was married to him for 35 years. I have to forgive and forget. I feel bad that he had no friends. I found out that he got engaged. Good for him. It has now been over six years since he got engaged. I don't know what they are waiting for. They have been living together almost from the start.

I believe he will probably retire after he is done paying me maintenance for 10 years which was up August, 2022. Now I am on full social security benefits and can work and make as much money as I want.

My lawyers told me that "You were a fighter. It was a nasty divorce. You are strong."

"After a divorce, it's a transition that can be very overwhelming . . . . . . a nagging feeling." This is something my lawyer told me.

There is a Beyonce song, "I'm a Single Lady." That was me!

I met a woman at a store where I buy my work scrubs. She is getting divorced after 35 years. Sound familiar? I asked her if she had a good lawyer and she replied, "Yes." I told her if she ever needed to talk, to call me; that I've been through it. Maybe I went through all of this to try and help someone else cope with it.

I thank God that I have my church friends, family and other friends. I keep plugging along.

I tried calling my ex-husband one day on his cell phone. There was no answer; surprise, surprise. I called the office and my older son answered the phone. He was now working for his Father in the company business which his Grandfather started. So, the business is in its third generation, which I'm sure would make Grandpa happy. No one told me my son was working with his Father. I asked him how it was going and he said, "Fine." This happened around eight years ago.

Since then I've talked to my son and he went on a business trip for training. He also got a company car. I hope it all works out. It's tough working for your father or any other relative. I remember when my ex first started working for his father; he quit a few times. Plus, my son and my ex-husband lived together, but our son finally moved out into his own apartment at 28 years old. Good for him.

I had talked to my ex-husband after our oldest son went to work for him and asked him about our other son, who felt left out of the family business, which is understandable. There was no need for another employee. I remember my ex-sister-in-law felt the same way when her brother, my ex-husband, went to work for their father. There were hard feelings.

I received a card from a friend. It read as follows: "You're one of the most amazing women on the planet," with a hand-written note: "You are an inspiration. Through all your issues you have been able to maintain your attitude and your faith and your great personality."

Forgiveness is a huge thing to learn during and after a divorce. This is something that is hard to do and takes a lot of time. When I used to see my ex-husband walking in front of my townhouse years ago when I was out and about in my car, I used to honk at him and he waived. It still hurt. I cried my eyes out. I can't explain it.

Forgiveness: I have a very close family member that got married and I was not involved in the wedding, ceremony, reception, nothing . . . There was not even a special seat for me at the church. I was hurt, but I have forgiven. You have to.

I have a niece/goddaughter, whose husband is a pastor. His mom asked his father for a divorce and I believe this was difficult for him. I heard that his parents each got remarried. Life goes on.

I know life can be so much worse.

CHAPTER 27

Communication with Ex-Sister-in-Law after the Divorce

E-mail to ex-sister in law:

Hi.

I don't know if you still have the same e-mail, but I am attempting.

Please do not respond to my e-mail.

I just wanted to tell you how I feel.

I know your family was not supposed to have any contact with me during the divorce.
But, it's been almost a year and I haven't heard anything from you and that really hurts.

We go back many years and I have sure found out throughout all of this who cares.

Just remember, there are 2 sides to every story.

Send my love to all. Hope all is well.

I've seen your mom a few times since all of this.

From her:

I understand where you are coming from, yet this is the first contact from you since way before the divorce. I contacted you several times when we heard about the situation and the pending divorce. I indicated that you were still a friend, divorce or no divorce, yet not a word from you since. I was honoring your silence, thinking perhaps it was too painful to talk to me. Yes, there are two sides to every story, and this is a prime example. As to your relationship with my brother, I know there are two sides to that story too. I know my brother's faults all too well. I thought you would contact us when you were ready but I didn't think you would do it in such an unkind and reprimanding manner.

It has always been a two way street, not just one,

I wrote back:

Thanks for your e-mail and I apologize.

I don't remember any of this.

It has been a very tough couple of years for me, to say the least, and there are two sides to every story and U R right.

I hope we can talk on the phone soon, if you want to, and I promise not to talk about your brother. When will you be in town next?

Hope all is well.

I love you all very much and miss you.

And she wrote:

Sure, maybe we could talk late next week; I will be out of town tomorrow-Monday. I don't have any of your contact information since your move; would you please send that to me? I will probably visit mom in the late fall, as you probably know I was just there. I had a short but nice visit and it was nice seeing your boys.

I told her that the following week would be great, and that we'd touch base as to when would be a good time with my new job and orientation. I also sent my contact info. . .

"If you come late fall, maybe we could get together with your mom if you want," I wrote. "I know you were just in town."

My ex-sister-in-law and I touched base one evening and caught up on everything. We were on the phone for two-hours. It was great. We had a lot of laughs. She knows how her brother is; my ex-husband. I told her a couple of things she didn't know anything about. For example, her brother wanted to put a home-equity loan on our house for a sports car after he left me. She also told me about old family friends who lost their mother. I sent my ex-husband an e-mail and asked him why he didn't tell me. After all, I informed him about our race-horse friend who died. What a jerk. He never responded.

I also told her that my son who lives with me was trying to find his way. I felt that he was jealous that his brother was working in the family business with his father. She totally understood because that was how she felt when her brother, my ex, went to work for their dad. She was told back then it was because she was a girl.

Also, both of our younger sons have Attention Deficit Disorder. Wow. They could be twins; same problems. It's nice to talk to someone who has the same problem with her son. She told me I can still call her boys my nephews.

My ex-sister-in-law and I did meet for lunch when she was in town in the fall. It was just the two of us and it was great.

Since then we have met for lunch and had a great time. Her son is and my oldest son got married three months later.

We saw one another when her Mom died the end of 2021. All was good. I got to see relatives I had not seen in years. My ex was actually nice to me. I got to see ole girlfriends we used to party with and we caught up. The luncheon was very nice. My Mom and nephew attended. I got to see both of my sons, my daughter-in-law and my sweet grandson, plus my two nephews on my ex-husband's side. A great celebration of the life of my Mother-in-Law.

My sister-in-law did a great job for the wake. She made beautiful posters with pictures. Her Mom's high school book was opened to a picture of her. There were a few of Mom's favorite Lladros which are very expensive figurines.

After the wake, about a month later, I received a package in the mail from my Sister-in-law. My Mother-in-Law wanted me to have three of her Lladros that were packaged up for years. Did that touch my heart. I have always loved them.

CHAPTER 28

Being a Christian-Emergency Bible Numbers

Something touched my heart one day. I was watching TV and there was a woman, Susan Rizzo Vincent, of "Drea's Dream." Her daughter had some kind of cancer and was in a long remission. Her daughter's dream was to teach dance, but she got killed by a drunk driver. This was her only child and she was divorced. She is now carrying on her daughter's dream and opened a dance therapy studio for pediatric kids with cancer.

How sad. It sure made me think about my life.

One day I was at the MacDonald's drive-through and there was a woman in a PT Cruiser who was stranded right where people were pulling in. I pulled over and asked her if she needed help. She told me right away that she could tell that I was a Christian. I replied, "Yes I am." I asked her to put her flashers on and then I told her I had to go through the drive-through to get something to eat as I was diabetic. While going through the drive-through, I asked that the manager call the police. This poor woman was on her way to work; a temporary job. She actually was working for Blue Cross/Blue Shield and I mentioned to her that I had just received COBRA information from them as I was in between jobs.

I then proceeded to pull my car behind her and also put on my flashers. I mentioned to her that I was just going to my friend's house to take care of his cat, so I wasn't in a hurry. I told her that I could drive her down the street to her job and I had a good mechanic who could call a tow-truck for her.

She called her insurance company and her job. Her boss told her to take care of her car. She was waiting for a tow truck to bring her home to Chicago, as this was in the suburbs. Thank goodness she got off of the highway before the tire bar broke off as she could not move her car. She asked me my name so that she could pray for me and thanked me. So, I was on my way.

I then drove to take care of the cat. On my way home, there was a PT Cruiser it front of me whose license plate was HEBRW something. Weird. Then I saw another one a few minutes later.

I met a gentleman at an Ace Hardware who lost his wife on December 24; which was also her birthday. It wasn't quite a year that she had been gone, but I gave him a hug and told him I would pray for him and his son. The couple were married for 20-years.

My Mom received a call from a distant cousin in Florida. She had been receiving chemo for cancer, and she was just told that it's too advanced to cure her, although they were continuing to give her the treatments. Along with that, we found out that her oldest son and his oldest daughter were shot and killed in a domestic violence shooting. What can we do as a family to comfort her? PRAY.

How does the Bible define a Christian?

The word Christian is used three times in the Bible (Acts 11:26; Acts 26:28; 1 Peter 4:16).

The Greek word "Christianos" is used which means a follower of Christ.

The word Christ-

Root of the word Christian-

Means the Messiah, Anointed One, and refers to Jesus Christ.

If you are a Christian, then you are a follower of Jesus Christ. But, I can attest to the fact that some people who claim they are Christians do not always show and act like that they are followers of Jesus. I have run into people like this throughtout my Lutheran, Christian life.

A Christian is someone who
is saved (Acts 11:19–23)

This part of Scripture starts out describing how Christians heard of the stoning of Stephen. They traveled far; went through the Eastern Mediterranean Sea, came to Antioch and preached the Gospel (of Jesus Christ). This resulted in a large number of Greeks living there. They believed the Gospel of Jesus Christ and being saved.

To be able to preach the Gospel and resulting in a large number of people being saved, you must first know the truth of the Gospel and trust Jesus Christ as your Saviour so that they can preach and understand. They call this understanding the clear Gospel and having "the hand of the Lord" to help people be saved. (2 Timothy 2:6-7.)

Ephesians 1:12-14; You receive salvation at the moment you receive the Holy Spirit.

1 Corinthians 2:9-16; The Holy Spirit gives you understanding of all the things of God.

2 Timothy 2:1-2; You teach others the Truth so they may be saved also.

3 Acts 26: 24-29; If you reject salvation through Jesus Christ, you cannot be a Christian.

A Christian is someone who is saved.

EMERGENCY BIBLE NUMBERS:

Upset	John 14
Weak	Psalm 18: 1-29
Lonely	Psalm 23
Sinned	Psalm 51
Worried	Matthew 8: 9-31
Anxious	Philippians 4:4-9
Unhappy	Colossians 3:12-17
In Danger	Psalm 91
Depressed	Psalm 27
Lack of Faith	Exodus 14
Others Unkind	John 15
Need Courage	Joshua 1
Need Direction	Psalm 73: 21-26
Seeking Peace	Matthew 11: 25-29

CHAPTER 29

Interview with Christians Who got Divorced

From a married couple from my church—

Her thoughts:

I never thought divorce would happen to me. I was the first in my family. I knew that being a Christian did not guarantee that our lives would be free of struggle and pain, but I just never gave it a thought.

I was brought up going to church my entire life. As a married adult, we were the couple with the two beautiful girls that sat in the front rows and looked like the perfect family. Although I was involved in some church activities and service opportunities, my walk with God was not as strong as it should have been. We were caught up in the activities of a busy life and the "material stuff." As a result we drifted apart and the marriage was no longer salvageable. I did find comfort in the grace and mercy of God and the people he put in my life to support me. It was during this time that I realized that the people I thought were my friends were really "acquaintances." What we had in common (neighborhood, income level, activities) was now gone and I no longer fit in. At this time, God saw my need and led me to a Christian singles group. The people I met there understood my situation, and I could count on them to really be there for me in the difficult times. It also gave me a new determination to recover from this loss and to be able to support others. You can either lay down and let sorrow overtake you, or you can get up and fight. I chose to fight. I would have to say that since that time I have experienced significant spiritual growth. I am more committed to Bible study and a personal relationship with my

Lord and Savior. I have stepped outside my comfort zone in the ministries I have participated in. I feel that as a result of this, any new challenges would lead me to God first, not relying on my own strength and then turning to God somewhere further down the road. I have learned to be open with people and strongly rely on the power of prayer. I have no problem sending out an e-mail asking for the prayers of people who love and support me. God is good and there is healing from the pain of divorce.

His thoughts:

My feelings about divorce were something I thought I would never have to contemplate. After all, I went to church, sang in the choir, was an ordained deacon and so forth. My wife and I weren't getting along very well, but I just thought that this would pass and we would be happy again. When I was told that my wife engaged an attorney and she wanted a divorce, my world collapsed. I couldn't believe it! The worst part of this was that I would no longer be a full time dad to my sons. I prayed, but once lawyers and courts get involved, the course is pretty well set.

My church home and fellow church members kind of pulled away from me. After all these years, I felt like I was being cast out. I went to church for a while, but I was increasingly uncomfortable there. I knew that God wouldn't desert me, but I still felt alone. I tried to find a new church home, but as a single Presbyterian, it seemed that congregations were less than friendly. No kids, no church, few friends—this was the saddest time of my life.

At this point in my life, it would have been enough, but the company I worked for was downsizing and guess what? I was on the downsize list. They were humane, however, and if you had enough time with them, you got a pension. Of course, now in addition to everything else, I had no job!

It would have been easy at this point to lose myself in worldly distractions, but being a Christian, this was not an option. I wouldn't say that my life was exactly Christ-like, but I would like to think that my religion guided me most of the time.

After my divorce was final and all monies were distributed, I bought an inexpensive condo. I started to rebuild my life. It took a while, but I always felt that Christ was helping me. When I calmed down and began working on my life, things started to happen. My old job was gone, but I found a better one as a consultant. I made more money as well.

Through it all, I never thought that God deserted me, but I just didn't understand what was going on. What good would come of this? A friend of my (soon to be ex) wife called one day and told me about a group called Helpmates that met at the local Lutheran church. In this group, I found that I wasn't alone, but that there were other Christian men in the same circumstance. It was in that group that I found some support and fellowship. It was here that I also met a woman and eventually married her.

My wife and I now have six of the most beautiful granddaughters anyone could ask for. We found a church home and lead a quiet life filled with an extended family. In closing, you really don't know how God will enrich your life, but if you're patient and listen, life seems to work out.

Yes, I agree with him. You need patience, help from family and friends, and God to see you through. While you are going through it, it is awful. But... better days were to come. And, he lost his job like I did. So we both got a double whammy!

God's Grace is the Foundation of the Future. Believe in HIM!

CHAPTER 30

Sermons (Note: need to cite Pastors)

PSALM 46:1—God is our refuge and strength, a very present help in trouble.

Pastor asked me for my permission to use my pre-divorce story in a Sermon: I told him, "Absolutely."

The Sermon . . . "What hurts? Where is the pain in your life?'

Jesus likes to go to places to help make things better. He went to prostitutes, lepers and outcasts. He went to places where things were bad. Jesus died for our sins. Go to Jesus to step in; he likes to do that.

The pastor used my life then in his sermon. "Someone in the congregation is going through a nightmare," he said. "Her husband left two years ago, his lawyer is procrastinating with the divorce, and they still are not divorced. He runs two businesses. He may be hiding assets. She has large legal bills. She has to sell the house she loves. Her kids won't talk to her. She lost her job after 25years. Her life hurts. It's the worst that things have ever been.

Jesus goes where things are the absolute worse, to make better. All better? Sometimes. . .

Jesus won't make everything all better. Jesus will make it better for us to deal with. Philippians: Ch. 4

"I can do all things in him who strengthens me."

Jesus will always give us strength when we go to him. He'll comfort us.

We have to expect trouble in this world. He has overcome the world and we can have his peace.

Another Sermon:

"Oh let not the Lord be angry."

Pastor: Do you ever want someone to get what they have coming? Ex-husband, neighbor, co-worker, boss?

Would it bring you joy to get back at them?

God talked to Abraham and wanted to wipe out Sodom and Gomorrah. God was going to let them have it. Abraham was important to God; Abraham's response: "Do you have to?"

50 good people—Wouldn't do it—God said OK
40 good people—Wouldn't do it—God said OK
30 good people—Wouldn't do it—God said OK
20 good people—Wouldn't do it—God said OK
10 good people—Wouldn't do it—God said OK

Abraham knew the people of Sodom and Gomorrah deserved it.

Acts Chapter 7—Stephen was the first Christian martyr (Verse 57). The people were stoning Stephen; he was dying. It killed him. "Lord, don't hold this sin against them."

Joseph: Genesis Ch. 50

Sold by his brothers as a slave; they attacked him, put him in a well, in prison. He was in authority to do whatever. (Verse 19) "Don't be afraid, I will provide for you and your children. He was kind to them and assured them and spoke kindly to them.

Miracle growth for your faith and you to grow.

Jesus Luke 23 verse. 24

Jesus was on the cross dying, "Father forgive them. They know not what they do."

Pastor: He doesn't want anyone to get what they deserve, steal—jail, kill.

Enforce laws of the land. Eternal consequences, we don't want what we deserve. Bring to the Lord. Lower the cross.

Pray for people—"Lord they need you to bring them to Christ."

After listening to this sermon, I felt a sense of peace. Good for us to pray for other people to get grace, ***not what they have coming***.

I received a fresh sense of appreciation and thankfulness for the blood of Christ that sets us free. Pray for others to come and know Jesus by interceding for other people and it will make it easier to live with.

The word of God is forever.

Proverbs 4:25-27

Look straight ahead and fix your eyes on what lies before you. Make a straight path. Don't get sidetracked. Keep your feet from following evil.

The Easter Sermon 2013:

Matthew 28: When Mary went to the empty tomb and the angels (in white) told her that Jesus wasn't there. Yes, he laid there, but he is not there now. The angels told Mary to go quickly and tell his disciples to go see Jesus. 500 brothers and then the Apostles saw Jesus. Don't fear death.

The message: Look forward. Let the future begin right now. Jesus keeps the motion going forward. Jesus was no longer in the "borrowed tomb."

Don't rehash the past. Nothing can take the resurrection from us. Don't be afraid of death. God has a room in his mansion ready for us where there will be no more pain, suffering; it'll be a great Heaven. This world is such a horrible place to live in right now; stabbings, bombings, illness . . .

What does this mean for us today? Remember that first Easter. Our lives are aimed to the future; **heaven**—no more sin, illness and pain; we will be with Christ. That is our goal. Jesus rose from the dead so we can be free from sin.

Don't stew over our sins. They are behind us.

Hebrews Chapter 12:

Don't think of the past. The race goes forward. Look to Jesus.

NOTHING can take the resurrection from us. Like Paul said, "Be content. Do all things through him who strengthens me."

Be the face-like life of Jesus.

LOVE THY NEIGHBOR SERMON.

The children in the congregation were asked if they remember Sesame Street: Big Bird, Elmo, Ernie, Bert, etc. The song was known as "Who are the people in your Neighborhood?"

God wants us to know our neighbors and serve, help, care and share.

At work one day, one of our resident's grandson's came to visit her. I saw that he had a book on Elmo. I sang him the song and he smiled.

The sermon was:

The last week of Jesus's life. The Road into Jerusalem—"King." Hosanna. A few days after his ride into Jerusalem and a few days before the Passover, Jesus knew what was going to happen.

Jesus was being "hammered" with questions and the Pharasees were trying to "trick him up." A lawyer (not civil law, but religious law) asked Jesus which of all the Commandments was the greatest as it was being debated.

Two tied for 1st place:

1. Love the Lord your God with all your heart, soul and mind.
2. Love they neighbor.

There are two rules that hang all the Law and if you follow these two, everything else will work out if these two Commandments are followed. You'll naturally hit all of the rest.

Even Pastors fall short of loving God 100% of the time.

Love they neighbor; the biblical meaning is love all of humanity. Anyone you are aware of is your neighbor.

Our Pastor said that he has a hard time practicing this Law.

1. He grew up poor. He loves the poor. Then why does he get annoyed when he is working on a sermon, for example, and he hears the same story from six poor people that come to talk to him in a row.
2. He loves kids. Why does he get annoyed with half of the kids on the block that live on his street?

You can love in "Theory," but it's hard to put that love into practice.
If you are having a good day, it's easier.
If you are having a not so good day; phone is ringing off of the wall or you are behind in your work, it is hard to put that love into practice.
Run to Jesus.
God wants you to love yourself in a "healthy way."
He sent his Son to die for us and to spend eternity with you.
He is there 24-7. That's Prayer.
God is your neighbor.
AMEN.

Sermon: Deuteronomy 23 vs. 7

RE: Jacob and Esau

That Sunday morning the Pastor had asked if anyone in the sanctuary would like to pipe in and talk about sibling rivalry. One woman started and said her brother threw her school books out the window and she threw his out the window. I discussed my relationship with my sister being estranged for many years.

Jacob and Esau were twins, but different (like me and my sister, even though we are not twins)

Esau was the oldest; very outdoorsy—me
Jacob was very quiet, a book worm—my sister.
Jacob had tricked Esau of both his birthright and inheritance.
Esau was going to kill Jacob after their dad died.
Their relationship never gets healed.
Jacob (ruled the nation of Israel)—Israelites
Esau (ruled the nation of Edom)—Edomites
They shared some borders and "hated" one another.
God said to Israel, "You shall not abhor an Edomite, for he is your brother."
Israel never tried, even though they were better people overall.

In the Book of Obadiah, it is all about God announcing the destroying of Edom.

Sibling rivalry. Even in the Bible.

I have had a long time ordeal with sibling rivalry. Time has healed this.

I saw a sticker on a car bumper that read, "Don't take your organs to heaven . . . heaven knows we need them here!

Psalm 46: "A Might Fortress is Our God."

[1] God is our refuge and strength,

an ever-present help in trouble.

[2] Therefore we will not fear, though the earth give way

and the mountains fall into the heart of the sea,

[3] though its waters roar and foam

and the mountains quake with their surging.[00]

[4] There is a river whose streams make glad the city of God,

the holy place where the Most High dwells.

[5] God is within her, she will not fall;

God will help her at break of day.

[6] Nations are in uproar, kingdoms fall;

he lifts his voice, the earth melts.

[7] The Lord Almighty is with us;

the God of Jacob is our fortress.

[8] Come and see what the Lord has done,

the desolations he has brought on the earth.

[9] He makes wars cease

to the ends of the earth.

He breaks the bow and shatters the spear;

he burns the shields[d] with fire.

[10] He says, "Be still, and know that I am God;

I will be exalted among the nations,

I will be exalted in the earth."

[11] The Lord Almighty is with us;

<u>**Wouldn't it be nice if we could just e-mail HIM our prayers?**</u>

www.God@heaven.pray!

Do not be anxious in anything because <u>**He is in control**</u>. These are just a few of the many teachings Jesus gives us that precedes our lesson for today.

A Firm Foundation Sermon

By our Associate Pastor—<u>**Directly Quoted by his Notes**</u>

Matthew 7:24-27BBB

The storms come to the wise man who is established in the ways of The Lord and the storms come to the foolish man who has relied on himself to figure his life out. When these storms come they either wipe you out or maybe knock off a shingle or take out a few shutters on your house. These storms come regardless of whether you are on the rock or on the sand. You know it and I know it; the storms come. At the end of these storms only one man remains and it is the one who has put God and his Salvation story as their foundation.

So how does this connect to our marriages, our friendships, our family relationships? Let's pretend for a moment that the house in the story is your relationship. Let's pretend that the thing you've worked so hard in putting up, building, painting, remodeling, this beautiful house is your marriage relationship or a relationship with a family member or close friend. Well, it may be presumptuous to say that this house that is your relationship is beautiful. Maybe the front porch light of your house needs to be changed. Maybe your house has some paint chipping off. Maybe your house has a window or two that needs to be replaced. Maybe your house needs a new roof. Maybe it isn't the exterior but more of the interior, the stuff people can't see that really needs the work. Maybe your house looks and feels more like a shack that is barely holding on and you look out your broken windows and see the storms coming and you think oh no, not again, there is no way we are making it this time.

I know that here at church we like to pretend that we have it all together so I won't ask you to raise your hand, but think for a minute. I want you to think about that relationship that has been on your mind so far during this sermon. No matter where you are at in this relationship, there is brokenness, that house is damaged in some way. I'm not sure to what degree and maybe you don't quite know, but the first important part of this process is to acknowledge that there is something that is lacking.

Maybe saying that there is something lacking is an understatement. All sorts of things can plague and poison our relationships. The things that we do to one another little by little put little nicks, and scrapes, and marks all over that house that is your relationship. Lying and those cutting remarks that put each other down breaks a few windows. Bitterness, arguing, and the withholding of forgiveness rip downs gutters and shingles from that once beautiful house. Infidelity, cheating emotionally or physically, and pornography can punch holes in the walls and ceilings. Through our sinfulness we can do a lot to our house on our own.

Sometimes things destroy our once perfect relationship house that we had no say in. Sometimes we deal with loss, unexpected death of loved ones that rips off shutters. Sometimes we are presented with strains on our relationships like disability, disease, depression, anxiety, things that deeply cut and wound that breaks up the floorboards of our house. There are so many things that come at us from all angles in our relationships that leave lasting marks, that tear us down, that wear us out, that make us feel like the whole house is just going to collapse in on itself. Is that you? What condition is your house in? Because if you are like most Americans, which statistics show Christians are no different in their marriage success rate than everyone else, then you may be facing some structural damage to that house.

You may be saying to yourself, "Pastor, that is them, that is the people next to me, across the aisle from me, the people at my work place, that is true of other marriages in my family, but not mine." If you feel all is good then God be praised, but things can be better. I'm not asking you to seek faults, but I want you to acknowledge that you are in a relationship with another human being. There are certain things that come with being a human being that makes it really impossible to have a perfect anything. Maybe it is little things that build up over time like bad communication, unfulfilled expectations, feeling unappreciated. Little things can build up and make just as much damage to your house. The deeper we get into these issues, the more in depth we talk about the attacks on our relationships, the easier it is to feel like all it takes is just one more storm maybe one more big gust of wind and this whole thing is gone, it's over, there is no way we will survive.

I don't want to leave us in despair here. I don't want to get too depressing in my talk here. Things may be bad, things may be terrible but there is a silver lining. What did Jesus tell us in his words for us today? He says anyone who hears these words of mine and does them will be like a wise man who built his house on the rock. And the rain fell, and the floods came, and the winds blew and beat on that house, but it. . . .did. . . . .

not. . . .fall. This house, despite the beatings it has taken in those storms, whether self-inflicted or unprovoked, did not fall. Why didn't it fall? The house had the structural integrity? The people who designed and built the house planned for such a storm and benefited from their own abilities? No. That house stood firm because it had been founded on the rock. It isn't even worth talking about the foolish man because I see it every day in the news, in the statistics, in my daily interactions in this world that enough people know what it is like to work and plan for this house that is their relationship only to forget the most important piece that is the foundation. We know what happens in those relationships but not with those who have the firm foundations that are the words of Jesus.

Practically speaking, I can think of the first and biggest step in setting our relationships on a firm foundation and I am going to tell you this today. In my short marriage, in my short years of life, I have found that the greatest success someone can have in relationships is when they are honest with who they are and who is really in control. These are the words that Jesus teaches in the earlier chapters leading up to his words in Matthew 7. This goes back to the whole acknowledging that you are in a relationship with, you are married to a human being. Human beings are not perfect. Human beings are inherently sinful. Human beings constantly seek their own gain, their own egos, what builds them up, what makes them feel the best and often times that leaves everyone else struck down in their path. It can be a pretty frustrating thing being married or in a relationship with a human being! The dangerous thing about relationships? There are TWO human beings involved. It is easy to see that others aren't perfect, others are inherently sinful, the world is broken but can you say that about yourself? Can you say I'm not perfect? Can you say I'm inherently sinful? Can you say I'm broken? Congratulations! You have just taken the first and biggest step in having a better relationship! It is almost like Alcoholics Anonymous or any other recovery program, the first step is acknowledging there is a problem!

So here is my solution for you today. If I were to give practical advice on how to improve your marriage, how to grow your relationships, then I would encourage you to do something that the church has been doing for centuries. The firm foundation in our faith comes from confessing that there is a God and I'm not it and this should be the same in our relationships. I think the biggest thing we can do is confess to one another each day that we are sinful, we are sorry for doing x, y, or z, and I seek your forgiveness. We do this almost every Sunday in the confession and absolution at the beginning of the service. It is a very good, very Christian practice to say "you know, I am a sinful human being and I am sorry, can you forgive me?" It is also a very good, very Christian thing for you to say, "I forgive you." I don't think we should say "it's okay" or "it's all good" or anything like that. There is power in the words, "I forgive you." I'm not saying this is a cure-all, a wonder drug that will make everything better or anything like that, but I'm saying this will get you there. It is our human nature to naturally gravitate towards a way of life, or patterns of behavior that promote our own ideas or our own egos so we need to consciously each day acknowledge these shortcomings and seek forgiveness. We each need to do this. No one is exempt from this practice. There are two human beings in your relationship. As Christians, people covered by the blood of Jesus, forgiven children of God, it is our duty, our responsibility, and our privilege to freely give that forgiveness that we have freely been given to others. Can I count on you to do that? It won't be easy. There may be things that have yet to be discussed that need confession and forgiveness. Please don't be afraid of these discussions, you will be stronger in the end. Your house is based on the firm foundation of Jesus Christ, the Son of God who died and rose again for you so that you may be forgiven, Jesus our Savior who has promised us his Holy Spirit who gives us the strength to forgive. This is a practice we should be having in our own devotional life and it is one we need to have with one another so that there are no hurts, so that lines of communication are opened, so that we know that forgiveness is there and it is free and you are willing to work toward that.

So, first I pray that you are wise and rest your relationship on this solid rock, this firm foundation that is Jesus Christ. Once you are wise, I pray that as the storms in life come, and they will come, they have come, they are coming, they will always be there this side of eternity, I pray that as these storms come that even though your house may take damage, you realize that you are founded on the rock. Your house will not fall. Please don't dismiss this as something you are far beyond. Please don't hear me and think "ha easier said than done" and completely ignore what you are hearing. You can start patching things up, it is not too late because you are still on that foundation. It is hard work, super difficult work. I am not underselling that there are deep hurts that take more than a few words to patch up, but I am telling you that you can get past this. It is worth the work, the communication, the confession, the forgiveness, the hard conversations are worth it as you start to pick up the pieces, hammer the shingles back down, and put those floorboards back in place. It may take more than just the two of you. Maybe you need a counselor to help you do this. Maybe you need Pastor or I to pray with you and help facilitate discussion. The point is that God wants this for you, he asks this from you, he actually demands it from you. He does this because this is what true God pleasing relationships are. A God pleasing relationship acknowledges that He is God and we are not. A God honoring relationship acknowledges that I am a human being, I'm married to a human being, and it is impossible to expect perfection. A relationship that points to God relies on his grace and love as we confess to him and one another that we screw up daily and we need forgiveness. Let's be real with each other. Let's stop hiding our faults, let's stop pretending like things are okay. Things aren't always okay but that is okay. The storms come, we know this. The point is that when they do we are grounded in forgiveness that puts our ego aside and lets God do the work of changing our sinful hearts. This is what our great, loving, merciful God who gave us this relationship wants for you! In Jesus name, Amen.

Dear Heavenly Father,

Thank you so much for who you are—our rock and our redeemer. You are the firm foundation that we rely on when all else seems lost. We first thank you for the relationships you have given us in our lives whether they be friends, family, or marriage. Day in and day out these relationships are attacked from within by our own doings and from the outside by the culture. We pray that you give us the courage in those moments to stop and first acknowledge that you are God and we are not. In those moments we pray that you give us the strengths to confess our shortcomings to you and to one another. We also pray that you give us the patience and the love to forgive one another. We hurt each other so often, intentionally and unintentionally. Open our eyes to our actions so that we can ask for forgiveness and be able to pick up the pieces of our broken relationships and start building them up again. We pray this is Jesus' name. Amen.

My note on this Sermon: It touched my heart and I cried, but I stand on a firm foundation. His love for me.

CHAPTER 31

The Lord's Prayer

Matthew 6:5-13

"And when you pray, you must not be like the hypocrites. For they love to stand and pray in the synagogues and at the street corners, that they may be seen by others. Truly, I say to you, they have received their reward. But when you pray, go into your room and shut the door and pray to your Father who is in secret. And your Father who sees in secret will reward you."

"And when you pray, do not heap up empty phrases as the Gentiles do, for they think that they will be heard for their many words. Do not be like them, for your Father knows what you need before you ask him. Pray then like this:

"Our Father in heaven,

Hallowed be your name.

Your kingdom come, your will be done,

On earth as it is in heaven.

Give us this day our daily bread,

And forgive us our debts,

As we also have forgiven our debtors

And lead us not into temptation,

But deliver us from evil"

This Prayer was taught by Jesus. It is a big deal. It's a "framework" for prayer. I prayed with my residents at work before they eat dinner and they love it. I let them participate in saying a prayer out loud or sometimes we have quiet time and say our prayer to ourselves.

CHAPTER 32

Rehearsal, Rehearsal Dinner and Wedding

All along, until two weeks before my son and future daughter-in-law's wedding, I was going to walk down the isle with my youngest son. Then I received a text message from my son that was getting married.

He asked me my opinion of walking down the isle with my ex-husband, his pop's. I was honest with him and told him that I would rather not. He responded by informing me that his pop's said it would be okay and if I did not walk down the isle with him, I would be considered as "A regular guest." Why didn't he tell me his pop's said, "Yes" first before asking me my opinion?

I responded by telling him that I would walk down the aisle with his pop's.

It was the night of the rehearsal and dinner. We were at the church all ready to start the rehearsal. The woman in charge came close to me and I, innocently, asked her how I was supposed to walk down the isle with my ex-husband. Was I to hold his hand? Walk arm in arm? How were we supposed to handle this?

She turned to me and asked me what I meant. I told her we were divorced. She proceeded to reply, "We can't have that."

She walked up front to talk to my son. He gave me a look. The woman went up to my younger son and asked him to go stand by me. He proceeded to ask me, "What have you done?"

I explained to him what transpired.

Then came the rehearsal dinner. My gentleman friend was with me and my ex-husband proceeded to say, "Hi, I am the ex." I talked to his fiancé and she was very nice. We were talking about their recent trip to Italy where we were supposed to go for our anniversary before we got divorced. She was holding a plate of food, them my ex said to her, "You need to eat your food."

I was drinking quite a bit that night. I drove to the hotel being followed by my man. He told me I was swerving.

The day of the wedding was almost perfect. The church was packed. Everyone looked gorgeous. My sister, from Arizona, read one of the readings. They were married!

Before we went outside to say congratulations to the bride and groom, I saw my ex and went up to congratulate him on our son getting married and hug him. He stepped back like I had the plaque.

At the cocktail party, I was greeting everyone, including his side of the family. I was having a senior moment and could not remember his cousin's name. I went up to him and whispered that I had a question for him that was confidential. I went up to whisper in his ear when he backed up again like I had the plague. I got very angry with him and asked him, "What is your problem?"

Everyone was having fun at the reception. I danced with my son and everything was great. I only had a few cocktails.

My ex's fiancé had brought her two daughters, but I never got introduced. They all left around two hours before the end of the reception which I thought was very strange and to this day have no idea why. Did he drink too much? I will probably never know.

My gentleman friend and I had stayed at the hotel and the next morning we met up with the bride and groom for breakfast.

Everything seemed fine.

Then the shit hit the fan.

My son and daughter-in-law had gone to Aruba for their honeymoon. I texted my ex to ask him when they were coming back and he was not sure.

They got back home and I texted my son and asked him how their trip was. He was very evasive for days. I finally asked him what was wrong. He replied that I knew what was wrong.

I asked him if it had something to do with his pop's and I not walking down the isle together and he responded, "Yes."

Finally after texting back and forth all day long, I found out that the woman in charge of the rehearsal at the church lied to him.

She told him that I told her I was supposed to walk down the isle with someone else. I never said that. I explained to my son how everything went down. He did not believe me. That was like a knife in my heart.

He told me after she talked to him at the rehearsal he was livid and his future wife had to calm him down as he was very angry.

I told him I said this all innocently, but he did not believe me.

He was upset at the wedding when we danced together, but never said a word to me.

My response to all of this was, "Why didn't you stop the rehearsal and talk about all of this?"

I was very hurt.

CHAPTER 33

Alcoholism

Months after my son and daughter-in-law got married, I began to drink a lot, morning, noon and night. I was drinking a half a bottle of pear vodka each day. I knew where all of the nearest liquor stores were and what times they opened in the morning.

I drank and drove. I was a mess. But I was still able to work. I was working in home health care. I drove clients around in my car under the influence. Shame on me. I was sick.

I would buy some small bottles of pear vodka and drink them down.

I was considered a functioning alcoholic.

I was hospitalized four times for drinking. The last time I drank, I had talked to my mom and she knew I was drunk. I was going to drive to my gentleman friend's house and she told me to stay put. I told her I was leaving to go over there.

Well. I never made it. My mom used her key to my house and walked into my house and found me flat on my back laying in a pool of blood with my head cracked open. I was rushed to the emergency room by ambulance and did not remember a thing. Mom asked me, only I don't remember, what I was doing on the floor. I responded, "Resting."

My sons and daughter-in-law sent me to a detox center for 3 days where I was locked up and could not go outside. I could not have a curling iron, which was very important to me. I could not make a phone call. I remember I had to be strip searched which was a horrible experience. Meetings all day long. Doctors. I recall a dr. asking me about my family history and I told him my father was bi-polar, a manic depressant. They had asked me if I thought I had it. "No way."

At detox, I was smoking and could not even have a cigarette. It was one of the worst three days of my life. I was able to get out of detox on Mother's Day to spend the day with my mother. I remember sitting outside on my front porch and the first thing I saw was a butterfly. Now butterflies mean something to me. Peace . . . hope . . . love . . . I thank God I never got into an accident or got pulled over for a DUI. I believe an angel was watching over me from Heaven, my dear Aunt CH.

My Mother came to visit me at the detox center and we talked. I was very embarrassed. After a few days I was able to make a phone call to my gentleman friend.

After the last hospitalization, my sons and daughter-in-law, my mom and gentleman friend stepped forward.

I had stitches on the top of my head. I was supposed to leave for a cruise with my gentleman friend and my sons did not want me to go. I did go and had to have my stitches removed on one of the islands we visited. I did not drink in front of my friend, but I did sneak off to the bathroom and snuck a few shots. Shame on me. I lied to him and everyone else.

I then went through extensive therapy meetings with alcoholics, drug addicts and suicidal people. It was tough. My sons had asked me to not drive for a while, so I agreed. They picked me up and brought me to and from the meetings. It was tough not driving, but I was glad they asked me to do it. They were always there for me, including my daughter-in-law, my mom and gentleman friend.

Then I got involved in AA (Alcoholics Anonymous) meetings. I had to find a sponsor, a therapist who I lied to about still drinking and cancelled some appointments. I also was going to see a psychiatrist who I saw for a while but then stopped as she gave me 40 mg. of a medication instead of 10 mg. What a big mistake.

My mother, bless her heart, bought me books on AA along with a meditation book which I read every morning in my car.

The first group meetings I had to attend for two weeks was very extensive. I was on a month medical leave from work. They would ask for urine samples occasionally, but you never knew when. I was supposed to be dismissed on a Friday. The day before I was called in and was asked if I had something to say. I started to cry. I had been drinking and was trying to fudge the system, but I got caught.

I went back into the meeting and raised my hand. I stood up in front of all of my friends and admitted to them what I had done. I told them not to try and fudge the system as they would get caught.

So, I had to go to a different place for another two weeks.

What a mess. I did not get anything done at home for months and months and months.

Alcoholism is a disease and it sure got me.

I remember being at my gentleman friend's granddaughter's house and urinated on her couch. He told her I was on a pain killer!I would go to his house drunk and passed out in his bed after he had made a nice dinner for us which I never ate.

I remember my gentleman friend was at his wits end and was afraid he was going to lose me. He begged me to quit drinking.

The bills I incurred were crazy. It took me a year to pay them off.

My sons and daughter-in-law came up with an idea of a voluntary breathalyzer for my car. They paid for the installation. I promised to keep it in my car for a year. My gentleman friend paid for the first six months of the rental fee and then I paid for the last six months. What a God send. It worked.

I had to take my car to the mechanic a few times during the year of having the breathalyzer and was very embarrassed about it. I would have to blow into the breathalyzer to start the car and off and on during driving. I would not let anyone else in the car with me except for loved ones and friends that knew about my alcoholism.

After I would drink, I would go on expensive shopping sprees. I am still trying to pay off my credit cards. This is very sad.

The Twelve Steps of Alcoholics Anonymous

The success of the AA program is due to the fact that an alcoholic, who no longer drinks, has an exceptional faculty for "reaching" and helping an uncontrolled drinker.

In the AA program, a recovered alcoholic tells their story of his or her own problem drinking, describes the sobriety he or she has found in AA, and invites the newcomer to join the informal Fellowship.

The heart of the suggested program of personal recovery is contained in Twelve Steps describing the experience of the earliest members of the Society:

1. We admitted we were powerless over alcohol—that our lives had become unmanageable.
2. Came to believe that a Power greater than ourselves could restore us to sanity.
3. Made a decision to turn our will and our lives over to the care of God as we understood Him.
4. Made a searching and fearless moral inventory of ourselves.
5. Admitted to God, to ourselves and to another human being the exact nature of our wrongs.

6. Were entirely ready to have God remove all these defects of character.
7. Humbly asked Him to remove our shortcomings.
8. Made a list of all persons we had harmed, and became willing to make amends to them all.
9. Made direct amends to such people wherever possible, except when to do so would injure them or others.
10. Continued to take personal inventory and when we were wrong promptly admitted it.
11. Sought through prayer and meditation to improve our conscious contact with God as we understood Him, praying only for knowledge of His will for us and the power to carry that out.
12. Having had a spiritual awakening as the result of these steps, we tried to carry this message to alcoholics and to practice these principles in all our affairs.

Newcomers are not asked to accept or follow these Twelve Steps in their entirety if they feel unwilling or unable to do so.

They will usually be asked to keep an open mind, to attend meetings at which recovered alcoholics describe their personal experiences in achieving sobriety, and to read AA literature describing and interpreting the AA program.

AA members will usually emphasize to newcomers that only problem drinkers themselves, individually, can determine whether or not they are in fact alcoholics.

At the same time, it will be pointed out that all available medical testimony indicates that alcoholism is a progressive illness, that it cannot be cured in the ordinary sense of the term, but that it can be arrested <u>through total abstinence from alcohol in any form</u>, not even smelling it. I remember attending church and received the bread and wine. I wasn't thinking about the wine. I should have asked for the juice. Even that little bit set me off!

#8 from The Twelve Steps—Make amends to all people I had harmed. My therapist some time later on told me he didn't think I was going to make it. He thought I was going to die. Wow.

When I talked to my Mother about what my therapist had told me, she agreed with him.

I have sat down with everyone and made amends to them all, my Mom, my gentleman friend, my sons and daughter-in-law, including my dear friend for drinking and cancelling with her because I got lost. And many other friends.

#12 from The Twelve Steps. I definitely had a spiritual awakening. I was laying in bed after drinking, but not heavily. I saw a foggy appearance of Jesus watching over me at the foot of my bed. Unbelievable, but it happened. That was a miracle.

To this day, whenever I am at a get together, my family and friends will ask me if it will bother me if they drink! My reply is, "Nope."

My youngest son came over and he told me he had a nightmare that I had started drinking again. He was going to call me to check in with me, but he didn't. I told him I would never have a drink again and that was a promise

I HAVE BEEN SOBER FOR FIVE YEARS AND HAVE NO DESIRE FOR ALCHOLOL! I AM VERY PROUD OF MYSELF.

CHAPTER 34

Baby Announcement and Baby Shower

One December on Christmas Day, I invited my Mom, sons and daughter-in-law over for brunch before I had to go to work. My oldest son came, but his wife did not. She was working. She is an RN (registered nurse) at a local hospital and he had to go pick her up early. She was sick and waiting for someone to relieve her. After he left, I mentioned to my Mom that maybe she was pregnant.

My birthday and my mom's birthday are a month apart. My son and daughter-in-law wanted to come over to my house and take us out to celebrate our birthdays. I didn't think anything of it. They came to the house and gave both of us a card. We were to open it together. Mom's was signed, "Congratulations to my future great-grandmother. We are pregnant!" Mine was signed, "Congratulations to my future grandmother. We are pregnant!" OMG. I jumped up and down and said, "I knew it." I said to my son, "I didn't know you had it in you!" What a happy day.

Now it was time to plan a baby shower. It was planned by me and my daughter-in-law's three sisters. It was a lot of fun planning. The shower was scheduled six weeks before her due date. The theme was baby elephants. It was a huge success. It was a beautiful, sunny day. My youngest son took over 300 pictures. The gifts were awesome. Great food. My daughter-in-law cried at the end. My younger son, who was taking pictures at the baby shower, actually got me and his dad together for a picture!

I was at the hospital with my mom on the day she was supposed to be released. I received a call from my daughter-in-law's oldest sister. I thought she was calling to check on my mom. I said, "Hello" and she said, "Hi Grandma!" I was in a state of shock. It was too early, by a week and it being their first baby. She had to have an emergency C-section.

My mom had been sick. I brought her to the dr. and they took a blood test. I stayed with her overnight. She was vomiting off and on all night. In the morning I told her we should go to the ER (emergency room). Just then the phone rang. The dr. told her that her sodium level was very low.

I took her to the ER. They immediately put her in ICU (intensive care unit). They told us that when the sodium level gets low, there is a chance of having a seizure. I stayed with her for hours and asked the nurse if I could leave for a while to clean up and check on my birds.

I was about a mile away from the hospital and the dr. called. He told me my mom had a mild seizure. I felt terrible I was not there with her. I got very angry at the nurse who told me it was safe to leave for awhile.

After I calmed down, I thanked God I wasn't there during her seizure.

My mom was fine. I rushed over to the hospital. I met up with my gentleman friend. Family and friends were gathered awaiting the announcement. My ex was there. My son came out smiling. I ran into the room. I had a grandson, with red hair like my son. What a precious moment.

So . . . I saw my grandson the day of his birth and the next day. I saw him a few times, including one time with my mom and my youngest son, his nephew. I texted my son and daughter-in-law every couple of days checking to see how things were going and to see if they needed anything.

My first visit to my son and daughter-in-law's house to see my grandson, they surprised me with a beautiful gift. It was a charm which read, "Mother established 1985" and "Grandmother established 2019." What a precious, thoughtful, beautiful gift. It even had a little heart on it. I love it. And my birth stone, an amethyst. Recently I had a t-shirt made to match.

My grandson was around six weeks old and I received the following text from my daughter-in-law: **Thank you for checking in. All is good. If that ever changes, we promise we will let you know. In the meantime it isn't necessary to check in with us every day/every few days. We will let you know if there's anything to report and we appreciate you understanding that we need some time and space.**

Wow. I felt hurt. I cried. I was just trying to help. Around a week or so later, I met up with my son, not talking about the text I received from his wife. He told me they had a lot of friends that wanted to see the baby, so I gave it some more time. She was going to be going back to work soon so I gave them their time and space.

"No promises but we can certainly try" is the comment I got from my son to see if I could come for a visit before going to Jamaica. Heard nothing.

I texted when I got back from my vacation stating the time of how long it had been since I saw my grandson.

My son texted, "I can do the math thanks. She (my daughter-in-law) doesn't need you to remind her of that. That's also not a reason you get to see the baby more and that also discredits (my ex-husband's fiance's name) relationship with the baby in the same sentence. Before you flip out that I mentioned (my ex-husband's fiancé's name) she has seen the baby 2x in his life. Once at their house and the baptism."

My son and I texted back and forth. I mentioned I was the only grandmother as my daughter-in-law lost her mother years ago. OMG. My son did not like that at all. He sent me mean text messages. I was upset.

We finally set a time to meet.

From my daughter-in-law:

"Sounds good! I think it's better to meet at at restaurant too in order to maximize our time together!"

We met about the comment about me being the only Grandma. I apologized to my daughter-in-law. I did not mean anything by my comment and that I was sorry she lost her mom years ago. All seemed good. I asked them if I could baby sit some time. I asked them if they were okay with me being sober now. My daughter-in-law told me they trusted me to babysit and knew I would never hurt my grandson.

I had invited her to a craft show with me and my mom months ago. She thanked me and told me maybe next time.

A month later I visited. I asked if we could set up a regular schedule; I was being bold. I was told they had to get back to a regular schedule. This was a few months after the pandemic. I texted my son that I needed a baby fix. I was told they were working on some things and would get back to me. I heard nothing.

When I asked my son if they were going to have a 1st birthday party, I was told, "Probably." Maybe because of the pandemic. I offered to help and was given a thumbs up!

I did not have a good feeling here. I prayed to God everything was okay. I have attempted visits with my mom. Their uncle has attempted, at the last minute. No go.

Praying.

Thank you, God. My prayers were answered.

I texted my son and asked him if everything was alright. He said it was. He asked me why I was asking. I told him it had been before the pandemic since his Grandmother (Great Grandmother to the baby and I saw the baby and it had been a month since my last visit. I told him we were concerned. I then asked him if something was wrong would it tell me. His response was, "Sure." I felt a little better as this entire situation was making me physically sick.

Within a few hours, Grandma and I got an e-mail of around 50 pictures taken a month ago by a professional. They were adorable.

Soon after that I received a text asking me my work schedule for the following week.

I saw my Grandson with my Mother. We were there for two hours. We got to play with the baby, talk with my son and daughter-in-law, had dinner together. It was awesome.

My daughter-in-law told us that two months prior she took a new position at the hospital. Instead of working three 12-hours shifts and not seeing her son awake these days, she took a new position and now works five days a week. She gets to do some teaching and some hands on as an RN. She seems to really like it. I am very proud of her.

Now I understand how very busy they are. My grandson goes to day care as his two cousins go five days a week and time is precious for them.

I spoke to my editor recently and we caught up on our lives. I told him I became a grandmother less than a year ago. I told him I only saw my grandson up to ten times since he was born. He told me he was sorry. My response was. "It is what it is. It is in God's hands."

Oh, but there is more to this story!

It was the day of my grandson's first birthday. Everything went off without a hitch. The food, decorations, gifts; they were all amazing. My mom did not attend due to the COVID-19.

My son and daughter-in-law waited two weeks before they went to visit Grandma/Great Grandma to make sure that no one got sick. It was on a Saturday. I received an e-mail from my mom telling me they were coming over with my grandson and would I like to come. I told her, "Sure." Well, that changed.

I sent a text to my son asking if it would be okay for me to come as Grandma invited me. His response was, "Oh I guess it's ok. Wasn't sure if she wanted some one on one time so we didn't mention it to you." I did not go.

Now it has been two weeks after the first birthday party. I texted my son and asked if I could have "A grandson fix." What I meant was a visit. Instead I received a video of him sitting in a bottom kitchen drawer throwing things out. It was adorable, but that was not what a wanted.

A few days later I sent another text asking if we could set up a day for me to see my grandson. The "Shit" hit the fan.

His response: "I'm seeing some old patterns popping through that I thought we discussed a while back. How can we set some boundaries?"

"We talked about how every 2 weeks isn't possible but we get texts 13-15 days after you saw him reminding us it's been 2 weeks. After 15 days the texts seem to ramp up (and become what feels like very manipulative) by adding Grandma into the conversation. Just trying to keep everything from boiling over."

My response: "And why isn't it possible for me to see him more often? U never explained that to me except u r busy. When he was born u needed time and space. Is that the reason or is it something else? I know there was the pandemic. I am hurt and sad. I have talked w u in the past and u say all is fine. Boiling over. That's why we need to clear the air. Most grandparents that live close by get to see their grandchildren often."

His response: "It's just not possible. We have many commitments. Family, friends, work, experiences we want to have with him, just not enough hours in the day. Who is most grandparents that you're talking about?"

My response: "Ok. Just grandparents in general. No problem."

Another one of my responses: "Just want to make sure u r not terribly mad at me, that's all. I just wud love to see him more. Now I understand. I apologize. Let me know when it is convenient. If you wud like to go out to celebrate yer anniversary, u have a baby sitter! Have a good day."

Another one of my responses: "P.S. I am not trying to be manipulative in any way. Simply stated, let me know when you have some time for me to have a visit. That's all. I know life is very busy. I guess my expectations of seeing my grandchild more often was not in the cards. I get it. Love, Mom."

I left them alone.

A few weeks later my son texted me and asked me if I wanted to come over for a visit.

Of course I did. I brought sandwiches for dinner from a local hamburger place down the street from where I grew up. It was a great visit. Before I left I talked to my son and daughter-in-law and told them I never wanted to stress them out. I understand you are busy.

I understood that her sister was getting married and there was the bachelorette party, the bridal shower, the actual wedding, and her niece's baptism. Busy, busy, busy.

I have texted my son a few times and it has been over a month and nothing.

Am I hurt? Yes. I don't understand. It is the COVID pandemic, but I have seen my grandson a few times since the pandemic started and all I can do is sit back, wait and pray.

I miss him terribly; I want him to know his Grandmother!

And . . . I have never changed his diaper.

And . . . I don't even remember what his bedroom looks like.

Update:

I received a text from my son two days before Thanksgiving inviting me over for dinner. Of course I went. All of my daughter-in-law's sisters and significant others were there along with her father. My mom did not go because of the pandemic.

It was great.

I wanted to hold my grandson, but he was fussy. My daughter-in-law said, "Oh go by grandma. She is a good grandma!" That touched my heart.

I got ready to leave and again offered to babysit. My son told me they just haven't needed it yet. He thanked me for coming and it was great to see me.

I am praying . . . .

And the story continues:

A few days before Christmas, my son texted me and asked if they could come over to my house that Saturday. I said, "Sure. I would love it."

I had snacks and ice cream and cookies and soda.

We celebrated my son's birthday, my daughter-in-law's birthday and Christmas.

My grandson enjoyed seeing my guinea pig and my birds and opening his presents.

What a great day.

I had given them as one of their Christmas presents a scrapbook of the baby shower. They loved it and I enjoyed making it.

They had given me last year for my birthday a picture frame where you download pictures and it changes automatically. My son got that all set up for me. It is one of the best gifts I have ever received. Every few seconds is a different picture of my adorable grandson and my granddog. I even get updated pictures!

I simply love it.

I texted my daughter-in-law on her birthday and she responded, "Thank you."

The second year of the pandemic... All three of us got together before Halloween and went to a farm. My grandson loved the petting zoo and feeding the animals. I loved it too. He giggled, we got some snacks, went on a hayride, bought pumpkins and took pictures.

I was in my glory!

Then we went out for dinner and I was again, on top of the world.

We got together at my Mom's house before Christmas to celebrate Christmas, my son's birthday and my daughter-in-law's birthday. The love of my life joined us along with my nephew and his girlfriend. We had a lot of fun. I picked up chicken dinner from a local restaurant along with sides and everyone enjoyed it.

We gave my grandson a wagon and many other cool gifts! I enjoy buying gifts for the little ones.

My son and daughter-in-law and grandson gave me a beautiful purple shawl, cool warm purple heavy duty socks, and a beautiful wooden birdhouse which I love.

Speaking of the color purple. . . it has always been my favorite color. My birthday is in February.

The violet is the flower of February, which I also love. It is also the state flower of Illinois where I live!

The birthstone of February is the amethyst, which is a type of quartz. The Greeks believed the stone would prevent drunkenness. Amethyst is Greek for "not intoxicated!" I found this interesting since I am a recovering alcoholic.

Today amethysts are associated with peace and inner strength.

Updated news: I met recently with my son, daughter-in-law and grandson for breakfast. I brought gifts for Halloween for my grandson and my son and daughter-in-law's anniversary a month prior.

My grandson softly said "baby." I had trouble hearing him because I had been very sick with a sinus infection and I asked him what he said. He repeated, "baby."

I looked at my son and daughter-in-law. They were smiling. She told me they were pregnant. Yeah. I am going to be a Grandma again.

Now I am waiting for them to tell my Mom and youngest son. Hurry up. I do not want to slip.

CHAPTER 35

Closing Comments

Something in my brain set me off down the road to alcoholism.

I believe it was seeing my ex-husband at my son and daughter-in-law's wedding, as sad as it is.

Alcoholism is a disease.

Alcohol is a poison.

I can't even take the bread and wine at church for communion. I have to drink juice instead of the wine as way back when I was sober for a short period of time, I accidently took wine as it has been a part of my life for years. It set me off and I began drinking again as I mentioned in a prior chapter.

The first time I was at an AA meeting, I had to state my name and that I was an alcoholic Now it was easy. I received my two year coin for being sober. It is a fantastic feeling. At the meetings they always clap for you and present you with your coin. I was fortunate to have my sponsor attend that day and she presented me with the coin she got when she was sober for a year. It touched my heart.

A prerequisite to joining AA is you have to get a sponsor. I have a great one. She was a good friend. The first one quit as I had remained drinking and was not serious at the time about following the program. I also lied to her.

I remember visiting my sister and brother-in-law in Arizona and them bringing me to an AA meeting. I also received a coin from them for being sober for four months. Yeah~I even made a shadow box with all of the coins I have received.

I thank everyone in my family, friends (including my church friends), and my gentleman friend for sticking by me throughout this tough time in my life. Also, thank you to my hairdresser for your love and support.

The angels were watching over me!

And, after eight years of being divorced, the last time I saw my ex-husband, he was very decent to me and wished me good luck as I hurt my back and broke my toe. He needed to step up to the plate and be nice to me as I granted him the divorce he wanted.

I am actually very happy and very blessed and thank God.

GOD brought me to it! GOD got me through it!

I am a grandmother for the first time. Alleluia.

Don't trust . . . .

I would not wish a divorce on my worst enemy.

It's like a death.

But . . . you get through it.

Have faith.

One out of two marriages ends up in divorce.

If you meet someone, be open with them. Ask questions about their sexual partners and if they have any STD's (sexually transmitted diseases). I have a friend who told me that. It's not the same world we live in like years ago. BEWARE!

BE CAUTIOUS.

"You don't know how strong women are until you put them in hot water like a tea bag, and they get stronger and stronger." I am not sure where I got this quote from.

I felt like a failure after my divorce. Time heals and you move forward.

I told a nurse friend at work that someone slit my tire. She told me God is watching over me and that God will protect me as our residents at work need me and I have a calling. It touched my heart.

Sometimes I get high anxiety. When I go to choir rehearsal and sing on Sundays, I feel such a sense of Peace (that's the name of my church.)

I was watching *The View* about a woman who lost three of her daughters (I don't know what happened). She and her husband were so depressed, of course, one of them wanted to commit suicide to be in heaven with their daughters. She wrote a book called, *I Will See You Again*.

I have a friend who has three daughters. She wanted to talk one day and I was happy to do so. She proceeded to tell me that her youngest daughter, who has high anxiety, a disorder known as agoraphobia, a condition where the sufferer becomes anxious in environments that are unfamiliar or where he or she perceives that they have little control. It is also called, "social phobia".

My friend's youngest daughter is gay, like my youngest son. Her daughter was supposed to stand up in her sister's wedding. She had the dress and the tickets to fly out of state. The family was ready to go. At the last minute, the daughter changed her mind. Needless to say, the sister that was getting married was upset and is not talking to her sister. She knows her sister is sick, but she won't talk to her. What happened to love? Forgiveness? She was raised in a Christian house. I told my friend that she needs to stay out of it. Time heals all wounds. I told her my sister and I didn't talk for almost ten years. It will get better.

My friend asked her oldest daughter to talk to the sister who got married about the youngest sister's illness, but the new bride didn't want to talk. She dropped the subject.

Every family has problems. Did God put me through everything to be able to help someone, like my friend. Just to talk?

I listened to my friend and told her I would pray for her and her family.

There are dating services out there for people who are 50 and over. I have a dear friend who met her husband through a dating service, so it can happen to you. There are sites such as Christian Mingle, and a special dating service for farmers.

It takes years to get over a divorce. I had a nightmare about my ex-husband. I can't explain it, but in my nightmare, we got back together. Why would I dream that? I would not get back together with him if he was the last man on earth! It may be because I am thinking of how the holidays used to be when our lives were good.

CareNotes from a pamphlet from church called "Healing the Wounds of Divorce."—Ruth and David Stipp; "All I wanted him to do was pay for what he had done to me emotionally. I felt cheated and angry. I was afraid of being on my own. I felt totally worthless and rejected. I had no hope of ever being happy again."

When people marry, they expect their bond to last forever. Ripping the bond apart through divorce is a devastating experience. Your problem seems all-consuming. As I mentioned, everything you see and hear reminds you of the breakup of your marriage; songs, people walking together holding hands, TV commercials, TV shows, sermons at church.

The song, "Eagles Wings," really gets to me every time:" He will lift you up on eagle's wings, bear you on the breath of dawn, make you to fly like the sun, and hold you in the palm of HIS hands". A real tear jerker. This song is usually sung at memorial services.

There is a song: Don't know who sang it: "Go through Hell B-4 you get to Heaven."

Our old Pastor just lost his wife after struggling for 16 years with a rare cancer. She had numerous bone marrow transplants. The doctors gave her 3-5 years to live, but because of the wonderful love and caring from her husband and love from her family, she survived for 16 years.

At the service, I cried. That's what love is supposed to be. I, unfortunately, along with many other divorced people, do not have that, and it HURTS.

Divorce is one of the most stressful situations a person can go through. In addition to a divorce, I had lost my job of 25 years, which is hard enough to go through, plus cleaning out my house and getting it ready to put up for sale AND changing careers and going back to school.

A tough part of a divorce—not seeing your ex-spouses family any more. Since I got divorced, I found out that two of my ex-husband's uncles died. Thank goodness my ex-husband's sister told me. This was tough for me.

Divorce affects everyone: Your kids, no matter what age they are; family, friends, neighbors—everyone.

When I see my ex-husband, I still get high anxiety and I feel like a knife is still stabbing me in the heart. But, it is getting a lot easier!

But . . . I did it with the help of God. And I stayed strong and didn't end up in the well of depression.

While we were separated and going to counseling and dating, I had false hopes. I thought that we had a chance of getting back together and there would be a happy ending. But, when my husband told me that he was worth a lot of money and that I would be "well taken care of," I knew that my marriage was over and I HAD to face it. I had to be honest with myself. I admitted to myself that I was getting divorced

Grief is ugly. You will have scars. But, you will also feel cleansed, unburdened and full of hope. It seems strange, but people who travel this jagged road are almost always enriched. They are more realistic, more compassionate, and more profoundly human.

This happened to me. I found a new career and I am more compassionate.

"Life breaks us all sometimes, but some grow strong at broken places."—Ernest Hemingway.

I turned to God. He is my greatest source of inner strength and loves me unconditionally. I turned to God for my bitterness and revenge factor. I felt that I was incapable of forgiving my ex-husband, but God has accomplished this in me. My compassionate pastor, friends at church, and others helped me tremendously.

Seek help if you need it. Everyone needs help at some time in their lives. You have to reach out to others to recover.

You can also regain your physical balance by exercising. Getting your adrenaline going helps tremendously.

Time does heal all wounds. My mom has always told me, "This too shall pass." Take as long as you need to come to a peaceful resolution about your divorce. You are not the only one. Divorce is not just an event in the courtroom. It is a process of recovering and you will begin to feel new.

Time has healed some wounds, but when I found out that my ex-husband had a girlfriend, it cut me like a knife. It's something I can't explain. I know I have a gentleman friend and my ex-husband deserves to be happy, but it still hurts, a lot. Like my mom told me, "Let it go," and she is right. I also talked to my patient, who is 84 years old and told her my feelings. She called it, jealousy, and she is right. "It is normal for you to have these feelings," she said. "After all, you were with him for 40 years." Now he is engaged and I will be seeing his fiancé at family events. It is better. I will be a little nervous, but God is good and I will get through this. After all, none of what happened is her fault. My thoughts, she can have him.

After working on this book, I have learned that there are books out there on divorce, helping kids through it, etc. One day I read in *USA Weekend*: "Dating After 50. It's never too late." That's a fact, Jack.

The Serenity Prayer:

God Grant me the Serenity to Accept the Things
I cannot Change

The Courage to change the Things I can and

The Wisdom to know the Difference.

Jesus is Lord . . .

MODEL OUR CREATOR!

LIVE . . . LAUGH . . . LOVE!

Prayer:

Dear Father,

Our world is so broken now since the pandemic started March, 2020. The COVID-19 has taken so many of our friends and loved ones. Please help us heal our world. Churches were closed, restaurants were closed, social distancing, masks. Will it ever end? Watch over us dear God. In Jesus name, AMEN.

When you go through deep waters.

I will be with you.

When you go through rivers of difficulty.

You will not drown.

When you walk through the fire of oppression,

You will not be burned up.

The flames will not consume you. Isaiah 43.2

God has a plan for us.

As Psalm 24:1 reads—Who may ascend the hill of the Lord?

    And know that time heals all wounds. You are happy again. You laugh again.
    Laughter is sunshine from God.

    Dear God,

    I pray that the COVID-19 pandemic will be over.

    I pray that a vaccine is found.

    I pray for peace, love, hope, grace . . . . . I listen to a radio station 97.9 FM called K-Love. It is a wonderful Christian station that cites scripture, sings Christian songs, talks to people with real life problems... they have pastors on call if you need to talk to anyone.

    What a great radio station sent from GOD!

My last and final prayer.

Dear Lord, Please watch over my youngest son who is going through depression issues and not happy at work. He is on Family Medical Leave (FML) for three months and help him through this long journey to feel better about himself and finally find a job he likes. In Jesus name. AMEN.

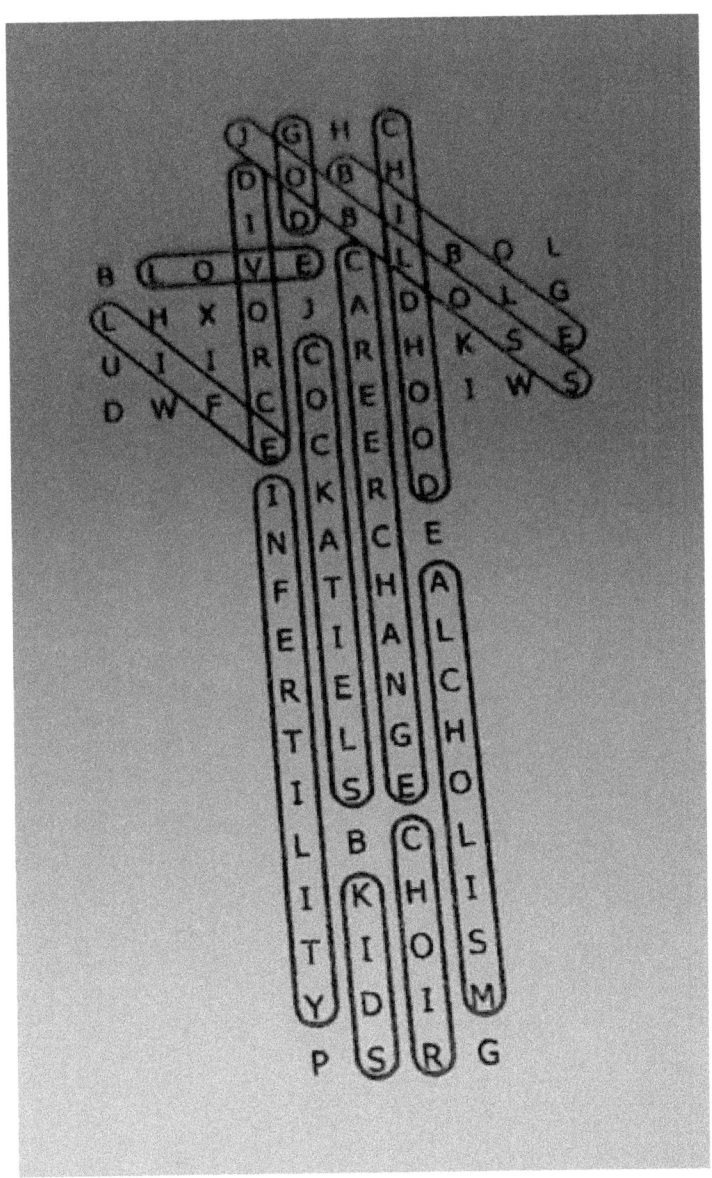

www.ingramcontent.com/pod-product-compliance
Lightning Source LLC
Chambersburg PA
CBHW051049160426
43193CB00010B/1125